An Ounce of Prevention:
A Course in Relapse Prevention

John Leadem, MSW, CSAT-S, CMAT
Shawn Leadem, MSW, CSAT, CMAT

An Ounce of Prevention:
A Course in Relapse Prevention
Copyright © 2009
John V. Leadem & Shawn M. Leadem

ALL RIGHTS RESERVED

No portion of this publication may be reproduced, stored in any electronic system, or transmitted in any form or by any means, electronic, mechanical, photocopy, recording, or otherwise, without written permission from the authors. Brief quotations may be used in literary reviews.

ISBN: 978-0-9835415-9-2
Second printing: January 2013

FOR INFORMATION CONTACT:
Leadem Counseling & Consulting Services, PC
668 Commons Way
Building I
Toms River, NJ 08755
732-797-1444

Please visit our website at
www.leademcounseling.com.
Online ordering is available for this and other products as well.

Table of Contents

Welcome	1
Section 1 – Course Overview	3
Introduction	4
Course Book Design	5
Review of All Six Sections	7
Prerequisites for Beginning This Self-Guided Course	9
Section 2 – Establishing a Foundation for Recovery	13
Introduction	14
Build Your Relapse Prevention Plan on Bedrock	15
Creating a Stabilization Plan	18
Section 3 – The Anatomy of Relapse	45
Introduction	46
Understanding Relapse As a Process	47
Phase 1 – Uncomfortable Feelings	53
Phase 2 – Time Travel	108
Phase 3 – Fragmentation	124
Phase 4 – Gathering Justification	141
Phase 5 – Eliminating the Witnesses	158
Phase 6 – Dry Drunk	168

Phase 7 – Relapse	176
Section 4 – Understanding the Symptoms of the Phases of Relapse	**195**
Introduction	196
Recovery – Like Relapse – Is a Process	197
Section 5 – Strategies for Interrupting the Relapse Process	**249**
Introduction	250
Relapse is a Process that Can and Should be Stopped	252
Section 6 – Personal Relapse Prevention Plan	**317**
Introduction	318
Relapse Prevention Planning Intensifies Recovery	319
Farewell	339
Endnotes	340
Glossary of Terms	341
Appendix A: Alcoholics Anonymous – The Twelve Steps	350
Appendix B: Feeling Words	351
About the Authors	356

Welcome

During our combined tenure in the *addiction** treatment field of over 49 years we have had the misfortune of working with a great many addicts that have relapsed into their active *addiction*. The ranks of our fallen fellows have come from all walks of life and their respective *drugs of choice* have included addictive substances as well as addictive behaviors. Some have paid with their lives, others with their marriages and careers and all with their self-esteem. While we have enjoyed the grace of sustained abstinence, our individual recoveries have not been without periods that closely paralleled the heartache of relapse. We have known times of such *dryness* where we could not explain why we had not relapsed and could identify nothing to be grateful for.

Our commitment to and acceptance of a higher power and a continual belief in the *Twelve Steps*, even though our commitment has sometimes wavered and we have not always practiced the steps perfectly, has led us to a better life. We are grateful to have remained sober long enough to learn some valuable lessons from our periods in the desert of recovery as well as a deeper understanding of ourselves by examining the misfortune of others. Our studies have brought us to an understanding that relapse is not an event but a process, that for most, begins long before we first reintroduce our *drug of choice*. This course has been written because we have learned that relapse is preventable and believe that other addicts and their families deserve to know why and how.

We hope that you are reading this because you have a strong appetite for personal growth and want to learn all you can about the progressive nature of relapse in order to avoid the hardship that a return to active *addiction* promises. If you have been led here because you are returning from the shadows of a relapse, welcome back. We have hope to share with you and a promise that it never has to happen again. Not ever!

We will be with you as you move through the process of building a relapse prevention plan because it is a journey that we are very familiar with.

Sincerely,

John & Shawn Leadem

* All italicized words or phrases will be described in the glossary at the end of the course. Words and phrases that appear in the glossary will be italicized every time they appear in the course so you are cued to refer to the glossary regardless of the section of the course they appear in.

Section 1

Course Overview

Introduction

If you have experienced any of the consequences of an addictive illness then you have known pain. *Addiction* hurts whether you are the addict, co-addict, or one of the victims of the behaviors associated with either disorder such as in the case of our children, employers, and neighbors to mention just a few. Every sphere of impact from our society as a whole to the addict who is at the epicenter of the disaster feels the cost of untreated *addiction*. You could fill a library with the works published that address the cost of *addiction*. A great deal of emotional and financial resources are invested every year to interrupt the addictive process and introduce those affected to therapeutic resources needed to stop the destructive cycle.

While it could be argued that more resources should be invested in intervention strategies designed to stop the progression of an *addiction* or to make treatment available to all who need it, we believe that far too little is being done to identify and interrupt the relapse process. We have found that far many more addicts are inspired to seek help by the changes they witness in recovering addicts than they are by attempting to scare them into recovery by focusing on the consequences of not getting help. Therefore, if we put energy and resources into relapse prevention, we can use recovery success to motivate others to seek help. In the same light, we believe that addicts who have an opportunity to identify and intervene on the symptoms of a relapse process are more likely to be motivated to make character changes with the promise of a positive outcome than they are driven to change by the threat of the harm that will come if they don't. We have chosen to write a course handbook with immense practical application rather than a critical review of the relapse prevention literature. While there are many fine treatment sources available to those who chose to get sober, there are few resources available for those who want to prevent a relapse. Additionally, it is unfortunate that most treatment programs place very little attention on plans for preventing relapse following discharge.

This course is intended to serve as a resource to both *addiction* treatment professionals and private families looking to sustain the hope they have found in the recovery process. We encourage your focus on relapse prevention because it is an insurance policy for your future. In the words Benjamin Franklin writing in Poor Richard's Almanac:

"An ounce of prevention is worth a pound of cure."

Course book design

The course is designed to be used individually, with the aide of a knowledgeable private *addiction* therapist, or with a group of clients working together under clinical supervision in an outpatient or residential treatment setting. The course book is formatted into six distinct sections that are intended to be completed in order because each of the sections build on the previous body of work that you have completed. Each of the sections begin with an introduction to the material that you will find in the coming chapter(s).

In Sections 2 through 6 you will be provided with Course Lessons that will introduce you to the key points to understand regarding the dynamics and prevention of relapse. These lessons will generally expand on the information you received in the Chapter introduction and guide you through the completion of each of the Course Assignments in the section you are working in. The Course Assignments should be completed in the Task order that they appear because they build on each other and will eventually generate the core material that you will focus on during the construction of your Individualized Relapse Prevention Plan. On occasion, we have added Concept Lessons for those times where we felt a visual diagram would make it easier to convey some of the more complex concepts found in this course.

Each of the assignment tasks that you undertake should be as thorough as you are capable of and include enough detail to communicate your answers fully. Do not hesitate to use actual examples of how the material applies to you even if the Task does not require it. This is your course and the more personalized your responses are the easier it will be to identify interventions to use that will help you to interrupt a relapse in process.

Please read all of the Course Lessons and accompanying Course Assignments in the section you are working on if you are working independently before completing any of the Course Assignments. If you are working with an individual therapist or in a treatment group your therapist is likely to group certain members together to work collaboratively and may select several Course Assignments to be completed before bringing the group members together to process their work. If you are working independently, please find members of your support group that you can share your insights with and obtain support and guidance from if you get stuck on a particular concept or assignment. If at any time in your work the material becomes too emotionally stressful, STOP, and get professional support or direction on how to proceed. While the assignments do not have any hidden triggers that are designed to set off an emotional reaction, you are likely to have them because the introspection that you will be undertaking can become emotionally painful at times. If you have any doubts about your emotional stability or ability to benefit from the course please seek professional guidance.

The final section of the course contains the format for you to enter your insights, plans, and strategies for preventing relapse. You are encouraged to share your plan with members of your support system. Take caution with loved ones who may not be emotionally prepared to receive the information that you will be imparting. If you have any doubts about the ability of those who you would share your work with to handle the contents, then do not share the work without first seeking professional supervision and guidance.

In the back of the course book there is a glossary of all the words or phrases that you will find *italicized* throughout the course book. Please refer to it as needed. You will also find an appendix that contains a robust selection of feeling words to help you to accurately express your feelings so others in your support system will better understand how to help you.

Leadem Counseling & Consulting Services (LCCS) will provide an ever-expanding library of recovery tools for you to use in your ongoing modifications to your plan. The LCCS Sobriety Tool Kit can be found by going to our website www.leademcounseling.com. Please review the contents of the kit frequently because we will be offering supplemental materials on a regular basis that have been withheld from this manuscript. The assignment samples and alternative intervention strategies that you will find there will greatly expand the offerings that you will find in the following chapters.

Lastly, remember that relapse is a process and not an event. If your coursework or the challenges of life exposes material that poses a threat to your sobriety or if you find yourself wanting to return to your *drug of choice*, pause the work in this course to get additional help from a knowledgeable *addiction* treatment professional. If you are unclear about where to find professional help or how to identify quality residential treatment programs, do not hesitate to call us at any of the contact numbers available on our website. We will now move to an introduction of each of the six sections.

Review of all six sections

An Ounce of Prevention: A Course in Relapse Prevention, can be used independently or in conjunction with a therapist. If you are working independently and become bogged down or confused please secure the help of a therapist with *addiction* treatment experience who has a working knowledge of the *Twelve Steps*. If you have difficulty finding such a person or believe that we can be of service to you, please do not hesitate to contact us at LCCS via our website: www.leademcounseling.com and we will help you to find the support you need.

The course guide is divided into six sections that are most helpful if you complete them in order. Each section builds on knowledge and insights obtained in the previous sections.

Section 1- Course Overview

This first section begins with an introduction to our purpose for writing this course. This introduction is followed by a highlight of each of the sections, which you are in now. This section concludes with important prerequisites for you to consider before beginning the course.

Section 2- Establishing a Foundation for Recovery

The second section begins with a review of the first three of the Twelve Steps, because there can be no meaningful intervention into a relapse process or recovery from an addictive disorder without a thorough grounding in the first three steps. The First Step requires a full understanding of the powerlessness and unmanageability resulting from an addictive disorder as the insight is critical to developing a sober life-style. When that understanding is supported by the acceptance found in the Second Step and the freedom made available in Step Three, the prospect of sustained recovery becomes very real.

This section continues with material that will help you to be sure that your recovery is stable before you begin examining the dynamics of relapse. Before concluding the section you will construct a plan for stabilizing recovery whether you are new to recovery or returning from a relapse. Additionally, if you are recovering in an unsupportive environment, points on how to remain safe are offered.

Section 3- The Anatomy of Relapse

The third section presents the core concepts critical to understanding that relapse is a process that can be detected, intervened upon, and prevented. Each stage in the relapse process is explored in depth. Writing assignments that can be completed alone or in a group are presented to help you to develop a personal understanding of each phase in the relapse process.

Section 4- Understanding the Symptoms of the Phases of Relapse

The fourth section will focus your attention on the identification of the symptoms in each phase of the relapse process that best fit your experience. You will be provided with a selection of common symptoms typically found in each relapse phase for you to choose from as well as space for you to add your personal creations. The symptoms you identify in this section will help direct you in the development of intervention strategies in Section 5.

The seven phases in the relapse process are: Uncomfortable Feelings, Time Travel, Fragmentation, Gathering Justification, Eliminating the Witnesses, Dry Drunk, and Relapse.

Section 5- Strategies for Interrupting the Relapse Process

The fifth section will direct your focus from your potential relapse symptoms to the construction of your personalized strategies for intervening on those symptoms. In other words, it is time to move from the problem to the solution. Sample strategies are offered for each phase and you are encouraged to create additional ones that really fit your life and challenges.

Section 6- Personal Relapse Prevention Plan

This last section brings all your exploratory work on identifying your personal potential relapse symptoms and the strategies you have created for addressing them into one clear plan.

The organization of the plan will help you communicate your needs to your support group and make it easy for them to help you remain accountable.

Prerequisites for beginning this self-guided course

There are no absolutes in this course except that you cannot work on a relapse prevention plan if you are still active in your *addiction*. Once you have established abstinence from your *drug of choice* you can begin to formulate a plan for recovery that ensures that you will remain that way. In order to have both your plan and you be successful you must begin the construction on a stable foundation. Section 2 of the course will guide you through the development of a plan to stabilize your foundation but first you must be sure that your thinking is clear and your motivation is focused.

Each one of us needs to take full responsibility for the quality of our own lives if we are going to establish and maintain a sober life-style – free of addictive substances and behaviors. The course you are embarking on can aide you in your efforts to regain emotional stability in your life if you have been spiraling out of control in addictive relapse cycles. If you have established a solid recovery program – free of relapse – but have not been able to get off the emotional roller coaster the course will help you identify and replace unproductive behavioral patterns that may be robbing you of the joy of *sober living*. *Sober Living* brings joy. The following points should be considered before continuing on with the course:

- You have successfully completed at least 10 – 14 days of sustained abstinence from your *drug of choice*

    The term abstinence is used in this course to refer to the act of denying yourself of your *drug of choice* in whatever form it comes. When your *drug of choice* is a substance such as alcohol it is relatively easy to monitor abstinence when compared to the challenge of defining or monitoring abstinence when your *addiction* is rooted in a process such as gambling, the pursuit of love, or overeating, to name just a few.

    If you are an alcoholic, abstinence is fairly easy to interpret – you are either *drinking* or not *drinking* and there is little confusion or gray areas to cloud the picture. However, even alcoholics have become unclear about their abstinence and have found themselves lost in the fog when they have failed to responsibly monitor drinks or foods that they ingest. Some will get into trouble and trigger a relapse as a result of using cough remedies that have high concentrations of alcohol in them that they were unaware of. Others will drink "non-alcoholic" beer claiming that they don't need to worry about the small percentage of alcohol in the beverage because the label reads "non-alcoholic beer." This is not confusion – this is DENIAL. "Non-alcoholic beer" that contains alcohol is for NON ALCOHOLICS.

    Your definition of abstinence may need to include a decision to refrain from other potentially addictive substances or behaviors in order for this course to be productive for you. If you are unsure about how you should be defining abstinence for yourself talk to members of your Twelve Step fellowship, a knowledgeable *addictions* therapist, and/or members of your family. If you get confused about the potentially contradicting definitions available from one Twelve Step organization to the next or simply want an additional opinion feel free to contact us through our website: www.leademcounseling.com.

    There is no universal length of sustained abstinence that is optimal for everyone to use as a foundation for beginning this important work. If you are in a supportive environment, 10 – 14 days may be satisfactory for the *cravings* and the physical discomfort associated with the termination of your *drug of choice* to ease its grip on you. We suggest that you secure input from your support group, a therapist, your family doctor or psychiatrist knowledgeable in *addiction* medicine, and/or a confidant of yours whose input about your readiness to undertake emotionally challenging work you would trust.

- You have a willingness to recover from your *addiction* using the concepts embodied in the Twelve Steps

    A thesaurus will offer words such as: readiness, eagerness, enthusiasm, motivation, and compliance as alternative ways of expressing willingness. We find that the alternate ways of relating that idea of willingness are actually great indicators that a person is willing.

    A readiness to use the Twelve Steps as the foundation for your recovery implies that you are standing at the ready to begin and not procrastinating and planning to undertake a particular step at some point in the future. A person who is eager and motivated to undertake the tasks embedded in the steps is seeking out direction and guidance anywhere it can be found to provide the support needed to complete the work. If you find yourself short on the motivation or incentive to do step work, spend some time talking to those who have been hurt by your *addiction* or lack of emotional sobriety. Their pain may inspire you to take action. The compliance needed is all about action, action, and more action. Thinking about change, wanting to change, needing to change are all positive but none of them will result in change. The only way to change is to comply with the steps and change.

    You may find yourself struggling with the idea of attending Twelve Step meetings because you find social situations too anxiety producing for you or you are fearful of the disapproval you think you will receive from your fellow group members. This fear is seldom realized but if it creates an insurmountable obstacle to returning to meetings do not avoid step work. While we are strong proponents of full participation in the recovering fellowships and have benefitted first-hand from the wisdom that can be obtained through participation in meetings, you do not need to go to meetings to work through the Twelve Steps. You can work the steps on your own, if you insist, but you cannot build a successful relapse prevention program without working through and incorporating the Twelve Steps in your life. You do not have to have completed all of the Twelve Steps but you should be aware of what each step is asking of you and what you are likely to gain from working each of the steps.

    Although this workbook should not be viewed as a step workbook the concepts of most of the Twelve Steps can be found woven into the form and function of this course.

- You have completed your stabilization plan

    Two different stabilization plans will be introduced in the coming chapters, which are designed for both the individual returning from a relapse as well as the beginner or individual with a stable recovery looking to enhance the quality of his or her interpersonal relationship and personal sense of well-being.

    If you are returning from a relapse into your active *addiction* after a period of sustained sobriety then it is likely that you have undergone a whirlwind of emotions ranging from anger with self and shame to hopelessness and defensiveness towards others. Relapsing after enjoying a period of abstinence and improved emotional stability can leave us feeling quite angry with ourselves and ashamed for having abandoned our recovery and perhaps some of the people in our lives. If this is not the first relapse or if we have no insights into how the relapse developed, the fear involved can leave us feeling hopeless and attempting to guard ourselves against criticism or that always painful question: "What happened, you were doing so well?"

If you are undertaking this course as a purely preventative measure and have been able to maintain abstinence without a problem but your emotional and *spiritual* recovery is lacking and your relationships are suffering you may feel just like the person described above. In your case the stabilization plan will focus on the supports and accountability that you will need in order to effectively take on the work of making the personality changes needed to improve the quality of your interpersonal relationships.

There will be those of you who have come to this course that are fortunate enough to be enjoying a stable recovery and maintaining meaningful and mutually supportive relationships with loved ones and members of your support group. For you, the course will serve to improve self-awareness and develop a deeper understanding of the social, emotional, and spiritual challenges that may threaten your recovery in the future.

- You have acquired a working knowledge of Steps One through Three

The first three steps of the Twelve Step recovery process are meant to establish a foundation for the more challenging recovery work that we find in Steps Four through Nine. It is wise to have completed at least a preliminary 1st Step prior to undertaking this course but for sure you need to have read the literature your fellowship has prepared for the first three steps and discussed your understanding of the principles involved with a support group member or therapist.

Section 2

Establishing a Foundation for Recovery

Introduction

Section 2 of the course is aimed at helping you to establish a sober foundation from which to build your Personal Relapse Prevention Plan. A meaningful, comprehensive, and enduring recovery plan of this type can only be created once the addictive process has been interrupted and the pangs of withdrawal have subsided. Simply put – you cannot openly and honestly work on a relapse plan if you are still relapsing or lost in the mental and emotional fog that can often accompany the first few weeks of recovery. Once abstinence has been established we can develop a reasonable and measureable plan for maintaining it and develop a well-rounded sober life-style. But as many of us have discovered, freedom from our *drugs of choice* will not produce sustained emotional and *spiritual* health without additional behavioral, emotional, and *spiritual* changes.

The foundation of any *addiction* recovery plan is prone to stress and fracture if careful attention is not paid to the development of a working knowledge of the Twelve Steps. For your reference, the steps are reprinted in their entirety in the glossary. A working knowledge of the Steps is obtained through the study, completion, and practical application of each of the Twelve Steps in all areas of your life.

We could not begin to conceptualize a relapse prevention model or write a plan that ignored the critical role that the Twelve Steps play in the development and maintenance of abstinence and emotional sobriety. While it is outside the scope of this work to detail task oriented strategies for completing each of the steps, it is prudent to take a moment to review the first three of the steps as they form the foundation for recovery. We currently offer *Clearing Away the Wreckage of the Past: A Task Oriented Guide for Completing Steps 4 through 7*[1], published by LCCS and it is available on our site: www.leademcounseling.com. Additionally, you are encouraged to read the literature available through your Twelve Step fellowship to enhance your understanding of how the steps can be used to prevent relapse.

If you have any questions about the security of your foundation for doing this work, check with your therapist, your family doctor, your family member or members of your support group. If you find yourself without meaningful sources of input to guide you, contact our office through our website for help to make that assessment.

What to Expect from the Following Chapters:

- Provide an overview of the first three steps of the Twelve Step process which if completed thoroughly will provide the bedrock you will need to complete your Personalized Relapse Prevention Plan

- Introduce plans for stabilizing your recovery whether you are returning from a relapse or just beginning the recovery process

- Provide key points of consideration if you are recovering in an unsympathetic environment

- Introduce ways in which your changed attitudes may inspire others to follow your lead

- Guide you through the completion of a personalized stabilization plan from which to build your recovery

Build your relapse prevention plan on bedrock

It can be difficult to stabilize your recovery following a relapse if you move too quickly from the problem to the solution like so many are apt to do. The early days following a relapse can involve great shame and self-condemnation as well as judgment from those around you. Many relapse survivors will want to move very quickly away from the scene of the accident and reestablish themselves in the social and emotional status that they had enjoyed prior to the relapse.

The Twelve Step recovery process that you begin in the first three steps can take you from loneliness and desperation to a place of genuine companionship and hope. We hope that you have come to this point in the journey with an appreciation for the many rewards that a life of sobriety makes possible. The first three steps of the Twelve Step process of recovery from addictive illnesses read:

1. We admitted we were powerless over (our addictive process) — that our lives had become unmanageable.[2]
2. Came to believe that a Power greater than ourselves could restore us to sanity.
3. Made a decision to turn our will and our lives over to the care of God *as we understood Him.*

Steps One through Three provide the foundation for the development of a way of life that leads the victims of the *addiction* from a solitary position of "I" to the united reliance on a fellowship of "we." The essential elements of the initial *surrender process*, which culminates in the Third Step, are summarized in the "ABC's" of recovery as referenced in *Alcoholics Anonymous* (p. 60)[3]:

(a) That we were alcoholic and could not manage our own lives.
(b) That probably no human power could have relieved our alcoholism.
(c) That God could and would if He were sought.

The First Step, said to be the only absolute requirement for recovery, requires an admission that your problematic behavior was neither a bad habit nor a cultural difference, but an *addiction*. The First Step requires an awareness that you did not behave the way that you did when you were active in your *addiction* because you are Irish, German, uncomfortably short, too fat, young and immature, or because you had an anger management problem. Everyone grows up with aspects of themselves, their culture, or their family that they might not like. These things or people we would like to change may very well have caused us pain – some of us a great deal of pain. These challenges, however, are not the reason we became addicted. In fact, the *defects of character* that some of us developed in order to cope with life actually caused us more problems than the original challenge or harm we experienced.

Our First Step declaration of unmanageability will require great humility because acceptance of defeat comes painfully slow to most of us. The stories, which describe our respective *bottoms*, vary greatly in both the breadth and depth of powerlessness and unmanageability. The tasks associated with the completion of a First Step will vary from fellowship to fellowship and sponsor to sponsor. While there is no universally accepted definition of *bottom*, you will know that you have hit yours by your willingness to acknowledge the need for help outside of yourself. The idea that "probably no human power" will suffice brings the need for further humility in the Second Step.

The Second Step, often over looked because it is thought to be an extension of the obvious dilemma already addressed in the First Step, is a vital step in the initial *surrender process*. Many newcomers will miss the implication that will, hopefully, become obvious with time. If all of our problems were related to our *addiction* and the problem was eliminated when we established abstinence, then why would there be a need for a Second Step?

The Second Step is not restating the obvious. It implies that our sanity is not restored merely because we resign ourselves to being powerless. Insanity is often defined as the tendency to do the same thing over and over again expecting the results to be different. The unmanageability that re-emerges for those who only establish abstinence is a painful example of this insanity. We need to do more than put the proverbial *cork in the jug*. The alcoholic who stops *drinking* but continues to romance the good old days and the food addict who avoids forbidden foods but gorges on salad have both put the *cork in the jug* but are still behaving like addicts. The recovering sex addict who merely stops the more socially unacceptable aspects of *acting out* behavior without replacing his or her reliance on external sources of pleasure will eventually find himself or herself *teasing the addiction*. The First Step does not signify surrender. For some it is barely more than a resignation to abstinence. The relief obtained from the admission found in the First Step will be short lived if not followed by the pursuit of a power greater than us. We have a great deal to change about the way that we manage our emotions and interact with others. We will need a power greater than our own to identify and make those changes.

The Third Step can introduce a real challenge to those of us who struggle with the idea of having a power greater than our own self. You do not need to believe in a supreme being. You only need to accept that your supreme solitary efforts have not enabled you to win the fight with your *addiction* single handedly. We are told that we cannot maintain sobriety on the power of our own will. "Willpower works about as well on *addiction* as it does on a bad case of diarrhea," ranted our sponsors. While they were ranting and raving we sometimes thought to ask whether or not there was a "good" case of diarrhea but we thought the wiser and were silent. We, like many, had a great deal to learn about the need for and the use of a Higher Power in our recovery.

Whether you believe in God; deny that God's existence is provable; or believe you can prove the non-existence of God; you will need to develop a relationship with a power greater than yourself. We cannot see ourselves clearly without the help of others and we cannot change what we cannot see. To make matters worse, we appear to be equipped with the ultimate weapon of self-destruction: free will. In the coming steps you will learn much about healthy uses for your willpower but for now it is important to remember that much of our injury has occurred because we are free to do as we please. Your sponsor might joke with you that "your best thinking has gotten you in this mess", but it is hardly a joke. Your thinking will need to change. The way you cope with your emotions will need to change. The way you interrelate with others will need to change. You will find that we are always changing. We are either moving forward or we are moving backward. The choice is yours. This would be a good time to exercise your *free will* to develop a God of your own understanding. The power greater than yourself can be your group conscience, a sense of a greater power of the universe, or the collective thinking and wisdom of those you trust. Please do not trust your recovery to yourself alone. We sometimes get defensive when our support group members challenge us to get out of our own heads. It is sound advice because our thinking can get us into a great deal of trouble. After all, our thinking occurs in a place where there is no adult supervision.

If you hit *bottom* you will have already suffered the lessons you would need to move beyond the powerlessness and unmanageability to acceptance of the need for a power greater than yourself to begin the healing process that will return your sanity. We have all paid our dues. The first three steps can be simply summed up as: "I can't, He can, and I'll let Him". The Third Step did not ask us to relocate ourselves from the pain of active *addiction* to the oppression of a violent or controlling deity. The Third Step invited us to turn our will and our lives over to the care of God as we understood Him. We will continue to enjoy the comfort of that care as we move through the house cleaning tasks that are associated with Steps Four through Nine.

You are encouraged to complete this course regardless of how far you have progressed in your step work. However, the course is not recommended if you have not established abstinence because the work involved requires clear thinking and the ability to be introspective. Before you continue – stop for a moment to examine the stability of your recovery foundation.

If you have been struggling with any of the emotional or *spiritual* concepts found in the first three steps then perhaps you would be better served to complete your work on the first three steps concluding with surrender before progressing with the coursework that begins in Section 3. There are fine materials offered by the various Twelve Step organizations for their members that you could benefit from regardless of whether or not you are affiliated with the fellowship whose material you are using. Regardless of whether or not you are prepared to begin the relapse prevention coursework, you are encouraged to develop a stabilization plan using the formats in the next chapter as a guide if they fit for you. If they do not fit, for whatever reason, then get professional help from a recognized *addiction* therapist to help stabilize your recovery.

Creating a stabilization plan

In this chapter you will be helped to create a plan to stabilize your recovery prior to beginning the tasks that the course asks of you. It is our hope that the two stabilization plans we have conceptualized for you will serve you as well as they have our clients over the years. For those of you wanting to stabilize your recovery following a relapse please continue on to the next paragraph below. If you are a newcomer using this guide exclusively as a preventative measure please skip to the course concept entitled "Formula for a stable recovery foundation for beginners". If you are a seasoned Twelve stepper looking to enhance the quality of your interpersonal relationships than feel free to make modifications to either of the stabilization plans so that you can put your focus on increasing the depth of your support group and heightening your level of accountability.

Stabilizing your recovery following a relapse

A decision to return to the recovery meetings or therapy following a relapse usually requires a great deal of courage. The degree of shame and guilt that you must overcome to begin again is directly proportional to the quality of life that your previous tenure in recovery has afforded you. If you had begun to get a glimmer of the joy that *sober living* could supply, then the challenges of returning can be very difficult. If you are returning from a relapse that followed years of abstinence and the fulfillment of recovery *promises* then the shame and self-anger can seem unbearable. Do not despair. There is hope, if you are willing to go to any lengths to achieve and maintain your sobriety.

In the following Course Lesson 2.1 you will find detailed descriptions of how you are expected to complete the corresponding tasks on your Stabilization Plan in Course Assignment 2.1. We encourage you to read the descriptions for all of the tasks before beginning work on your stabilization plan. To begin the creation of your stabilization plan you can proceed to page 20.

Formula for a stable recovery foundation for beginners

If you are new to the recovery process, welcome. You have undoubtedly paid your dues for membership in your recovery fellowship. You may be coming with a sense of foreboding because of the shame and regret associated with the powerlessness and unmanageability you have endured, but do not fear. Desperation may have brought you to the recovery rooms, but it is the joy and freedom of *sober living* that will make your journey through this course worth your while and keep you coming back for more.

If you are a newcomer and are taking this course as a proactive measure in your recovery, you are to be commended. Many addicts do not think about strategies for preventing a relapse in the early days of recovery because they are so close to the pain of their last *drunk* that they cannot imagine ever returning to active *addiction*. If you have struggled with your powerlessness over your *drug of choice*, then the relief that you will have derived from abstinence may have led you to believe that the hard part of recovery is over. We have heard many newcomers and relapse victims assert boldly that they "will never *drink* or *drug* again" because it is the "furthest thing from their mind" or they are certain that "to return to active *addiction* is a death sentence" and they "really want to live." While it is a good thing to have a healthy respect for the power of your *drug of choice*, do not comfort yourself into believing that fear will keep you sober. It will not. Your commitment to abstinence is a beginning but fear of returning to the past is not an insurance policy against relapse.

In time you will most likely discover that stopping was the easiest part of the recovery process. If you have not been introduced to the concept of the disease model for explaining *addiction*, it might be new information for you that we suffer with a disease of the body, mind, and spirit. Abstinence begins to address some of the physical aspects of recovery but the emotional and *spiritual* healing that is required for long-term sobriety does not flow directly from abstinence. Seasoned recovery members are quick to note that while they might have "come for their drinking" they ended up "staying for their thinking." And so it is with most of us. We come to recovery wanting to quell the storm of active *addiction* and discover that we are emotionally and *spiritually* ill and that we will need to address the emotional and *spiritual* aspects of our disease if we are to keep our disease in an arrested state. Do not be too alarmed if the honeymoon of early recovery has begun to fade. You are discovering that the easy part of the recovery process is establishing abstinence and the challenging parts of recovery are found in the lessons you will learn about getting comfortable in your own skin. This course will help you do that without having to relapse first – because it is not required.

You will hear many times during this course that relapse is not a part of the recovery process because it is a dangerous sinkhole left open if you believe that a relapse is normal and to be expected. You will see members of your group, whom you have come to admire, relapsing and you could become confused. You will witness some people return from a relapse with <u>seemingly</u> little in the way of consequences for their decision to return to their *drug of choice*. Do not consider that the hardship others face with relapse means that it is normal because you might encounter a pattern of people relapsing during your initial introduction to recovery. Likewise avoid assuming that those who relapse without apparent problems are free of consequences. It is more likely that you are comparing your insides to someone else's outside appearance. As you get to know people who have relapsed you will learn it never gets better in active *addiction*. It always gets worse. To begin the creation of your stabilization plan please turn to page 30.

Course Lesson 2.1 - Stabilizing Plan for Recovery Following Relapse

Returning from a relapse can be quite challenging and potential weaknesses in your previous or current recovery plan could give rise to another relapse before you can fully understand what has just happened and get back on your feet. It is common to hear suggestions that you should treat relapse like a fall from a horse and get right back in the "saddle." A quick return to the support and acceptance available in the Twelve Step rooms is certainly advisable as are efforts to reconnect to trusted members of your support group. It is not, however, a good idea to return blindly to the strategies for maintaining sobriety that you had been relying on in the past because something was wrong if you relapsed.

The following tasks are especially important if you are returning from relapse after a period of sobriety as they are intended to create and/or fortify your foundation. In Course Assignment 2.1 you will be asked to formalize a preliminary recovery plan. The items to be addressed in the plan are listed below for your review.

IMPORTANT:

The following descriptions of the various tasks in this lesson are presented to introduce you to the actual written work you will complete in the Course Assignment that follows this lesson. Do not write anything until you reach the assignment.

When you have completed the lesson be sure to share your findings with members of your support system and your therapist if you are working with one.

~ Task 1 ~

Describe any health problems that resulted from your relapse or may have occurred during your relapse process and how you plan to address them:

Developing a plan for addressing your overall physical health as well as specific health concerns will play an important role in the development of a solid foundation for your recovery. Be cautious about taking any potentially addictive medications. It is wise to check out your medication protocol with a physician certified by the American Society of Addiction Medicine. In the days or months prior to your relapse or during the course of your relapse you may have developed health problems or concerns that have been ignored. Threats to your physical health will have a negative impact on your overall sense of well-being and should be addressed before they create lasting consequences or chronic conditions.

Establishing and maintaining a plan to promote your physical well-being and overall fitness will be an invaluable recovery tool. Make sure that your physician approves your plan and that your plan does not become compulsive in nature. Your fitness program should not interfere with your attendance at meetings, therapy, work and family obligations, or completely dominate your free or recreational time.

Course Lesson 2.1 - Stabilizing Plan for Recovery Following Relapse (Continued)

~ Task 2 ~

What steps will you take to develop or enhance the breadth and depth of your support system or make better use of the support you currently have:

Your recovery support system is an integral part of a healthy recovery process. The core of your support system could be a sponsor but should not be restricted to just one person. It is wise to have several people, from the Twelve Step fellowship you are involved with, to be a part of your support system. The role of a support group member or sponsor is to share experience, strength, and hope with you regarding how they have managed to develop a sober life-style for themselves. It is advisable to stay in regular contact with members of your support system even if you do not find yourself in emotional need. Frequent contact will make it easier for you to reach out to them should the time come that you do need help. Just as in active *addiction*, the development of rituals and habits helps to ensure that we engage in the behaviors that the rituals are built around. When we practice reaching out we will be able to reach out when we need help.

It is also important to work steadily at enhancing the depth of your relationships with them because the *antecedents* to a given trigger or point of discomfort often have their roots in past *traumatic experiences*. It will be valuable to you to invite the members of your support system into the deeper recesses of your life story as it will enable them to help you to identify when you are likely to become ensnared in emotional traps in recovery.

~ Task 3 ~

How do you plan to make regular attendance at Twelve Step oriented recovery meetings your number one priority:

Attend a minimum of one Twelve Step meeting a day for the first 90 days in addition to other recovery activities. If that is impossible then every day should include either a Twelve Step meeting or a recovery activity but never less than four meetings per week for 90 days (multiple meetings in one day are not a substitute for the expectation that you attend at least one meeting per day for four days). If the recovery axiom is true, that we have a daily reprieve from our obsession with our *drug of choice*, than it is not advisable to try getting three meetings into a 24 hour period and wait 48 hours or more until the next meeting. Our reserves need to be replenished daily and sometimes more often if we are experiencing difficulties.

Course Lesson 2.1 - Stabilizing Plan for Recovery Following Relapse (Continued)

~ Task 4 ~

Describe your plan for completing the first three steps of the Twelve Step program as quickly as possible. If you have already completed Steps One through Three describe what you learned about yourself, your relapse, and/or how the insights gained may help you to prevent a relapse in the future:

The first three steps of the Twelve Step program create the foundation. The First and Second Steps are best done in writing and shared with the important members of your support group, your therapist, and when appropriate, members of your immediate family. The Third Step is where personality change begins. The surrender inherent in the Third Step is critical to the process of developing healthy strategies for coping with the emotional challenges of life. It represents a paradigm shift that can be as pervasive as the one that occurs when we begin the free-fall into the addictive process.

If you have already completed the first three steps, discuss the insights you have found to be the most valuable to you through the consideration of the following points:

- Describe the example of powerlessness that you waged the greatest effort to control during the progression of your illness
- Highlight the most costly price you paid during the evolution of your unmanageability in physical, emotional, and *spiritual* aspects of your life
- Describe one event in your recovery following abstinence when someone attempted to intervene on your "insane" thinking or behavior that you failed to accept. Describe the outcome of your denial
- Describe, in simple terms, the power greater than yourself, that you used in completing the Second Step

~ Task 5 ~

List the threats to your personal or recovery safety and describe your plan for remaining safe:

If you are in any personal danger or fear that there are imminent threats to your sobriety, develop a plan with your therapist or sponsor or intimate family member that will diminish or eliminate the perceived or real threat.

If you are recovering from a love or sex *addiction* you should consider contacts from prospective relapse partners to be an imminent threat to your sobriety. An invitation to a holiday event where food is going to be the central focus could pose serious threats to your efforts to maintain a sober food plan if you are a recovering food addict. The acceptance of a prescription for potentially addictive pain medication following a surgery can represent a clear and present danger for individuals recovering from a substance *addiction*. The list of possible examples is endless as would be the plans needed to diminish or eliminate the threats associated with them. It is safe to assume that you need a plan for addressing all threats seen by you or those who love you.

Course Lesson 2.1 - Stabilizing Plan for Recovery Following Relapse (Continued)

~ Task 6 ~

List the behaviors you display or the perception that others have of you that has generated the concern about your potential for dangerousness to yourself or others and what you plan to do or have done about them:

If you or any one else is concerned about your potential for dangerousness to yourself or others, make arrangements to get an immediate medical evaluation by going to the nearest hospital emergency room or calling emergency response centers such as 911 in the USA or your local hospital emergency room. Here are some indicators of the need for immediate evaluation:

- verbal intimidation or threatening comments issued with the intent to instill fear in others
- statements of intent to harm self
- statements of intent to harm another
- any deliberate attempt to damage or destroy work or personal property
- difficulty de-escalating emotions following a disagreement or conflict
- poor behavioral control due to frequent drug or alcohol use
- impaired judgment
- pre-occupation with incidents of violence
- pre-occupation with weapons (especially firearms with high lethality capabilities)
- giving away valued treasures and keepsakes to others
- legal history or workplace history of assaultive or combative behaviors

Place a check alongside every item that applies to you on this page and copy the items checked onto your list of behaviors on Task 6 of the Course Assignment on page 27. Additionally, describe what your plan is for addressing the concerns.

~ Task 7 ~

List any threats to your sobriety that are related to your economic health and how you plan to address these problems:

Review your income and expenses to establish a clear and honest picture of your financial status in order to develop a plan for creating economic stability. We are not talking about a fear of economic security; we are talking about actual economic instability. If your expenses exceed your income and there are not long-term cash reserves available to you, steps must be taken to close the gap by either reducing your expenses, increasing your income, or securing economic support from others. The stress associated with attempting to live beyond your income is sure to threaten your sobriety and make any plans for relapse prevention difficult.

Course Lesson 2.1 - Stabilizing Plan for Recovery Following Relapse (Continued)

~ Task 8 ~

List the meetings or people to whom you need to disclose your relapse:

If you are returning from a relapse it is critical that you draw from the support and acceptance of your fellow recovering addicts. If you conceal your relapse from members of your local recovery community, your secrets will eventually make it impossible for you to receive that support. It is difficult to imagine that others are genuinely accepting of us when we are not presenting the truth.

~ Task 9 ~

Take a quick inventory of the degree to which your relapse may have threatened your job security and what steps you will take to address these problems:

Discuss your current employment situation with your therapist and/or trusted member of your support system to determine whether or not your relapse or the associated behaviors have compromised your employment standing in any way. It is common to learn, after the fact, that our job performance has been negatively affected by the behavior associated with a phase in the relapse process. Examine your situation closely with your therapist or close family member to be clear about any immediate threat to your current employment and develop a plan for minimizing the damage or prevent future consequences. Do not confuse this stabilization task with Ninth Step amends.

The Eight and Ninth Steps are intended to focus your attention on the amends that are needed from you to all the people or institutions you have harmed during the course of your active *addiction*. Task 9 is asking you to determine if any immediate corrective action is needed to address threats to your job security. For example, if your *addiction* has left you unproductive at work and/or caused injury for your employer it may be wise to conduct a quick inventory of your wrongs that you can address in a timely fashion along with corrective measures. It may not be wise to wait until you get to your formal Ninth Step. This stop-gap amends effort, while not a complete Ninth Step, could make potential disciplinary measures that are being considered behind the scenes, unnecessary.

~ Task 10 ~

List any legal problems that developed during, or as a result of, your relapse and how you plan to address these problems:

If there have been any civil or criminal behaviors prior to your return to sobriety, secure legal counsel. The stress associated with the threat of legal consequences looming on the horizon will make it difficult to focus your mind and spirit on your recovery.

Course Assignment 2.1 - Stabilizing Plan for Recovery Following Relapse

Please complete the following tasks and review the results with your therapist or members of your support group. If you have not been able to establish and maintain abstinence for more than 10 days you might consider seeking more personalized and or intense treatment for your *addiction*.

When you have completed the tasks for this assignment proceed to page 42.

IMPORTANT:

If you find that you need more space please feel free to continue the writing on a separate piece of paper.

~ Task 1 ~

Describe any health problems that resulted from your relapse or may have occurred during your relapse process and how you plan to address them:

_____

_____

_____

_____

_____

~ Task 2 ~

What steps will you take to develop or enhance the breadth and depth of your support system or make better use of the support you currently have:

_____

_____

_____

_____

_____

Course Assignment 2.1 - Stabilizing Plan for Recovery Following Relapse (Continued)

~ Task 3 ~

How do you plan to make regular attendance at Twelve Step oriented recovery meetings your number one priority:

___

~ Task 4 ~

Describe your plan for completing the first three steps of the Twelve Step program as quickly as possible. If you have already completed Steps One through Three describe what you learned about yourself, your relapse, and/or how the insights gained may help you to prevent a relapse in the future:

___

Course Assignment 2.1 - Stabilizing Plan for Recovery Following Relapse (Continued)

~ Task 5 ~

List any threats to your personal or recovery safety and describe your plan for remaining safe:

_____

_____

_____

_____

_____

_____

~ Task 6 ~

List the behaviors you display or the perception that others have of you that have generated the concern about your potential for dangerousness to yourself or others and what you plan to do or have done about them:

_____

_____

_____

_____

_____

_____

Course Assignment 2.1 - Stabilizing Plan for Recovery Following Relapse (Continued)

~ Task 7 ~

List any threats to your sobriety that are related to your economic health and how you plan to address these problems:

___

___

___

___

___

___

___

~ Task 8 ~

List the meetings or people to whom you need to disclose your relapse:

___

___

___

___

___

___

___

Course Assignment 2.1 - Stabilizing Plan for Recovery Following Relapse (Continued)

~ Task 9 ~

Take a quick inventory of the degree to which your relapse may have threatened your job security and what steps you will take to address these problems:

_____

_____

_____

_____

_____

_____

_____

_____

~ Task 10 ~

List any legal problems that developed during or as a result of your relapse and how you plan to address these problems:

_____

_____

_____

_____

_____

_____

_____

Course Lesson 2.2 - Formula for a Stable Recovery Foundation for Beginners

The following tasks should be reviewed and addressed in your Stable Recovery Foundation for Beginners. The Tasks to be addressed on the plan are listed below for your review.

IMPORTANT:

The following descriptions of the various tasks in this lesson are presented to introduce you to the actual written work you will complete in the Course Assignment that follows this lesson. Do not write anything until you reach the assignment.

When you have completed the lesson be sure to share your findings with members of your support system and your therapist if you are working with one.

~ Task 1 ~

How do you plan to make regular attendance at Twelve Step oriented recovery meetings your number one priority? List the Twelve Step meetings you plan to attend and describe the recovery activities you plan to engage in:

Attend a minimum of one Twelve Step meeting a day for the first 90 days in addition to other recovery activities. If that is impossible then every day should include either a Twelve Step meeting or a recovery activity but never less than four meetings per week for 90 days (multiple meetings in one day are not a substitute for the expectation that you attend at least one meeting per day for four days).

List the Twelve Step meetings you plan to attend and the recovery activities you plan to engage in.

~ Task 2 ~

What steps will you take to develop the breadth and depth of your support system or make better use of the support you currently have:

In the early days of recovery it is easy to become preoccupied with repairing all the damage done at once. Go slowly and first make your recovery and development of a support system a priority. Attend a minimum of one Twelve Step meeting a day for the first 90 days in addition to other recovery activities. In the beginning it is safer to schedule your life around your meeting schedule than it is to try and fit meetings into your life schedule.

Keep in mind that there may have been other victims of the *addiction* who need attention as much as you do. Many newcomers will find daily meeting attendance a challenge when their loved ones express dissatisfaction with the time that it is taking away from contact with them and the needs of the family. Many a spouse has begun to sound like a *Twelve Step widow or widower* when the meeting and fellowship time appears to be creating as much deprivation as the behaviors associated with active *addiction* did. The time you spend in meetings and around the fellowship is most necessary but balance, even in the early days of recovery, is also quite

Course Lesson 2.2 - Formula for a Stable Recovery Foundation for Beginners (Continued)

important. Many recovering addicts will find such warmth and acceptance in the Twelve Step rooms that home seems to be unfamiliar and at times an unwelcoming place. You will find that you can create balance between home, family, work, and recovery if you put recovery first without hiding in the fellowship.

A meeting a day can take one to two hours, including traveling time, but it does not require three to five hours out of your day or evening. It is not unusual to discover that the extra time spent at meetings and other fellowship experiences is driven by a desire to avoid the discomforts associated with home and family that many face in the early days of sobriety. Many an active addict has found himself or herself so absorbed in the pursuit of their *drug of choice* that the tasks associated with living have been long ignored and assumed by others. Sobriety should include efforts to take a responsible place in the family and romantic relationship. Tasks should not be ignored and fractured romantic and family relationships should not be avoided. There might not be much that you can do in the beginning but your avoidance will probably make everything that you have done worse. You can be purposefully involved in the fellowship every day without it requiring all of your free time.

Your recovery support system is an integral part of a healthy recovery process. The core of your support system could be a sponsor but should not be restricted to just one person. It is wise to have several people from the Twelve Step fellowship you are involved with in your support system. The role of a support group member or sponsor is to share experience, strength, and hope with you regarding how they have managed to develop a sober life-style for themselves. It is advisable to stay in regular contact with members of your support system even if you do not find yourself in emotional need. Frequent contact will make it easier for you to reach out to them should the time come that you do need help. Just as in active *addiction*, the development of rituals and habits helps to ensure that we engage in the behaviors that the rituals are built around. When we practice reaching out we will be able to reach out when we need help.

It is also important to work steadily at enhancing the depth of your relationships with them because the *antecedents* to a given trigger or point of discomfort often have their roots in past *traumatic experiences*. It will be valuable to you to invite the members of your support system into the deeper recesses of your life story as it will enable them to help you to identify when you are likely to become ensnared in emotional traps in recovery.

Describe the actions you plan to take to develop the breadth and depth of your support system.

Course Lesson 2.2 - Formula for a Stable Recovery Foundation for Beginners (Continued)

~ Task 3 ~

Secure a medical evaluation of your physical health and follow directions to address any physical problems that may have developed as a result of your active addiction or that have been ignored because of impairment to your reason, logic, and judgment. Describe any health problems you are having and what your plan is for addressing them:

It can be emotionally challenging to confide in your physician about the exact nature of your *addiction* because many of our stories can have really dark chapters that we might want to keep secret. If you are not comfortable with a candid discussion with your family doctor than secure a consultation with another physician that you can tell the whole story to. If your doctor is someone you can trust but you find him or her struggling with your self-diagnosis, do not dismiss the reaction you are experiencing. It may be ignorance or denial of his or her identification with your story. Encourage your physician to speak with your therapist or secure professional consultation on the matter. Do not make the reaction that your physician experiences your fault or their resolution of conflict your responsibility.

Be cautious about taking any potentially addictive medications. It is wise to check out your medication protocol with a physician certified by the American Society of Addiction Medicine. In the days or months prior to the start of your recovery you may have developed health problems or concerns that have been ignored. Threats to your physical health will have a negative impact on your overall sense of well-being and should be addressed before they create lasting consequences or chronic conditions. Developing a plan for addressing your overall physical health as well as specific health concerns will play an important role in the development of a solid foundation for your recovery.

Establishing and maintaining a plan to promote your physical well-being and overall fitness will be an invaluable recovery tool. Make sure that your physician approves your plan and that your plan does not become compulsive in nature. Your fitness program should not interfere with your attendance at meetings, therapy, work and family obligations, or completely dominate your free or recreational time.

Describe any health problems that you are having and what your plan is for addressing them.

~ Task 4 ~

List any addictive behaviors or processes that you or anyone has ever had concern about and describe what your plan is for addressing those concerns:

Even if you have decided not to begin this work with a therapist secure the consultation of an addiction therapist who is knowledgeable about the treatment of multiple addictions to assess whether or not your recovery efforts related to the addiction you are currently treating are being compromised by other addictions. It is common in our ranks to find men and women who

Course Lesson 2.2 - Formula for a Stable Recovery Foundation for Beginners (Continued)

struggle for years with a pattern of chronic relapse who are suffering with multiple *addictions* that are confounding the recovery efforts of the *addiction* that they initially thought was their only problem. If you are just now entering recovery for the first time, it would be wise to secure an evaluation to assess the potential that exists for you to become cross-addicted to other addictive substances or processes, or to determine if you are currently suffering with multiple *addictions* that you have been unaware of or have failed to address.

We encourage you to secure the services of a knowledgeable *addiction* treatment professional with extensive experience in treating primary *addictions* and has a working knowledge of the Twelve Steps and how to integrate them into your therapy work.

Additionally, do not hesitate to consult with your family physician or a psychiatrist if you have a history of emotional problems unrelated to *addiction*. In much the same way that we can suffer with co-occurring disorders such as depression and alcoholism we can develop treatment plans to address multiple problems at the same time.

In this task you are being asked to list any addictive behaviors or addictive processes that you or anyone has ever had concern about for you and describe what your plan is for addressing those concerns.

~ Task 5 ~

Alert your loved ones who are knowledgeable of the symptoms of your addiction that you are developing a plan for remaining sober and share it with them if they are willing to receive it from you. Who do you plan to discuss your recovery plan with and why:

If you believe that your loved ones have been negatively impacted by the progression of your *addiction* or believe that they would like to serve in a supportive role in your recovery, it would be thoughtful to advise them of your commitment to develop a recovery plan that focuses on relapse prevention as a method for building a solid foundation. When you have completed your Personal Recovery Plan in Section 6 of this course it would be wise to review it with your spouse, romantic partner, or close family member in the presence of your therapist if you have one. If you intend to review your plan with a loved one then consider securing the services of a knowledgeable *addictions* therapist to help guide the process. There are circumstances in which it would not be wise for you to open up fully to those you love about the nature of your progression in *addiction* or the challenges that you are experiencing or anticipate in recovery. A thorough review of all the possible exceptions to this task is outside the scope of this course. It is always wise to get professional counsel in these matters if you have any doubt about the appropriateness of the suggested task for you. If you need assistance and would like to contact us, please feel free to do so by going to our website at www.leademcounseling.com.

If your loved ones have any interest in gaining more personal information about the nature or purpose of the Personal Relapse Prevention Plan that you are developing, encourage them to participate in a joint session with you and your therapist so the components can be explored in greater detail. Additionally, secure contact information for them about how they can find support for themselves in the *Anon* group that matches your Twelve Step fellowship and encourage them

Course Lesson 2.2 - Formula for a Stable Recovery Foundation for Beginners (Continued)

to secure therapy from a licensed professional with an in-depth background in the treatment of addicted people and their families.

Who do you plan to discuss your recovery plan with and why?

~ Task 6 ~

Complete Step One as quickly as possible and share your findings with your therapist and support group members. Describe what plan you intend to use to complete your First Step and how you intend to process your findings with your therapist and support group members:

While most Twelve Step programs promote the notion that no one is capable of maintaining perfect adherence to all of the *spiritual* principles found in the Twelve Steps, all agree that the first step must be done absolutely. The decision that each one of us has made to admit personal powerlessness over our *drug of choice* and that we have made an acknowledgement that our lives have become unmanageable as a result of that powerlessness are two critical steps in the recovery process. Without a clear and absolute understanding of the powerlessness and unmanageability there will be no lasting change and most likely frequent relapses.

Describe what plan you intend to use to complete your First Step and how you intend to process your findings with your therapist and support group members.

~ Task 7 ~

Establish an immediate plan for your personal and recovery safety that you review with your support group and at least one member of your family. List the threats to your personal or recovery safety and describe your plan for remaining safe:

It can be very difficult if not impossible to give the needed attention to the development of your Personal Relapse Prevention Plan if you are not feeling safe. The plan for establishing and maintaining your personal safety at physical, environmental, and psychological levels can become very challenging. Take time with your therapist, sponsor, or trusted family member to examine the real and present threats to your safety. You need to be free of danger (safe) to undergo the emotional and *spiritual* changes that recovery demands.

List the threats to your personal or recovery safety and describe your plan for remaining safe.

Course Lesson 2.2 - Formula for a Stable Recovery Foundation for Beginners (Continued)

~ Task 8 ~

List the behaviors you display or the perception that others have of you that has generated the concern about your potential for dangerousness to yourself or others and what you plan to do or have done about them:

If you or any one else is concerned about your potential for dangerousness to yourself or others, make arrangements to get an immediate medical evaluation by going to the nearest hospital emergency room or calling emergency response centers such as 911 in the USA or your local hospital emergency room. Here are some indicators of the need for immediate evaluation:

- recent or present thoughts of wishing you were dead or wanting to kill yourself
- verbal intimidation or threatening comments issued with the intent to instill fear in others
- statements of intent to harm self
- statements of intent to harm another
- any deliberate attempt to damage or destroy work property
- difficulty de-escalating emotions following a disagreement or conflict
- poor behavioral control due to frequent *drug* or alcohol use
- impaired judgment
- pre-occupation with incidents of violence
- pre-occupation with weapons (especially firearms with high lethality capabilities)
- giving away valued treasures and keepsakes to others
- legal history or workplace history of assaultive or combative behaviors

Place a check alongside every item that applies to you on this page and copy the items checked onto your list of behaviors on Task 8 of the Course Assignment on page 40. Additionally, describe what your plan is for addressing the concerns.

~ Task 9 ~

Accept professional guidance to define and undertake steps to secure your current employment if it has been threatened by your addiction. Avoid making your employment or sense of economic security a priority over your recovery. Describe your concerns regarding job or economic security and what your plan is for addressing it:

Discuss your current employment situation with your therapist and/or trusted member of your support system to determine whether or not your *addiction* associated behaviors have compromised your standing in any way. It is common to learn, after the fact, that our job performance has been negatively affected by the behavior associated with a phase in the relapse process. Examine your situation closely with your therapist or close family member to be clear about any immediate threat to your current employment and develop a plan for minimizing the damage or prevent future consequences. Do not confuse this stabilization task with a Ninth Step amends or even a Tenth Step.

The Eighth and Ninth Steps are intended to focus your attention on the amends that are needed from you to all the people or institutions you have harmed during the course of your

Course Lesson 2.2 - Formula for a Stable Recovery Foundation for Beginners (Continued)

active *addiction*. Task 9 is asking you to determine if any immediate corrective action is needed to address threats to your job security. For example, if your *addiction* has left you unproductive at work and/or caused injury for your employer it may be wise to conduct a quick inventory of your wrongs that you can address in a timely fashion along with corrective measures. It may not be wise to wait until you get to your formal Ninth Step. This stop-gap amends effort, while not a complete Ninth Step, could make potential disciplinary measures that are being considered behind the scenes, unnecessary.

It is common in early recovery to look around at the functional areas of our lives and identify that we have really short changed our employers in the course of our disease's progression or that there are economic consequences that we imagine would be quickly remedied if we were to burn the midnight oil at work. Unless there is imminent job jeopardy, avoid making your work and economic recovery the priority. Your priority needs to be developing and maintaining a sober life-style and that will take time.

You will hear, in time, references to the *promises* of recovery as introduced in the recovery text *Alcoholics Anonymous*. One of the *promises* that attracts a lot of attention for newcomers is the promise that the "fear of economic insecurity will leave us." In the early days our fear of economic insecurity can generate wide and depressive mood swings. While it is important to intervene on depressive moods and maintain overall emotional balance, it is not advised to make your net worth ledger sheet the priority. Review your income and expenses to establish a clear and honest picture of your financial status in order to develop a plan for creating economic stability. We are not talking about a fear of economic security; we are talking about actual economic instability. If your expenses exceed your income or your long-term cash reserves, steps must be taken to close the gap by either reducing your expenses, increasing your income, or securing the economic support from others. The stress associated with attempting to live outside of your means is sure to threaten your sobriety and make any plans for relapse prevention difficult.

Describe your concerns regarding job or economic security and what your plan is for addressing it.

~ Task 10 ~

Obtain legal counsel if there are any real or potential legal consequences of your active addiction and take immediate steps to terminate any behaviors that might cause you legal consequence. Identify the legal concerns that you have and what your plan is for addressing them:

Secure legal counsel if there have been any civil or criminal behaviors prior to your return to sobriety. The stress associated with the threat of legal consequences looming on the horizon will make it difficult to focus your mind and spirit on your recovery.

Identify the legal concerns that you have and what your plan is for addressing them.

Course Assignment 2.2 - Formula for a Stable Recovery Foundation for Beginners

Please complete the following tasks and review the results with your therapist or members of your support group. If you have not been able to establish and maintain abstinence for more than 10 days you might consider seeking more personalized and/or intense treatment for your *addiction*.

IMPORTANT:

If you find that you need more space please feel free to continue the writing on a separate piece of paper.

~ Task 1 ~

How do you plan to make regular attendance at Twelve Step oriented recovery meetings your number one priority? List the Twelve Step meetings you plan to attend and describe the recovery activities you plan to engage in:

_____

_____

_____

_____

_____

~ Task 2 ~

What steps will you take to develop or enhance the breadth and depth of your support system or make better use of the support you currently have:

_____

_____

_____

_____

Course Assignment 2.2 - Formula for a Stable Recovery Foundation for Beginners (Continued)

~ Task 3 ~

Secure a medical evaluation of your physical health and follow directions to address any physical problems that may have developed as a result of your active addiction or that have been ignored because of impairment to your reason, logic, and judgment. Describe any health problems you are having and what your plan is for addressing them:

_____

_____

_____

_____

_____

~ Task 4 ~

List any addictive behaviors or processes that you or anyone has ever had concern about and describe what your plan is for addressing those concerns:

_____

_____

_____

_____

_____

_____

Course Assignment 2.2 - Formula for a Stable Recovery Foundation for Beginners (Continued)

~ Task 5 ~

Alert your loved ones who are knowledgeable of the symptoms of your addiction that you are developing a plan for remaining sober and share it with them if they are willing to receive it from you. Who do you plan to discuss your recovery plan with and why:

_____

_____

_____

_____

_____

~ Task 6 ~

Complete Step One as quickly as possible and share your findings with your therapist and support group members. Describe what plan you intend to use to complete your First Step and how you intend to process your findings with your therapist and support group members:

_____

_____

_____

_____

_____

Course Assignment 2.2 - Formula for a Stable Recovery Foundation for Beginners (Continued)

~ Task 7 ~

Establish an immediate plan for your personal and recovery safety that you review with your support group and at least one member of your family. List the threats to your personal or recovery safety and describe your plan for remaining safe:

_____

_____

_____

_____

_____

_____

_____

~ Task 8 ~

List the behaviors you display or the perception that others have of you that has generated the concern about your potential for dangerousness to yourself or others and what you plan to do or have done about them:

_____

_____

_____

_____

_____

_____

_____

Course Assignment 2.2 - Formula for a Stable Recovery Foundation for Beginners (Continued)

~ Task 9 ~

Accept professional guidance to define and undertake steps to secure your current employment if it has been threatened by your addiction. Avoid making your employment or sense of economic security a priority over your recovery. Describe your concerns regarding job or economic security and what your plan is for addressing it:

_____

_____

_____

_____

_____

_____

~ Task 10 ~

Obtain legal counsel if there are any real or potential legal consequences of your active addiction and take immediate steps to terminate any behaviors that might cause you legal consequence. Identify the legal concerns that you have and what your plan is for addressing them:

_____

_____

_____

_____

_____

Getting sober in an unsympathetic or unsupportive environment

Your planning efforts for stablizing your recovery must always consider the environment that you are getting sober in because the level of support available to you may have a negative or positive impact on how you meet the challenges of early recovery. Please do not mistake this caution or the recommendations below to mean that you can only get and maintain sobriety in the most optimal environment for you. We can and do get and maintain sobriety in the worst and best of times, places, and circumstances.

The physical, emotional, and *spiritual* challenges endured by those we love and are emotionally engaged with are usually quite significant. It may take some time to address the fractured structure of our relationships. Some might never heal and that is tragic, but many seemingly lost relationships have been mended in the course of recovery for countless others before you. However, every relapse into active *addiction* reduces the likelihood of healing and reconciliation. The swath of the *addiction's* destruction can be wide and deep, and a declaration of abstinence and a promise to change is not necessarily going to alter the minds and the hearts of the people who have shared in your tragic unmanageability of body, mind, and spirit. The environment that you are getting sober in may not be supportive or safe for you in the early days. If you believe that you are trying to get sober in an unsympathetic or unsupportive environment consider the following when you are developing your stabilization plan:

- If your family and friends have withdrawn from you, do not force yourself on them, as you are likely to threaten their security and people can behave poorly when they feel threatened.
- If your current living environment includes other active addicts, consider a temporary change in your living arrangements until you are stable, especially if the other parties involved are unwilling to abstain from their addictive behavior after you have presented your request.
- Secure help from members of your support group to establish a *clean house*. It is usually safer to keep all prospective *drugs of choice* outside of your living environment. We understand that you can easily leave the home to secure your *drug of choice* but your immediate surroundings should be free of opportunities to relapse if possible.
- Be careful not to remain in an environment that you find physically threatening. It is wise to secure a *safe house* prior to a time that you might need it. If there is a threat of physical abuse or anyone is behaving in a way that you find dangerous to them or others – get safe and call the police.
- If someone in your inner circle of family or friends begins to inquire about your recovery behaviors invite him or her to attend a therapy session with you. You can also provide him or her with the contacts he or she will need in order to obtain information about your *addiction* or help for his or her problems from a professional who is experienced in the treatment of *addiction* as a primary illness and who has a working knowledge of the Twelve Steps.

While the environment that you are restarting or initiating your recovery in may not be supportive at the moment, it can change. The people in your life may have no reason to trust you, your commitment to recovery, or the changes you are making at the present time but they are likely to feel differently in the weeks and months to come. Some relationships may never heal but we have found that more times than not, the emotional, behavioral, and *spiritual* changes that we make in our recovery have become a source of attraction to those who had previously lost trust in us. Consider the following points regarding the benefit of developing yourself as a source of attraction rather than attempting to promote others to take a risk with you.

Attraction – rather than promotion

Your peace of mind may be challenged by the distress you feel in the relationships with people that you care for. While it may be true that the progression of your *addiction* has generated great consequences in the lives of others, it is not in your power to fix them. Your changed behavior will help them to feel less threatened and that, in and of itself, can promote healing. In time you are likely to have opportunities to point those you love in the direction of help. Do not try to impose your help on them for, unless they have complete trust in you, it is likely to backfire. You, however, may be able to inspire them to seek help. Recovery wisdom supports the potential benefit to be derived from becoming a source of *attraction rather than promotion*. Implementation of the following points may cause those close to you to be attracted to your program for *sober living*:

- Sustained abstinence from your *drug of choice* will help to reduce the threat level perceived by those around you
- Make the changes necessary in your schedule to enable you to be dependable
- Your commitment to bring the results of your step work into your daily life and personal relationships will show others that change is possible in all areas of your life
- Demonstrate your acceptance of the full and total responsibility for the quality of your own life
- Always treat your loved ones with the same dignity and respect that you would a newcomer to your Twelve Step group

Section 3

The Anatomy of Relapse

Introduction

In Section 1 of this course we provided you with an overview of the course and introduced the importance of understanding relapse as a process rather than an event. The plans for stabilizing your recovery before proceeding with an analysis of the progressive nature of relapse was encouraged in order for you to form a solid foundation from which to conduct the introspective work that this section asks of you.

Section 3 will help you to understand and analyze the path that a recovering addict takes to a relapse and expose each of the phases in the process to a detailed examination for you to review. The model you will be using to develop your Personalized Relapse Prevention Plan in Section 6 has evolved from our core professional belief that relapse, as a process, can be prevented if identified and intervened on early enough.

Make sure that you take your time as you move through this section because the information obtained and the self-awareness acquired is vital to the successful completion of your Personal Relapse Prevention Plan.

It is also important for you to remain emotionally supported as you undertake the lessons and complete the assignments because a good deal of the material is likely to stir up a wide variety of stressful emotions. It is especially important to stay in close contact with your support system as you are moving through the course if you chose to undertake the work without the benefit of a knowledgeable *addictions* therapist. If at any time you find yourself becoming depressed or feeling overwhelmed by the material STOP your work and consult with your support network or obtain professional input about the wisdom of your moving forward without a therapist.

What to Expect from the Following Chapters:

- Provide you with a general introduction to each of the seven phases in the relapse process in order to better understand how they are relate to each other

- Present an in-depth examination of how each of the phases in the process might impact an addict struggling to maintain a stable recovery program

- Contain Concept Lessons, Course Lessons, and Course Assignments that present conceptual as well as practical information to help you personalize your understanding of the challenges found in each of the phases of relapse

---

Understanding relapse as a process

A relapse into active *addiction* is a preventable syndrome and not a predictable aspect of recovery. Proponents of the position that relapse is a common phenomenon in the recovery process from *addiction* would have you believe that relapses are expected and that most people recovering from an addictive illness will "fall short" of "perfection" from time to time. Some supporters of this idea are quick to reference the "program" as teaching that we cannot expect perfection. The original Twelve Step recovery text *Alcoholics Anonymous*, when referring to the challenges of working the Twelve Steps, would appear, on first glance, to support the notion of understandable relapses in the following position:

> "No one among us has been able to maintain anything like perfect adherence to these principles. We are not saints. ... The principles we have set down are guides to progress. We claim spiritual progress rather than spiritual perfection" (p. 60).

On the surface it would seem that the encouragement to aim for *spiritual* progress rather than *spiritual* perfection supports the idea that relapse just happens. While we believe that relapse can happen when one has not developed sufficient emotional and *spiritual* tools for coping with life's challenges, we do not believe that it should be expected or that one should reserve his or her right to "fall" from time to time. We do not believe that the program supports the eventuality of relapse, just the opposite. The author of *Alcoholics Anonymous* cautions that: "If we are planning to stop *drinking*, there must be no reservation of any kind, nor any lurking notion that someday we will be immune to alcohol" (p. 33).

It is true that none of us is perfect. We are not suggesting otherwise. However, our abstinence must be perfect. The First Step must be taken without reservation or qualification. If you reserve the right to relapse, then you will. There are many challenges in life that were once answered with an addictive substance or behavior but that can and will change if we are willing to go to any lengths to achieve and maintain sobriety. A particular path that one follows to a relapse may have highly individualized trigger points and each person's life can introduce seemingly unique challenges. The path to *sober living* is clearly marked in the Twelve Steps. We have prepared this guide to enable you to plot the specific course you might follow to a relapse so you can prevent it. Relapse is preventable. While there is no one path to avoid, there are predictable phases that we pass through before we reach the decision to resign (not lose) our sobriety and choose to relapse.

This chapter will serve as an introduction to the seven phases in the relapse process through brief descriptions of each phase followed by a graphic flow chart of the relapse process for you to refer to later in your individual planning work.

Phases of relapse – highlights

In this guide the phases of relapse are presented to reflect both a progressive as well as an inter-reactive process. First, the model holds that an individual's movement through the relapse process is progressive in nature and will always result in a return to active *addiction* if it is not interrupted. The second defining feature is that behaviors and experiences associated with any of the phases can trigger the symptoms of any of the other phases. By way of example consider the following inter-reactive scenario:

> John is terminated from his job and is angry and feels rejected (Phase – Uncomfortable Feelings)
>
> He denies any concern when questioned by his colleagues and claims he was looking for a change anyway (Phase – Fragmentation)
>
> His dishonesty with colleagues leaves him feeling rejected and alone because he is on his own again just like when he was a kid (Phase – Time Travel)
>
> He drives past a bar he used to frequent on his way home before he got sober and thinks to himself "maybe no one will blame me if I *drink*" (Phase – Gathering Justification)
>
> He is greeted by his wife at the door who is in tears about her fear of their financial security. John gets angry at himself for causing her pain and feels like the "loser that my father said I was" (Phases – Uncomfortable Feelings & Time Travel) and concludes that his wife is like all the rest of them and only cares about herself (Phases – Time Travel & Gathering Justification)
>
> He tells his wife that he will take care of everything and that there is nothing for her to worry about and covers up the hurt he is feeling (Phase – Fragmentation) but secretly believes that no one understands him (Phase – Gathering Justification) and besides she does not care about him any more than his sponsor does who never seemed to understand how difficult his boss was (Phase – Eliminating the Witnesses)
>
> He thinks to himself that he is going to start going to the gym on Tuesday night (his home-group meeting night) to play ball with his high school buddies (Phase – Eliminating the Witnesses) by cutting off his home-group contacts
>
> He blows off his commitment to take a sponsee to a meeting and plans to meet up with his friends for an hour or two of basketball followed by steak sandwiches at the bar next to the gym (Phases – Eliminating the Witnesses & Dry Drunk)

The above scenario occurs in under two hours. In that short period of time John has moved in and out of every phase in the relapse process except an actual relapse. Hopefully John will arrive home with his sobriety intact. If he wakes up sober he will start the day with all of the emotional discomfort of the previous day. It is likely that he will wake up in some phase of the relapse process.

Relapse is understood by many recovering people to be a progressive process despite the claims by some that they had no indication that they were "in trouble" and that they were "struck" with a compulsion to use addictive substances or engage in addictive behavior, and they relapsed without provocation or warning. The progressive process generates increasingly greater consequences in the form of physical, emotional, and *spiritual* costs that build during one phase and seem to flow into the next like a tsunami before it crashes on land. The phases can progress rapidly or gradually from emotional discomfort to relapse once time travel has begun.

At other times or in other sufferers, the phases appear to react to each other in a way that resembles a funnel cloud as it whirls at great speeds collecting debris and wreaking havoc. The interactive nature of the phases generally is not as easy to identify until the relapse has occurred and you are surveying the damage from the rear view mirror.

Please refer to Concept Lesson 3.1 - The Path of Relapse: A Progressive Process, for a flow chart depicting the anatomy of the relapse process that begins with uncomfortable feelings as you review the summaries noted below that introduce you to each phase of relapse.

Uncomfortable Feelings

The presence of uncomfortable feelings does not signal a relapse but you will not have a relapse without them. We know this to be true because we relapse with a design on changing the way we feel. Since every addicted person has learned to alter their feelings with addictive substances or behaviors, relapse prevention will require that alternative ways of coping with emotional challenges be learned and practiced. Uncomfortable feelings can trigger time travel regardless of the individual's tenure in recovery or emotional and *spiritual* well-being. Uncomfortable feelings that are not anesthetized will "wake up" other uncomfortable feeling memories.

Time Travel

Our feeling memories of the past can flood our current reality and make it difficult for us to maintain objectivity about what we are experiencing in the moment. Time travel can be triggered by a vast number of variables such as illness, emotional intimacy, and threatening events, to name a few.

Fragmentation

When the ways that we Think, Feel, Speak, and Act do not match up we are fragmented because we present a distorted picture of who we are and what we are trying to communicate. The act of maintaining an openness, which allows selected others to see who we really are, can be one of the greatest challenges in recovery from an addictive illness. When my insides match my outsides I am on my way to overcoming fragmentation.

Gathering Justification

No one really relapses because it seemed like "the thing to do at the time". Everyone who relapses must find a way to make it OK. The justification, real or imagined, must be established to return to active *addiction*. In the course of gathering the justification we start putting emotional distance between us and other people.

Eliminating the Witnesses

First, we push people away to avoid the pain of seeing ourselves the way that others see us. Before long, a sense of isolation develops that threatens our emotional security and increases the attraction that relapse has for us.

Dry Drunk

The *dry drunk* phenomenon represents the level of behavioral, emotional, and *spiritual* toxicity that often leaves observers to suspect that the addicted person has already relapsed.

Relapse

This phase in the relapse process represents the addict's return to active *addiction*. A relapse can stop with a single event or continue for the duration of the addict's life that is far too often terminated prematurely.

Concept Lesson 3.1 - The Path of Relapse – A Progressive Process

Relapse is a preventable syndrome and not an inevitable aspect of recovery! Relapse, as a process will build momentum as it carries physical, emotional and *spiritual* discomfort from one phase to the next. In time all of your relationships will be negatively impacted by the behaviors associated with the relapse process. Your ability to spot yourself in a particular phase will grow with practice and will be greatly enhanced by engaging others in your Personal Relapse Prevention Plan efforts.

If you are not practiced at tracking your mood swings or monitoring your behaviors and the coping strategies that drive them, it might appear that there are no patterns at all. Do not give up. It takes time. You will learn a great deal about what steers the patterns of your life if you continue with this work.

It is also important to remember that you will not always start a relapse process in the Uncomfortable Feelings phase. Those of us who suffer with post traumatic flashbacks or *panic* attacks can appear to go from comfort to severe discomfort with the blink of an eye. A quick review of the spiraling phases of a relapse process is intended to orient you to the common course of relapse and help you to identify when your sobriety might be in jeopardy.

The path of relapse is depicted in the figure below as a cyclical process that begins with emotional discomfort at phase #1 - Uncomfortable Feelings - and progresses to phase #7 - Relapse. In reality we can appear to start at any point in the process and crisscross back and forth between points. In fact, during a Dry Drunk phase, the addict might appear to be operating from many phases at the same time.

John was experiencing a dry drunk in the vignette depicted on page 45. Take a moment to re-read it now. His behaviors appeared to be self-destructive and although there was no odor of alcohol, you would swear he was intoxicated. He was at odds with everyone. The kids were driving him crazy and he felt under-valued at work (Gathering Justification). He rebuffed his wife's concerns because she was a "control freak" who was acting just like his mother (Time Travel). He claimed to want help to get out of the emotional mess he was in but (Fragmentation) dismissed Elaine's encouragement to return to his twelve step meeting because everyone there was "hopelessly addicted to meetings" and "his sponsor was a hypocrite" (Eliminating Witnesses).

Avoid the tendency to view the 7 phases in the spiral as if they were doors that you pass through from one phase to the next. As you learn more about yourself, you will begin to identify when you are in a particular phase. When you find yourself reacting to a situation as if you were 8 years old, you are probably experiencing time travel. Whenever you identify yourself as being at one of the points on the spiral, begin to ask yourself and others if the symptoms of any of the other phases are posing threats to your recovery.

The symptoms of each of the phases in the relapse process will be explored in depth in the upcoming chapters.

The seven phases in the relapse process are depicted in the cycle on the next page. Important features of each phase are listed in the center and are numbered according to the phase they describe.

Concept Lesson 3.1 - The Path of Relapse – A Progressive Process (Continued)

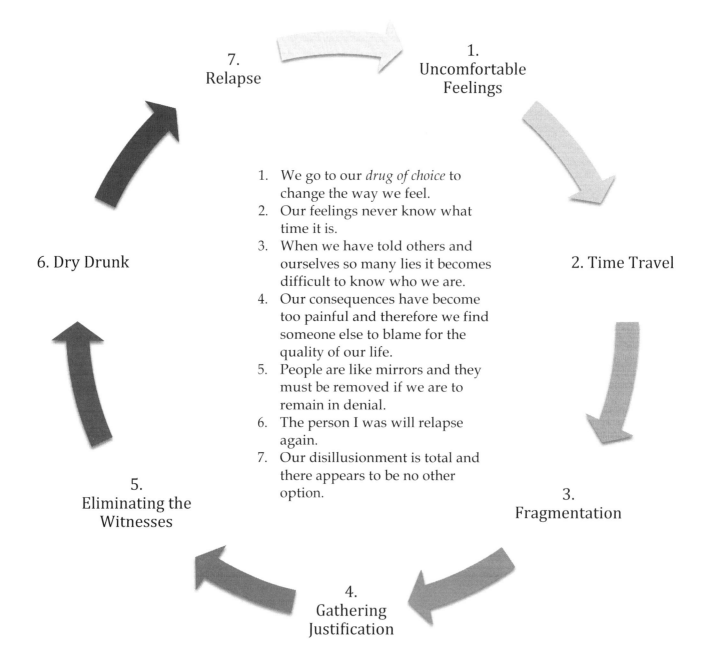

1. We go to our *drug of choice* to change the way we feel.
2. Our feelings never know what time it is.
3. When we have told others and ourselves so many lies it becomes difficult to know who we are.
4. Our consequences have become too painful and therefore we find someone else to blame for the quality of our life.
5. People are like mirrors and they must be removed if we are to remain in denial.
6. The person I was will relapse again.
7. Our disillusionment is total and there appears to be no other option.

Phase 1 - Uncomfortable feelings

We do not believe that uncomfortable feelings like anger, fear, or rejection lead to relapse any more than feelings of love, affection, and acceptance. Our feelings have little or no impact on whether or not we remain sober. Certainly we must work to develop our emotional sobriety if we intend to derive the benefits of *sober living* that have been promised in *Alcoholics Anonymous* in pages 83 and 84. So why, you are asking, have the authors placed Uncomfortable Feelings as the title of the first phase in the process of relapse? The answer is really quite simple.

We relapse, in whatever form it takes, in order to change the way we feel and for no other reason! We do not *drink* again or overeat or gamble away the mortgage payment because we are rejected or hurt. We return to our *drug of choice* because we have chosen to not address those and other uncomfortable emotions in healthy ways. When we stuff our feelings, they do not seem to stay put. Pressure of some type begins to build and the thought that "one small indulgence of my *drug of choice* can't hurt" seems to make sense. That build up may take minutes, weeks, or years but eventually an addict will seek relief from the pain of living with all those pent up emotions. It is inevitable that we will have an emotional discharge or collapse, which will move us closer to an actual relapse but it is not necessary.

All addictive substances or addictive behaviors have the potential for physical and/or psychological dependency by virtue of the potential impact that the substance or behavior has for altering our mood or feelings. If an addicted person uses a mood altering substance or engages in an addictive behavior, the choice will be driven by a desire to change the way he or she feels. The addicted person, in the throws of withdrawal, will be driven to the addictive substance or behavior, in varying degrees, by the desire to reduce withdrawal symptoms. One level of withdrawal will generate a mild desire while others will be severe and seemingly impossible to resist. One could argue that the addicted person has no choice in the matter and the disease is making all the decisions, but it is really more complicated than many of the recovery culture's explanations offered such as, "the disease made me do it" or "it was the addict in me" that relapsed.

The negative aspects of withdrawal can generate a strong motivation to continue using the substance or engaging in the addictive behavior, but there is also a drive, powered by our *defects of character*, to change the way we feel when we are uncomfortable, that is contributing to the likelihood that we will relapse. We are a species that has learned to worship at the shrine of the instant cure. Discomfort of any kind is to be eliminated. We are told that certain headache remedies are preferred over others because they are formulated to reduce the suffering associated with nighttime headaches versus those intended for the relief of daytime headaches. Is there really a difference between AM and PM headaches? We are bombarded by advertising campaigns that entice us to purchase their products because the product will enhance the quality of our life. Soap commercials are still warning consumers that if they fail to use Wisk they may suffer the embarrassment of "ring-around-the-collar". It would seem to us that consumers could avoid the shame of a dirty shirt collar if old dirty neck bathed properly.

All kidding aside, it is important to understand that our obsession with the elimination of discomfort might be generating more discomfort than anyone could adequately medicate. We have learned to go to great lengths to escape from pain. We who have suffered the pain of *addiction* have come to understand that many so-called pain relievers only cause more pain. Pain, whether its origin is physical or behavioral, is trying to tell us something. When we tell the doctor that something hurts the symptoms are analyzed as clues to the mystery. The symptoms of physical pain are accepted markers of an underlying problem. Unfortunately, many of us have learned to move quickly away from emotional pain as if it was the problem and an addictive substance or addictive behavior is the solution. Emotional pain is a symptom and not the problem to be removed.

If you consider relapsing it is not likely to be accompanied by an expectation that more pain will come, as is illustrated in Concept Lesson 3.2 - What We Expect from Returning to Our Drug of Choice. Most people who recover from relapse report that the choice to return to their *drug of choice* was preceded by an expectation that they would feel better. This chapter will help you look beyond the simple notion that a relapse decision is merely the product of irrational or deluded thinking. A decision to relapse after a period of sobriety is both irrational and delusional but most people do not make the choice to sabotage their success or to punish themselves as is so often said. Consider the following example:

> Joe's brother and several other family members were mourning the loss of their loved one due to a prescription medication overdose. In their eyes, Joe had it all; a great family, a loving and forgiving wife, a chance to regain his integrity, and was close to a full economic recovery from his bankruptcy. To them Joe just could not handle success! That was his problem. Joe actually had many other problems that he kept secret from everyone for he was sure that no one could ever accept him if they knew the truth.

Relapse is most often reported to be chosen with an expectation of an improved emotional state. However, people who have conducted personal research on the outcome of relapse and lived to tell us about it assure us that it does not generate a sustained emotional state – anything but.

Hindsight affords us the 20/20 clarity to see that what results from relapse is greater discomfort, as illustrated in Concept Lesson 3.3 - What Happens When We Return to Our Drug of Choice? Instead of removing the emotional pain with addictive substances, behaviors, or other distractions, become willing to find out what the pain is trying to tell you. The next two Course Assignments are designed to help you hear what your pain is trying to tell you.

What we expect from returning to our drug of choice

Most people returning from a relapse are usually quick to report that "it has not gotten any better out there," even in the cases where the addict remained active for years before returning to recovery. The authors have never heard reports that support the delusion that a particular *drug of choice* is going to make life pain free. Every single relapse reveals the same reality – it always gets worse and never better no matter what the fantasy perception promises.

The fantasy perception promises that we will feel more powerful and/or less vulnerable. We expect we will be more desirable or more fully alive. The delusion points toward freedom from boredom and relief from depression or anxiety. We expect to socialize more comfortably and speak our minds in eloquent and compelling communication. Have you ever expected more pain or irreparably broken relationships when you launched into the sea of *intoxication*?

Concept Lesson 3.2 - What We Expect from Returning to Our Drug of Choice

This figure illustrates what we expect from our *drug of choice* when we are experiencing uncomfortable feelings and looking for relief. Take, for example, an addicted person who is feeling overly anxious and wants relief because he does not know how to cope with the anxiety. The addict expects the *drug of choice* will bring relaxation, calm, and/or peace of mind. The top left circle "Uncomfortable Feelings" represents the emotional challenges we face that can threaten our *sobriety* depending on how we cope with them. These uncomfortable feelings evolve from uncomfortable circumstances, events, and uncomfortable relationships with people. The bottom left circle represents the object of your addictive illness or *drug of choice*. The larger circle to the right of the arrow (->) symbol represents what we expect to feel as a result of the re-introduction of your *drug of choice*.

It may seem odd to think of positive outcomes but for right now that is exactly what we are asking you to do. Most of you are probably thinking that I cannot imagine ever *drinking* or binging on sweets again because you can readily recall the harms that your *addiction* has caused you and others. The vast majority of relapse sufferers that we have worked with did not relapse with a plan to end up in jails, institutions, or death. But sadly enough we have known many who have suffered such fates.

When people relapse they tend to think "it", whatever "it" is, is going to make things better and it never really works out that way in the long run. So please work with us here and continue to examine the expectations that you or others have when they consider returning to their *drug of choice* in the lesson below.

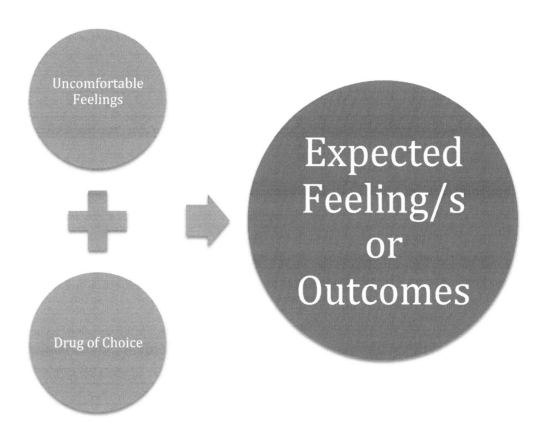

Course Lesson 3.1 - What We Expect from Returning to Our Drug of Choice

In the next Course Assignment you are asked to focus your attention on what you have historically expected from your *drug of choice*. Most of us do not expect painful consequences. We expect to feel more socially comfortable or better able to communicate. We imagine ourselves as being enhanced by the use of a substance or as the result of participation in a behavior. Many of us have the tendency to believe that the *drug of choice* is allowing the real ME to emerge and we are generally surprised when a seemingly positive relationship with a mood altering substance or behavior generates unwanted consequences. The loss of the magical relationship with our *drugs of choice* is a real surprise for many of us and creates a genuine sense of loss and grief, but we will not be examining those dynamics in this lesson. We are not asking you to examine the consequences of a magical relationship that has gone bad. In fact we want you to ignore the negative consequences for the purpose of this assignment.

Focus your attention on an experience during your active *addiction* when you were actively engaged with your *drug of choice* and imagining that your use or *acting out* was going to be a positive experience. Complete the following tasks that you can share with your support group members or therapist.

IMPORTANT:

The following descriptions of the various tasks in this lesson are presented to introduce you to the actual written work you will complete in the Course Assignment that follows this lesson. Do not write anything until you reach the assignment.

When you have completed the lesson be sure to share your findings with members of your support system and your therapist if you are working with one.

~ Task 1 ~

Name uncomfortable or challenging feelings:

Identify a single *using episode* from the past and place all the feelings that you remember or could imagine experiencing before you began using. The use of a mood altering substance or mood altering behavior is always intended to alter our mood. We never engage in a *drug of choice* without some feeling experience that we expect will be improved. It is safe to assume that since mood altering substances or behaviors move us in the direction of euphoria, the feelings we were having before taking a *drink*, overeating or viewing pornography, to name but a few of the options, were necessarily less comfortable than the anticipated outcome.

~ Task 2 ~

Name your drugs of choice:

Use the same episode as identified in Task 1 and indentify the names of your addictive substances or addictive behavioral descriptions. If your *drugs of choice* were substances such as *drugs* or food, describe the quantities consumed, the methods of consumption, and the patterns of use in an effort to create a graphic picture for your therapist or support group to better

Course Lesson 3.1 - What We Expect from Returning to Our Drug of Choice (Continued)

understand you. If your *drugs of choice* were behaviors such as those found in sex and gambling *addictions* describe in general terms the behaviors that represented your *acting out*.

~ Task 3 ~

Expected feelings or outcomes:

Use the same episode as identified in Task 1 and enter the feelings or outcomes you expected from the use of your *drug of choice* and share your work with your support group members or therapist. Remember to focus your reflections on what you expected to come from your engagement with your *drug of choice* and not any negative consequences that may have occurred.

Course Assignment 3.1 - What We Expect from Returning to Our Drug of Choice

Complete the following tasks with as much detail as possible. If you find you are having a difficulty identifying the feelings you were experiencing for the scenario you chose to write about please refer to Appendix B for a list of feelings words.

IMPORTANT:

If you find that you need more space please feel free to continue the writing on a separate piece of paper.

~ Task 1 ~

Name uncomfortable or challenging feelings:

___

___

___

___

___

~ Task 2 ~

Name your drugs of choice:

___

___

___

___

___

Course Assignment 3.1 - What We Expect from Returning to Our Drug of Choice (Continued)

~ Task 3 ~

Expected feelings or outcomes:

What happens when we return to our drug of choice?

A minor recovery slogan that has faded from popularity in recent years declares: *It is the first drink that gets you drunk!* The ominous warning was intended to caution the newcomer who was having fanciful ideas about having just one alcoholic *drink* and believing that it would be safe. The warning was adopted by many Twelve Step members from various fellowships to be a caution against slipping into relapse after fooling themselves into believing that they could handle "just one more time".

While it is a time-honored recovery truth that the first use or action with your *drug of choice* is the one that gets you *drunk*, the authors have not found it to be so. We have never gotten intoxicated on one *drink* of any alcoholic beverage or toxic on any single addictive behavior. We have found instead that the first *drink* or action of our addictive behavior generates emotional discomfort in the form of guilt, shame, and remorse. Guilt requires a few *drinks* to muffle the alarms being raised by our conscious. A *drink* or two helps to ease us into the shadows as we recoil from the searchlight of shame. The shadows, as we all know, do not protect us from the waves of painful remorse over what we have sacrificed and – you guessed it – a few more *drinks* are needed for the pain the first *drink* was supposed to relieve. *Intoxication* is frequently the end point that an addict finds himself or herself at when he or she starts out to have "just one drink" or to buy "one" lottery ticket. It is the first one that makes *intoxication* possible. In the spirit of keeping it simple, do not take the first *drug* or addictive action and you will not end up intoxicated and wondering how it all went bad again.

One of your author's, (the older bald one), would hear almost daily about the horrors that follow the first *drink* from the old timers. There was such threat associated with the first *drink* that one would assume that one *drink* would cause the sky to fall or at least drastically change life as we know it. In fact, that is usually not even close.

People who relapse are surprised when the first *drink* or addictive behavior does not bring about the cataclysmic event that our support group had prophesized about. Some relapsing addicts will go on for days or weeks having just "a little bit" before they end up in a full blown relapse. Our fellows in recovery and clients have told us that shame and guilt is sometimes supplanted by the relief or bewilderment that came when they were not initially sucked into the bowels of hell following the "first one". Those whose relapse is short and seemingly inconsequential often relapse again or succumb to a rapid succession of relapses which continue for months or years before the crash because their decision to relapse again did not immediately return them to the pain of the past unmanageability – but it will. It always does. One of the authors was treated to an axiomatic pearl of recovery wisdom over lunch with Ruth Fox, Founder of the American Society of Addiction Medicine.

Dr. Fox believed you could "not turn an alcoholic back into a social drinker any more than you could turn a pickle back into a cucumber". Once we have been pickled by an addictive illness," she believed, there was "no way to restore a person to a state which permitted social drinking." We have found that there is no way to eliminate an addictive illness, only its symptoms. It is a hallmark symptomatic feature of *addiction* that an addict can return to his or her *drug of choice* after a period of sobriety but not with impunity. There will always be a cost.

A return to our *drug of choice* never makes it better. The scouts in our ranks who venture out to see if they can use safely return riddled with the arrows of *addiction* following a return to their *drug of choice*. They are shot through with legal problems, fractured relationships, and financial hardship. They left in search of an easier, softer way and those who were able to return to recovery often did so with injuries or consequences that had never been a problem for them in the past. Unfortunately, for many of the scouts, exploration taught others more than they themselves had learned. They had redefined the problem with life as something other than their *drug of choice*. We learned from them that when life is difficult the problem is not the failure to use a *drug of choice* socially or in moderation. The problem of living can never be solved with a "solution" that generally creates more living problems.

A simple premise regarding *addiction* is useful to remember:

> When a substance or behavior is used to reduce or eliminate a problem and the use causes problems more than once and you are not able to TOTALLY eliminate the substance or behaviors, then you are probably addicted to it or them.

> Many alcoholics drowning in a vat of denial will proudly proclaim, during a diagnostic evaluation, that they "have given up drinking forever, many times without a problem". This proclamation is offered as evidence to dispel any concerns about being alcoholic. Most are stunned to hear that social drinkers hardly ever claim to have such absolute control over the *drug*. Social drinkers generally do not find a need to "give up booze" forever because it never causes them the problems that lead an alcoholic to swear off alcohol.

Concept Lesson 3.3 - What Happens When We Return to Our Drug of Choice?

This figure illustrates what actually happens when an addicted person re-introduces his or her *drug of choice*. If you recall the example offered in Concept Lesson 3.2 you will remember that the addicted person hoped to receive relief from the discomfort when he or she relapsed. Unfortunately, the addicted person does not receive relief or the relief is short-lived. Usually his or her level of discomfort will increase. Perhaps you can identify but have had a hard time understanding why this phenomenon occurs. You will gain more insight as you progress through this course. If you have any questions make sure you ask your support group or therapist for a more personalized explanation.

Now let us take a more focused look at what happens when the "solution" to our problems creates problems in the next Course Lesson 3.2

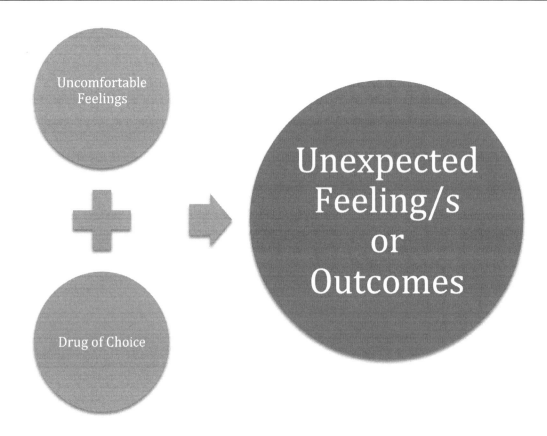

Course Lesson 3.2 - What Actually Happened When You Returned to Your Drug of Choice?

The next Course Assignment is intended to briefly examine the actual outcome of the *using episode* that you introduced in Course Assignment 3.1. If the *using episode* did not turn out the way that you expected and there were immediate consequences, it will be easy for you to complete the tasks below. If the event did not generate easily identifiable consequences or the consequences were delayed, the tasks below may be challenging.

If your relapse behavior resulted in immediate consequences it would be helpful to provide as much detail in your response to each of the Tasks that you need to communicate your experience to others. If you are having difficulty completing Tasks 2 and 3 because the relief from your decision to relapse was initially greater than the costs that followed, you might consider choosing another event. If you opt to continue with the example that you selected than it might be necessary to get help from a knowledgeable witness in your life to help you identify what the costs that eventually followed from your decision, however delayed or seemingly unconnected they might appear to be.

A decision to relapse after a period of recovery of either internally or externally imposed abstinence will always lead to a point of realizing that our *drugs of choice*, while they once produced relief, eventually became *rapacious creditors*. If you are still struggling to see that every *using episode* generated a bill that would need to be paid, then ask yourself how it is that you have come to be reading or undertaking this course.

Focus your attention on a *using episode* during your active *addiction* that followed a period of abstinence that was imposed by others or self prescribed and complete the following tasks that you can share with your support group members or therapist.

IMPORTANT:

The following descriptions of the various tasks in this lesson are presented to introduce you to the actual written work you will complete in the Course Assignment that follows this lesson. Do not write anything until you reach the assignment.

When you have completed the lesson be sure to share your findings with members of your support system and your therapist if you are working with one.

~ Task 1 ~

Name uncomfortable or challenging feelings prior to relapse:

You could pull the uncomfortable feeling/s you identified in Course Assignment 3.1 and place them into the space provided or focus on a different episode in which you were uncomfortable and had expected relief from returning to your *drug of choice*. Remember, we are asking for you to focus on the discomfort you were in before you relapsed, not the discomfort that followed the relapse.

Course Lesson 3.2 - What Actually Happened When You Returned to Your Drug of Choice? (Continued)

~ Task 2 ~

Describe your relapse behavior:

Use the same episode as identified in Task 1 and write examples or precise descriptions of your specific behaviors in the space provided regarding the relapse portion of the incident during the episode.

~ Task 3 ~

Unexpected uncomfortable feelings or outcomes:

Use the same episode as identified in Task 1 and enter the uncomfortable feelings or consequences that developed as a result of your relapse in the space provided. If the costs from that specific event are not readily apparent to you, then highlight several of the consequences that eventually drove you to get help. Construct a timeline to trace the consequences back to the use of substances or behaviors to alter your mood that you have described in Tasks 1 and 2.

Course Assignment 3.2 - What Actually Happened When You Returned to Your Drug of Choice?

Complete the following tasks with as much detail as you find necessary to accurately communicate your experiences as it relates to the identifications you made in Course Assignment 3.1.

IMPORTANT:

If you find that you need more space please feel free to continue the writing on a separate piece of paper.

~ Task 1 ~

Name uncomfortable or challenging feelings prior to relapse:

_____

_____

_____

_____

_____

~ Task 2 ~

Describe your relapse behavior:

_____

_____

_____

_____

_____

Course Assignment 3.2 - What Actually Happened When You Returned to Your Drug of Choice? (Continued)

~ Task 3 ~

Unexpected uncomfortable feelings or outcomes:

Challenges to your recovery

If you hang around the Twelve Step recovery rooms long enough you will eventually be introduced to a seemingly ominous threat to your recovery that is lurking in the shadows to rob you of your sobriety. It is known by many names such as – *the addict within* or the *addiction*. Many folks envision *addiction* as being a force that is separate and distinct from the addicted person. You will be warned by the proponents of the *addict within* school of thought about an *addict self* or an *addictive force* within you that you will always have to struggle with. The most outspoken will claim that "your disease wants you dead but will settle for a relapse." To the contrary, we believe that your disease does not have a mind of its own. It is not a separate entity from you or us that is "out in the parking lot doing push-ups" while you are safely inside meetings. The disease process, when it is active, is right there inside our minds and spirits. When we are irritated and judgmental of a group member who "tells the same story that he has told at least 100 times before," we have entered the relapse process. When I am blaming others for the distress or irritation that I feel at a meeting because "they aren't doing it right", I am experiencing elements of the two phases of relapse process depicted in Concept Lesson 3.1 referred to as Gathering Justification and Eliminating the Witnesses. In the next chapter, the authors will take you through an in-depth review of these phases, as well as the other phases introduced in the same Concept Lesson.

We are people with an *addiction*. We are not people being hunted down by an *addiction*. Our *addiction* is not waiting in the parking lot for us to leave a meeting so it can mug us. The threats that we face in recovery are not on the outside of us like gangs roaming around a "bad" neighborhood. The threats to sobriety are entirely an inside job. The "addict who is stuck in his head and consumed with his own thoughts is in a dangerous neighborhood" or so goes the recovery joke. Actually the old joke has some real wisdom in it. The methods that we have developed for coping with life generate the threats that place us in a "bad neighborhood." We are cautioned by our sponsors to be mindful of the potential impact of *people, places, and things,* but they are not the real problem. *People, places, and things*, however menacing or tempting they might seem, will never cause us to relapse. The problem is that we have learned to cope with challenging feelings, situations, events, and people in such a way that our *drug of choice* becomes attractive and for some, yet unknown reason, our bodies respond differently to the introduction of an addictive substance or behavior than normal people. We would appear to have acquired a taste for our poisonous *drug of choice* that social users and social actors cannot seem to tolerate. It probably does not help matters that our *drugs of choice* appear, for a time, to be just the medicine we need to tolerate or "live life to the fullest".

Our disease, like that of the diabetic, can be arrested but it cannot be cured. We can arrest our *addiction* regardless of the nature of our *drug of choice* and develop a recovery plan that supports a sober life-style. Every addicted person, who is constitutionally capable of and committed to being honest with themselves and others, can establish and maintain sobriety once abstinence has been secured. Since relapse is usually preceded by an expectation of a positive alteration in our mood, as identified in Course Lessons 3.1 and 3.2, it is critical that we understand the origin of the emotional challenges. The emotional challenges in our lives, that evolve as the result of the way that we cope with uncomfortable feelings, situations, events, and people can give rise to a desire to return to the *drug of choice*, as you will see in the coming chapters.

Course Lesson 3.3 - Identifying the Sources of Challenges to Your Recovery

In this assignment we are asking you to identify the sources of challenges that you are experiencing presently or may have faced in your recovery. Please remember that we are not suggesting that these challenges are reasons for a relapse. There is no reason for a relapse. These life challenges can be of the same variety and intensity as those experienced by non-addicts. It is important to note here that recovering addicts are not threatened by a set of life challenges that are unique to addicted people. All people lose loved ones, suffer losses in income and social-standing, miss out on opportunities for fame and fall short of performing at the level of an Olympiad. As recovering addicts, we may cope with challenges in ways that are maladaptive much like our non-addicted counterparts. We can blame others for our own errors and claim that others are responsible for the poor quality of our lives in much the same way that non-addicted people do. These and other *defects of character* are not the exclusive domain of addicts.

The critical difference lies in what happens when these maladaptive coping strategies fail to produce the desired result. For some, as yet unexplained reason, recovering addicts will begin to think about their *drug of choice* as a solution to the emotional distress, which can accompany life challenges.

When an addict reaches for his or her *drug of choice* because the character defects fail to lessen the emotional distress – all bets are off about how severe the outcome will be. A non-addict could also choose *drinking*, gambling, over-eating or pornography as a way of coping with life but they are likely to wake up in a very different place than the addict when the mood-altering experience is over.

If you are suffering with *addiction* the consequences will be greater, longer lasting, and there will be a pattern of reoccurrence despite a desire for the outcome to be different. The following descriptions are offered to introduce you to the tasks involved in this assignment.

IMPORTANT:

The following descriptions of the various tasks in this lesson are presented to introduce you to the actual written work you will complete in the Course Assignment that follows this lesson. Do not write anything until you reach the assignment.

When you have completed the lesson be sure to share your findings with members of your support system and your therapist if you are working with one.

~ Task 1 ~

The first task is to identify the feelings that you have had or might have difficulty coping with:

List the feelings that have historically caused or presently cause you concern or you have had difficulty coping with in the past. Do not focus exclusively on the more uncomfortable emotions such as anger, fear, and rejection. Many of us have experienced as much difficulty coping with feelings of love and tenderness as we have had with hate and revenge. If you are having difficulty identifying the feelings please refer to the extensive list of feelings words located in Appendix B.

Course Lesson 3.3 - Identifying the Sources of Challenges to Your Recovery (Continued)

~ Task 2 ~

Identify the situations you find uncomfortable, that you have felt challenged by, wished you would have handled differently, or avoided altogether:

Focus your energy on the identification of situations from the past, the present, and future that have been or could be uncomfortable. A situation, as used in this course material, refers to unplanned circumstances that occur in day-to-day life, that are not necessarily expected and are usually unscheduled. Once again we are not asking for a narrowly focused list of the painful situations like funerals and dark alleyways. Some of us would find rough neighborhoods less threatening than a surprise birthday party given in our honor.

~ Task 3 ~

List examples of specific past events you felt challenged by or wished you had handled differently:

An event, as used in this course material, refers to a planned circumstance such as dental checkups and spring-cleaning as well as calendar events such as birthdays and holidays. Although events such as the disastrous family vacation may occur with such regularity so as to appear to be commonplace they should be treated as events and not situations. We are not asking for general sets of circumstances like family birthday parties.

~ Task 4 ~

List the specific people and personality types that you have or would likely be uncomfortable with:

Include the role that each specific person plays in your life. When describing personality types include a simple description of their behavior using descriptors such as bully or predator.

Phase 1 - Uncomfortable feelings

Course Assignment 3.3 - Identifying the Sources of Challenges to Your Recovery

Briefly list or describe examples of the feelings, situations, events, and people that have been uncomfortable or challenging for you in your recovery efforts.

IMPORTANT:

If you find that you need more space please feel free to continue the writing on a separate piece of paper.

~ Task 1 ~

The first task is to identify the feelings that you have had or might have difficulty coping with:

_____

_____

_____

_____

_____

~ Task 2 ~

Identify the situations you find uncomfortable, that you have felt challenged by, wished you would have handled differently, or avoided altogether:

_____

_____

_____

_____

_____

Course Assignment 3.3 - Identifying the Sources of Challenges to Your Recovery (Continued)

~ Task 3 ~

List examples of specific past events you felt challenged by or wished you had handled differently:

_____

_____

_____

_____

~ Task 4 ~

List the specific people and personality types that you have or would likely be uncomfortable with:

_____

_____

_____

_____

Uncomfortable or challenging feelings

If we relapse into active *addiction* it will occur in response to a desire to alter the way we feel. Generally a relapse is preceded by a desire to move away from an emotional experience of discomfort toward a state of relief or euphoria. The discomfort may be associated with feelings of love and intimacy as well as feelings like anger and rejection. Some will claim that others had left them with no alternative way to ease the pain, while others rationalize that the return to their *drug of choice* was an understandable and a perfectly human way of celebrating good fortune. Some of us have developed strategies for coping with uncomfortable or challenging feelings over the years that do little to actually relieve the discomfort we are feeling and often intensify the distress many times over; yet we continue to use the same methods.

The person who relapses to numb the pain of living may be fooling himself, but those around him are clear that he is merely changing seats on the Titanic, especially when the pain of living was caused by *addiction*-related consequences. The alcoholic's job promotion that requires champagne to fully experience the joy is working from a mandate that is deeply embedded in the self-delusion. Really joyful people do not need a central nervous system depressant (champagne) to celebrate good fortune. The sex addict's spouse who strikes back at her partner's betrayal by having sex with a stranger is likely to be understood only by those familiar with the use of acts of self-degradation. The partner was the victim of the betrayal and now has become the target of her own revenge but she does not see it. She just wants to feel better.

The person who has known rejection or betrayal by a family member or close friend is just as likely to be uncomfortable with feelings of vulnerability and tenderness as they might be with sadness, loneliness, or grief. An individual who happens into a social situation that he finds intimidating because of the tone of a person's voice or the physical posturing which is forecasting the potential for aggression can experience the same degree of discomfort when he is being praised by a family member or friend. The nature of the feeling or the circumstances in which it was felt is not necessarily what drives the discomfort.

The uncomfortable emotional state that you find yourself in may have little to do with the situation or circumstances at hand. If you have been hurt in the past and the current situation or behaviors being displayed trigger your memories of the past, you can feel hurt in a situation that does not warrant the reaction that you are having. How we feel at a given moment may not seem justified or rational to others, but it will not change the sensations we are experiencing or the discomfort that arises.

Much could be said about the role emotional pain plays in the behaviors that are developed to cope with it. In many ways the addict is not much different from any of the non-addicts who struggle with strategies for managing the feelings that they experience. The difference between them and us is found in the cost levied for the use of maladaptive strategies for coping with discomfort. Active *addiction* leads to one of three places: *jails, institutions, and death*. We cannot afford the luxury of common folk. We are uncommon in the extreme. The following Course Lesson and Course Assignment will help you to examine your patterns with regard to the management of uncomfortable or challenging feelings.

Course Lesson 3.4 - Identifying Uncomfortable or Challenging Feelings from the Past

Uncomfortable or challenging feelings are neither good nor bad, neither negative nor positive, and neither productive nor unproductive. Anger is no more negative an emotion than love is a positive one. What makes a feeling uncomfortable is the challenge we experience in dealing with it. Anger can cause havoc for you if the only way that you know to deal with it is hurting someone or breaking something. Fear can become a rapacious predator if your response is to run away or pretend that you are not feeling it. Love has threatened many of us into isolation when we avoided the exposure it demanded. Rejection can become a way of life if the strategy we use for coping with the discomfort it brings is to precipitate a rejection to fulfill the prophecy we expect is our fate anyway.

You will be asked to describe one of the most challenging feelings you have encountered in recovery that you are not satisfied with and the way that you dealt with it or the outcome that followed. The following expanded description is offered to aid you in your completion of tasks associated with Course Assignment 3.4.

IMPORTANT:

The following descriptions of the various tasks in this lesson are presented to introduce you to the actual written work you will complete in the Course Assignment that follows this lesson. Do not write anything until you reach the assignment.

When you have completed the lesson be sure to share your findings with members of your support system and your therapist if you are working with one.

~ Task 1 ~

Name the feeling:

Describe the feeling in simple terms that you have experienced during recovery that left you dissatisfied with the way that you coped with it or the outcome that followed.

~ Task 2 ~

Describe the event or situation in which it occurred:

Describe the event or situation in simple terms that you have experienced during recovery that left you dissatisfied with the way that you coped with it or the outcome that followed. Your description can include specific details related to dialogue or behavior if it helps you to present the event in a way that others will understand without having been there themselves. Remember that the focus here is on communicating what made this feeling particularly challenging.

Course Lesson 3.4 - Identifying Uncomfortable or Challenging Feelings from the Past (Continued)

~ Task 3 ~

Describe the way you handled it:

Describe in detail how you handled the uncomfortable or challenging feeling in that particular situation or event. If you were hurt and pretended that you were not hurt, describe how you acted to cover up what you were feeling. If you felt rejected in the situation or event or by the people involved, describe how you addressed the rejection. If you answered the perceived rejection with an attack on others be clear about what you did and said. Do not focus your energy on whether or not your behavior was justified.

~ Task 4 ~

Describe what the outcome was and how it left you feeling:

Describe what the outcome was for the way that you dealt with the emotion in terms that address tangible, emotional, and *spiritual* outcomes if possible. Conclude by describing how you were left feeling as a result of the way you dealt with the uncomfortable or challenging emotion and not as a result of what others did or failed to do during the event under examination.

Course Assignment 3.4 - Identifying Uncomfortable or Challenging Feelings from the Past

Describe one of the most challenging feelings you have encountered in recovery where you are not satisfied with the way that you dealt with it or the outcome that followed.

IMPORTANT:

If you find that you need more space please feel free to continue the writing on a separate piece of paper.

~ Task 1 ~

Name the feeling:

~ Task 2 ~

Describe the event or situation in which it occurred:

Course Assignment 3.4 - Identifying Uncomfortable or Challenging Feelings from the Past (Continued)

~ Task 3 ~

Describe the way you handled it:

___

~ Task 4 ~

Describe what the outcome was and how it left you feeling:

___

Uncomfortable or challenging situations

The list of potentially uncomfortable or challenging situations is incalculable because every life situation or set of circumstances can generate the kind of discomfort that we, as addicts, have sought relief from in our *drugs of choice*. One aspect of the *spiritual* malady that many of us suffer with is rooted in a propensity to blame other people, places, and events for the quality of our lives. Again, common people behave in some of the same ways but our delusional system, confounded by the *intoxicating* nature of our reaction to our *drugs of choice*, raises the blame game to an art form and most of us are grand masters.

It is not enough to say that there are an infinite number of potentially troubling situations that we might encounter as we "trudge the road to happy destiny" and we should be careful of the potholes. We, as addicts, cannot afford to take blind chances with situations that history has told us will be difficult without a plan for insulating ourselves from harm. This course is largely devoted to the development of a better understanding of the recovery terrain that lies ahead and how to deal with the uncomfortable or challenging situations before they confound us.

The examination of uncomfortable or challenging situations will be covered in two separate Course Lessons 3.5 and 3.6. Course Lesson 3.5 will deal with situations that you have faced in the past. Following the lesson you will be asked to complete two examples of situations in the past that you found uncomfortable and how you coped with them in Course Assignments 3.5 (Part 1) and 3.5 (Part 2).

Course Lesson 3.6 will shift the focus from the past to the future. We are not asking you to focus on problems that have not happened yet but to look into the future at situations that could arise that you would want to handle differently than you might have in the past. You will be asked to complete one assignment, Course Assignment 3.6, which asks you to imagine what challenging situations you might have to face in the future. Feel free to copy the Course Assignment sheet and complete as many as you believe you will benefit from, but you will only be asked to complete one.

Course Lesson 3.5 - Identifying Uncomfortable or Challenging Situations from the Past

Uncomfortable or challenging situations can generate potentially overbearing emotional challenges in recovery that could threaten your emotional sobriety.

The following Course Lesson and two separate Course Assignments, titled Identifying Uncomfortable or Challenging Situations From the Past (Part 1) and (Part 2), will introduce a model for increasing your ability to identify uncomfortable or challenging situations and to critically examine how your methods of coping with them have impacted you. Additional benefit will be derived from the insights you may gain that could influence the changes you may make in the future should you find yourself in a similar situation.

Describe the typical setting for each situation providing enough detail so that a reader, with some knowledge of you, would understand what you are communicating. After the description of each setting, write a brief description of what the outcome was and how it left you feeling about the examples from the past. The following expanded description is offered to aid you in your completion of tasks associated with Course Assignments 3.5 (Part 1) and 3.5 (Part 2).

IMPORTANT:

The following descriptions of the various tasks in this lesson are presented to introduce you to the actual written work you will complete in the Course Assignment that follows this lesson. Do not write anything until you reach the assignment.

When you have completed the lesson be sure to share your findings with members of your support system and your therapist if you are working with one.

~ Task 1 ~

Describe the situations:

Describe two separate situations in Course Assignments 3.5 (Part 1) and 3.5 (Part 2) from your past in which you have found yourself experiencing emotional discomfort. If possible avoid references to events such as a surprise birthday party, religious holidays, or the death of a loved one as they are events. Situations, as used in this course, refer to episodes in your life that could be commonplace, such as a crowded two-hour bus ride or getting lost in route to an important event.

In this task you are asked to describe such variables as the setting, the people involved, participants, and the time of year or day. Describe only one situational example per Course Assignment sheet to avoid confusion when communicating your experience to others.

~ Task 2 ~

Describe the feelings you experienced and the thoughts that dominated your thinking:

Describe what you were thinking and feeling during a past situation you found challenging or uncomfortable.

Course Lesson 3.5 - Identifying Uncomfortable or Challenging Situations from the Past (Continued)

~Task 3~

Describe the way you handled it:

Describe in detail how you handled the uncomfortable or challenging situation in the past. When you are examining a past situation consider these points: if you were hurt and pretended that you were not hurt, describe how you acted to cover up what you were feeling; if you felt anger or rejection in the situation or by the people involved, describe how you addressed the uncomfortable emotions you experienced; if you answered the perceived rejection with an attack on others, be clear about what you did and said. Do not focus your energy on whether or not your behavior was justified.

~Task 4~

Describe what the outcome was and how it left you feeling:

When you are describing a past situation focus on what the outcome was and how you were left feeling as a result of coping strategy you employed. Remember, we are not looking for a description on how you were harmed by the situation or the way that others behaved in it. We are looking for you to describe how you felt in detail about the outcome of the way that you behaved. In both examples you complete, conclude by describing what you know about how other people felt about the way you handled yourself.

Course Assignment 3.5 (Part 1) - Identifying Uncomfortable or Challenging Situations from the Past

Complete the following tasks using only one situation from the past that you found uncomfortable or challenging.

IMPORTANT:

If you find that you need more space please feel free to continue the writing on a separate piece of paper.

~ Task 1 ~

Describe the situation:

_____

_____

_____

_____

_____

~ Task 2 ~

Describe the feelings and the thoughts that dominated your thinking:

_____

_____

_____

_____

_____

Course Assignment 3.5 (Part 1) - Identifying Uncomfortable or Challenging Situations from the Past (Continued)

~ Task 3 ~

Describe the way you handled it:

_____

_____

_____

_____

_____

_____

_____

~ Task 4 ~

Describe what the outcome was and how it left you feeling:

_____

_____

_____

_____

_____

_____

_____

Course Assignment 3.5 (Part 2) - Identifying Uncomfortable or Challenging Situations from the Past

Complete the following tasks using only one situation from the past that you found uncomfortable or challenging.

IMPORTANT:

If you find that you need more space please feel free to continue the writing on a separate piece of paper.

~ Task 1 ~

Describe the situation:

~ Task 2 ~

Describe the feelings and the thoughts that dominated your thinking:

Course Assignment 3.5 (Part 2) - Identifying Uncomfortable or Challenging Situations from the Past (Continued)

~ Task 3 ~

Describe the way you handled it:

_____

_____

_____

_____

_____

_____

_____

~ Task 4 ~

Describe what the outcome was and how it left you feeling:

_____

_____

_____

_____

_____

_____

_____

Course Lesson 3.6 - Identifying Uncomfortable or Challenging Situations in the Future

We would not want you living in a world of projections about the future or stuck recounting the past life challenges over and over again but there is wisdom to be gained from studying the past and preparing for the future. Hopefully you have gained insights from examining the uncomfortable or challenging situations from your past that can help you to cope differently with situations that will arise in the future.

The following Course Assignment will continue with the model used for examining situations from the past but the focus will shift to those situations that are likely to arise during the coming months.

The following expanded description is offered to aid you in your completion of tasks associated with Course Assignment 3.6.

IMPORTANT:

The following descriptions of the various tasks in this lesson are presented to introduce you to the actual written work you will complete in the Course Assignment that follows this lesson. Do not write anything until you reach the assignment.

When you have completed the lesson be sure to share your findings with members of your support system and your therapist if you are working with one.

~ Task 1 ~

Describe the situation:

Describe one situation in Course Assignment 3.6 that is likely to arise in the months to come that you would have reason to expect that you would find uncomfortable or emotionally challenging. If possible avoid references to events such as a surprise birthday party, religious holidays, or the death of a loved one as they are events. Situations, as used in this course, refer to episodes in your life that could be commonplace, such as a crowded two-hour bus ride or getting lost in route to an important event.

In this task you are asked to describe such variables as the setting, the people involved, participants, and the time of year or day. Describe only one situational example per Course Assignment sheet to avoid confusion when communicating your experience to others.

~ Task 2 ~

Describe the feelings you might experience and the thoughts that might dominate your thinking:

Describe what you might be thinking and feeling during that future situation that you might find challenging or uncomfortable.

Course Lesson 3.6 - Identifying Uncomfortable or Challenging Situations in the Future (Continued)

~ Task 3 ~

Describe the way you would expect yourself to handle it:

Describe in detail how you would expect yourself to handle the uncomfortable or challenging situation should it occur. When you are examining the projected situation consider these points: if you are hurt and pretend that you are not hurt, describe how you might act to cover up what you were feeling; if you felt anger or rejection in the situation or by the people involved, describe how you might address the uncomfortable emotions you experienced; if you answered the perceived rejection with an attack on others, be clear about what you did and said. Do not focus your energy on whether or not your behavior would be justified in the future situation.

~ Task 4 ~

Describe what the outcome might be given the way you plan on coping with it and how it could leave you feeling:

Remember, we are not looking for a description of how you might be harmed by the situation or the way that others behaved in it. Since you are writing about some future situation, describe how you would imagine yourself handling the discomfort and the feelings you would expect to be experiencing because of how you behaved. Also, detail the consequences that you might expect to follow your handling of the situation. Lastly, describe how you would expect others to react to your coping strategies.

Phase 1 - Uncomfortable feelings

Course Assignment 3.6 - Identifying Uncomfortable or Challenging Situations in the Future

Complete the following tasks using only one uncomfortable or challenging situation you would expect to find yourself in at some point in the future.

IMPORTANT:

If you find that you need more space please feel free to continue the writing on a separate piece of paper.

~ Task 1 ~

Describe the situation:

_____

_____

_____

_____

_____

_____

~ Task 2 ~

Describe the feelings and the thoughts that might dominate your thinking:

_____

_____

_____

_____

_____

Course Assignment 3.6 - Identifying Uncomfortable or Challenging Situations in the Future (Continued)

~ Task 3 ~

Describe the way you imagine handling it:

_____

_____

_____

_____

_____

_____

~ Task 4 ~

Describe what the outcome might be and how it might leave you feeling:

_____

_____

_____

_____

_____

_____

Uncomfortable or challenging events

Each of us face a great many social events in the course of recovery that were once the catalyst for power-driven forays into some of the most toxic episodes in our active *addiction*, or so they seemed to be the leavening for a grand *binge*. Recovery wisdom suggests that we can go anywhere and into any situation or attend any event that common people do as long as we have a good reason for being there and we are in fit *spiritual* condition.

You will be invited to many events and unknowingly wander into a few more that would seem to be appropriate for you to attend. Some will seem so because of the sense of obligation that you feel to attend, and others because they appear harmless. Still others will seem necessary for work or to fulfill family or societal obligations, but in all cases you are advised to determine that you have a good reason for being there and the conditions of the event are in harmony with the sober life-style that you are developing for yourself.

In Section 5 – Strategies for Interrupting the Relapse Process you will have the opportunity to prepare specific intervention plans for events that have been historically uncomfortable or challenging as well as those you anticipate having discomfort with based on the personalities that will be in attendance or the emotionality that you will bring to the event. The following Course Lessons and Course Assignments will begin analyzing past and future events in order to help you determine if there is, in fact, a good reason for you to be there and an increased awareness of your level of *spiritual* preparedness.

The examination of uncomfortable or challenging events will be covered in two separate Course Lessons 3.7 and 3.8. Course Lesson 3.7 will deal with situations that you have faced in the past. Following the lesson you will be asked to complete two examples of events in the past that you found uncomfortable and how you coped with them in Course Assignments 3.7 (Part 1) and 3.7 (Part 2).

Course Lesson 3.8 will shift the focus from the past to the future. We are not asking you to focus on problems that have not happened yet but to look into the future at events that could be scheduled that you would want to handle differently than you might have in the past. You will be asked to complete one assignment, Course Assignment 3.8 that asks you to use your imagination to select a challenging event you might have to face in the future. Feel free to copy the Course Assignment sheet and complete as many as you believe you will benefit from, but you will only be asked to complete one.

Course Lesson 3.7 - Identifying Uncomfortable or Challenging Events from the Past

The events of our past would be easy to recall with a specific date and time if we had kept a journal every day of our lives. Since most of us do not have a diary of the events we have encountered since reaching the age of consent, this assignment may take some reflection. Feel free to confer with other support group members, a trusted family member, or your therapist if you need help with jogging your memory or identifying challenging events.

In the Course Assignments for this lesson we want you to select at least two uncomfortable or challenging events from your past, in Course Assignments 3.7 (Part 1) and 3.7 (Part 2), which left a lasting impact on you. You will first set the place and date of the event. Then you will identify the people present and what behaviors were emotionally disturbing to you and continue with the impact it has had on the quality of your life today.

After you have completed the first four tasks, look into the future and list upcoming events that might be similar to the past events that you analyzed and bring your findings for discussion with your support group and therapist.

IMPORTANT:

The following descriptions of the various tasks in this lesson are presented to introduce you to the actual written work you will complete in the Course Assignment that follows this lesson. Do not write anything until you reach the assignment.

When you have completed the lesson be sure to share your findings with members of your support system and your therapist if you are working with one.

~ Task 1 ~

Describe the past events with an estimation of the date and time or period of the year in which they occurred:

Describe two events from your past in Course Assignments 3.7 (Part 1) and 3.7 (Part 2), where you found yourself experiencing emotional discomfort. In this task you are asked to describe such variables as the setting, the people involved, participants, and the time of year or day. Describe only one example per Course Assignment sheet to avoid confusion when communicating your experience to others.

~ Task 2 ~

Identify the people involved and what was disturbing about their behaviors:

You are being asked to describe each person's specific behavior. If you fear that you will breach the confidence of anyone you name, give them an alias and conceal or alter the specific behaviors that might reveal the identity of the real person. If you have any questions, ask your therapist about how to proceed.

Course Lesson 3.7 - Identifying Uncomfortable or Challenging Events from the Past (Continued)

~ Task 3 ~

Describe how you handled the uncomfortable or challenging event:

Describe in detail how you handled the uncomfortable or challenging events in the past. Consider these points: if you were hurt and pretended that you were not hurt, describe how you acted to cover up what you were feeling; if you felt anger or rejection in the situation or by the people involved, describe how you addressed any uncomfortable emotions you experienced. If you answered the perceived rejection with an attack on others, be clear about what you did and said. Do not focus your energy on whether or not your behavior was justified.

~ Task 4 ~

Describe what the outcome was and how it left you feeling:

Explain the outcomes that you associate with the event and those you believe are connected to the way that you handled yourself. Focus on how your method of coping with the discomfort left you feeling. Remember, we are not looking for a description on how you were harmed by the situation or the way that others behaved in it. We are looking for you to describe, in detail, how you felt about the outcome of the way that you behaved. Finally, describe how others reacted to the way that you behaved.

~ Task 5 ~

Similar past events:

This task moves the focus from the event that you have been analyzing to other similar events in your past. List the events that come to mind with only as much detail as you will need to recall the story when it comes time to share it with others. Please keep it simple and make just a brief summary that will guide you in sharing the stories with others. You may not have enough space on the sheets provided. You can add loose leaf attachments if you need.

Course Assignment 3.7 (Part 1) - Identifying Uncomfortable or Challenging Events from the Past

Describe one uncomfortable or challenging event from the past.

IMPORTANT:

If you find that you need more space please feel free to continue the writing on a separate piece of paper.

~ Task 1 ~

Describe the event:

_____

_____

_____

_____

_____

_____

~ Task 2 ~

Identify the people involved and what was disturbing about their behavior:

_____

_____

_____

_____

_____

Course Assignment 3.7 (Part 1) - Identifying Uncomfortable or Challenging Events from the Past (Continued)

~ Task 3 ~

Describe the feelings you experienced and the thoughts that dominated your thinking:

~ Task 4 ~

Describe the impact that the event has had on your life up to the present time:

Course Assignment 3.7 (Part 1) - Identifying Uncomfortable or Challenging Events from the Past (Continued)

~ Task 5 ~

Similar past events:

Course Assignment 3.7 (Part 2) - Identifying Uncomfortable or Challenging Events from the Past

Describe one uncomfortable or challenging event from the past.

IMPORTANT:

If you find that you need more space please feel free to continue the writing on a separate piece of paper.

~ Task 1 ~

Describe the event:

_____

_____

_____

_____

_____

_____

~ Task 2 ~

Identify the people involved and what was disturbing about their behavior:

_____

_____

_____

_____

_____

_____

Course Assignment 3.7 (Part 2) - Identifying Uncomfortable or Challenging Events from the Past (Continued)

~ Task 3 ~

Describe the feelings you experienced and the thoughts that dominated your thinking:

_____

_____

_____

_____

_____

_____

_____

~ Task 4 ~

Describe the impact that the event has had on your life up to the present time:

_____

_____

_____

_____

_____

_____

Course Assignment 3.7 (Part 2) - Identifying Uncomfortable or Challenging Events from the Past (Continued)

~ Task 5 ~

Similar past events:

Course Lesson 3.8 - Identifying an Uncomfortable or Challenging Events You Might Face in the Future

We suspect that even though it might be easier to predict the future with a crystal ball it would probably not be wise or comforting to do so. The idea of planning for our future by critically examining our past is not a new one. Our past successes and failures are full of lessons for us to learn from if we are willing to study without defensiveness. Additionally our examination of the behavioral patterns that we have observed others following in the past might tell us something about what we might need to prepare for in future encounters with them.

It is important to remember, however, that the past does not dictate the future. People change and our reactions to certain types of events can change. We look to the past for clues about what to plan for. Clues – not evidence. What has happened in the past is not proof of what will happen next week or years from now.

Feel free to confer with other support group members, a trusted family member, or your therapist if you need help with jogging your memory or identifying challenging events. In the Course Assignment for this lesson we want you imagine one uncomfortable or challenging event that has either been scheduled or is likely to arise in the future to examine.

Feel free to copy the Course Assignment sheet and complete as many as you believe you will benefit from, but you will only be asked to complete one.

IMPORTANT:

The following descriptions of the various tasks in this lesson are presented to introduce you to the actual written work you will complete in the Course Assignment that follows this lesson. Do not write anything until you reach the assignment.

When you have completed the lesson be sure to share your findings with members of your support system and your therapist if you are working with one.

~ Task 1 ~

Describe event:

Describe at least one event that you could imagine experiencing at some point in the future that you suspect will leave you feeling uncomfortable or that you would find challenging to your recovery. While you are free to make copies of the sheet to record several different events, please describe only one example per Course Assignment sheet to avoid confusion when communicating your experience to others.

Course Lesson 3.8 - Identifying an Uncomfortable or Challenging Events You Might Face in the Future (Continued)

~ Task 2 ~

Identify the people involved and what might be disturbing about their behavior:

Describe the people by personality type or by name and their relationship to you who are likely to be involved in the event. Describe the behavior that the people are engaged in that you might find disturbing. Provide enough detail to enable a reader with no real knowledge of your life be able to understand what would be happening as if the reader were there observing it all.

~ Task 3 ~

Describe the feelings you might experience and the thoughts that could dominate your thinking:

Describe the feelings that you expect you will have during the event and the thoughts you would be having about the people, the event, or yourself. You are encouraged to consult the list of feelings we have provided in Appendix B. The thoughts you would be having might be more difficult to identify so feel free to examine past life experiences when you found yourself in similar events and what self-talk and intellectual processing you would have been engaged in.

~ Task 4 ~

Describe the impact that the event might have on your life:

Describe the impact or effect that the event might have on your life in the hours, days, and weeks after the event is concluded. By impact we mean the feelings that you would be left with, the ways in which any of the relationships in your life might change as a result of the event, or the new challenges that you would have to face in your recovery.

Course Assignment 3.8 - Identifying an Uncomfortable or Challenging Events You Might Face in the Future

Describe one uncomfortable or challenging event that you would expect to find yourself in at some point in the future.

IMPORTANT:

If you find that you need more space please feel free to continue the writing on a separate piece of paper.

~ Task 1 ~

Describe the event:

_____

_____

_____

_____

_____

~ Task 2 ~

Identify the people involved and what might be disturbing about their behavior:

_____

_____

_____

_____

_____

Course Assignment 3.8 - Identifying an Uncomfortable or Challenging Events You Might Face in the Future (Continued)

~ Task 3 ~

Describe the feelings you might experience and the thoughts that could dominate your thinking:

_____

_____

_____

_____

_____

_____

~ Task 4 ~

Describe the impact that the event might have on your life:

_____

_____

_____

_____

_____

_____

Uncomfortable or challenging people

The authors have often joked that we would not have any *defects of character* at all if we lived alone on a deserted island. While it might be true that most character defects relate to relationship expectations, self-imposed isolation is not a sober solution for us because we believe we were born with a hard-wired *spiritual* desire for others. We are not suggesting, even in jest, that other people are our problem – just the contrary. We believe that emotional freedom and well-being is impossible unless we take full responsibility for the quality of our own lives. In the following Course Assignment we are asking you to identify the people in your life by name or personality type that you currently find uncomfortable or would expect to find uncomfortable to be around or challenging to deal with. We are not asking for you to describe the motivation for their behavior or to defend yourself.

The motivation for a person's behavior has little to do with the way that you respond to it. Besides, all too often we have been wrong about the true nature of the driving force behind the people we found uncomfortable or challenging to be around. There is always a story to explain the function of behavior we find offensive or hurtful. We cannot be sure what motivates others to behave in a certain way but we, with work, can develop a clear understanding of what stimulates our own behavior. We must!

Your investment toward the development of strategies for responding rather than reacting to uncomfortable or challenging people will be rewarded many times over. The foundation for the strategies you will begin to develop in this course and continue to revise in the Sixth and Seventh Steps begins with an increased awareness of the patterns that exist in your interactive relationship with them. The Course Assignment that follows provides a simple way of launching the examination that will take on a more detailed format in the Fourth Step.

Course Lesson 3.9 - Identify the People in Your Life That You Have Been or Might Become Uncomfortable with or Find Challenging

In the next assignment you will be asked to identify people that you have been uncomfortable with in the past, currently find uncomfortable to be around, or that you might find challenging in the future.

There are many reasons that we become uncomfortable around other people. We are not looking to find people that make you uncomfortable. We do not believe that other people are responsible for how we feel about life or ourselves. It is not blame that we are wanting to post. We are encouraging this exploration so you can tag the people that you have come to associate with discomfort. If you are more aware of who these people are, you will be alerted to guard yourself from slipping into the relapse process by learning how to deal soberly with the discomfort.

IMPORTANT:

The following descriptions of the various tasks in this lesson are presented to introduce you to the actual written work you will complete in the Course Assignment that follows this lesson. Do not write anything until you reach the assignment.

When you have completed the lesson be sure to share your findings with members of your support system and your therapist if you are working with one.

~ Task 1 ~

Identify the people in your present life that you are likely to be uncomfortable around:

You are asked to identify the people in your present life that you are uncomfortable with or find it uncomfortable to be around and describe the role that they play in your life. Additionally describe the nature of the discomfort by describing what happens to you when they are around or when you think of them.

~ Task 2 ~

Select one real person and one personality type from Task 1 and describe how you cope with your feelings and how you behave when you are in their company:

This task asks you to provide examples of the common strategies you use to cope with uncomfortable people. You should not invest any energy justifying your behavior. It is unnecessary and not productive to explain why you behave the way that you do when certain people are around. Feel free to include samples of all the different strategies you use to cope with your feelings around these people. Make sure at least one of your examples explains the coping strategy that you most regret after the fact.

In this task you will have space to describe a real person and a personality type. A personality type refers to the way that you perceive the person's behavior or attitude that you are uncomfortable with. It is likely that the personality type that you would select to include in this task is similar to the people that you have already named but that is all right. Do not worry about

Course Lesson 3.9 - Identify the People in Your Life That You Have Been or Might Become Uncomfortable with or Find Challenging (Continued)

what name to assign to the description of the personality. Some examples in case you need them would be people who are pushy, people pleasers, bullies, care takers, micro managers, those that are too needy, etc.

~ Task 3 ~

*Name the people in your active addiction that you were uncomfortable around and have blamed for your use of an addictive drug of choice. Place a star * alongside the real people that are still in your life today:*

This task is intended to help you make a clear identification of the people who you blamed in the past for your use of an addictive *drug of choice* and what you were uncomfortable about at the time. This awareness is important because there are times when a desire to relapse in the present or future will be associated with a particular person or personality type from your past that you have unresolved conflict with. This insight makes you aware of the situations or events that you should prepare for and have a plan for coping with in case you encounter similar personality types.

~ Task 4 ~

Name one real person and one personality type in your present life whom you suspect are uncomfortable when they are around you and describe how he or she behave and what they are likely to be feeling:

This task will help you to develop awareness of the people in your life with whom there is likely to exist a mutual incompatibility. You can use this insight to guide you should you prefer to work on the conflict or merely avoid in-depth contact.

You are asked to identify one real person and one personality type in your present life whom you suspect are uncomfortable when they are around you and describe how you think they cope with their discomfort. You are free to add more specific people or types on loose leaf paper you can attach.

~ Task 5 ~

Describe any similarities you see in the way that you cope with the uncomfortable people you have identified:

Recovery wisdom suggests that we are most likely to spot the *defects of character* in others that we can most identify with personally. Look at the coping strategies being employed by the people whom you perceive are uncomfortable with you. Describe wherever possible the coping strategies that you can identify within yourself.

Course Assignment 3.9 - Identify the People in Your Life That You Have Been or Might Become Uncomfortable with or Find Challenging

Describe people you find uncomfortable to be around or challenging to cope with that you interact with some regularity.

IMPORTANT: If you find that you need more space please feel free to continue the writing on a separate piece of paper.

~ Task 1 ~

Identify the people in your present life that you are likely to be uncomfortable around:

Name or role in your life	Nature of your discomfort
1.	1.
2.	2.
3.	3.
4.	4.

~ Task 2 ~

Select one real person and one personality type from Task 1 and describe how you cope with your feelings and how you behave when you are in their company:

Name of a real person and your coping strategy:

_____

_____

_____

_____

_____

Course Assignment 3.9 - Identify the People in Your Life That You Have Been or Might Become Uncomfortable with or Find Challenging (Continued)

Describe a personality type and your coping strategy:

_____

_____

_____

_____

_____

_____

_____

_____

_____

~ Task 3 ~

*Name the people in your active addiction that you were uncomfortable around and have blamed for your use of an addictive drug of choice. Place a star * alongside the real people that are still in your life today:*

Name or role in your life	Nature of your discomfort
1.	1.
2.	2.
3.	3.
4.	4.

Course Assignment 3.9 - Identify the People in Your Life That You Have Been or Might Become Uncomfortable with or Find Challenging (Continued)

~ Task 4 ~

Name one real person and one personality type in your present life who you suspect are uncomfortable when they are around you and describe how he or she behave and what they are likely to be feeling:

Name of a real person and his or her coping strategy and perceived feeling around you:

___

Describe a personality type and his or her coping strategy and perceived feeling around you:

___

Course Assignment 3.9 - Identify the People in Your Life That You Have Been or Might Become Uncomfortable with or Find Challenging (Continued)

~ Task 5 ~

Describe any similarities you see in the way that you cope with the uncomfortable people you have identified:

Phase 2: Time travel

Time travel refers to a physical, emotional, and intellectual phenomenon that can occur when an emotional stressor is encountered on the road to relapse into active *addiction*, which is intensified by previous life experiences. Consider the following example:

> John has been uncomfortable since he stopped compulsively over-eating two months ago. He finds himself at lunch with his co-workers attempting to shrug off the jabs he is receiving about ordering a salad. At the point that his friend Bob jokes that John could probably do without the salad because he has packed on enough fat to get him through a winter hibernation, John begins to time travel. His mind races back to the 5th grade gym class where he is next in line for the rope climb. Mr. Jock, the gym teacher, rings a bell he has hidden as John approaches the rope. He announces that his action is in honor of John who will never see the top of the rope to ring the bell himself. The class roars with laughter as John jumps at the rope but is never able to propel himself off the mat and up the rope.
>
> There is nothing John could do to handle the emotions of the experience at the restaurant with his co-workers because he was back in elementary school feeling powerless and shut down.

When time travel occurs it will diminish your ability to cope with the challenges of present moment situations or relationships.

The notion that our feelings never know what time it is, is more than a light hearted reference to the tendency for us to feel bombarded by the emotional memories of prior life experiences. Our feeling memories of the past can flood our current reality and generate or reinforce the perception that a trusted friend or loved one is trying to hurt us.

A time travel experience is an emotional flashback. When we are time traveling we are emotionally reacting to a present life situation or event as if it contained the elements of an earlier time in our life. The emotional flashbacks that occur during time travel might cause us to view the behavior of someone in our current experience as being more than similar to the actions of someone from our past. When we are time traveling we will react to the present person as if he or she was the individual that we struggled with from our past. We imagine that our spouse is our mother or that a friend is an enemy from the past. Additionally, feelings from our past seem to have an effect on our physical reaction to a present day stressor. In the midst of a quiet disagreement with someone, we can begin to feel physically threatened and develop a sense of danger, which is actually rooted in some past memory. The present physical threat that we feel can cause us to view others as dangerous when in fact they do not pose any real threat to us in the moment.

Feeling memories are more readily accessible to us than the factual details of the events that are related to the flashback recall we are experiencing. The visual memories or pictures of the events in question can be the most difficult to retrieve. This phenomenon is particularly disheartening for many of us because we tend to mistrust our feeling memories and require picture proof of authenticity of the feelings we are having or a living witness to the event to testify to the authenticity of our feeling. When the barrage of feeling memories is positive, like the anticipation of returning to a favorite vacation spot, the round trip journey from present to past is a pleasurable one. It is unlikely that others will be hurt or feel rejected by our euphoric recall related to an enjoyable vacation experience even when packing and commuting hassles were lost in the recall processes. When the journey from past to present is unpleasant it generates dysphoric recall. The luncheon situation described above triggered a painful time travel experience, which left him at the luncheon with his colleagues experiencing dysphoric recall. He was not surrounded by taunting 5th grade students and a heartless teacher. The adult men at his lunch table would have responded appropriately if John objected but he had no way of knowing that.

Dysphoric recall can precipitate or exacerbate a sense of being in danger or unsafe. It is important that each of us learns to detect when time travel is negatively influencing our perception of reality. The following is offered as a highlight of the dynamics that might be involved as we move through the usual trajectory or path of time travel. In addition, Concept Lesson 3.4 (p. 112) has been prepared with a visual depiction of these dynamics and the way in which each of the dynamics compound the power of the reaction the addict is having.

Understanding the trajectory of time travel

The four elements of time travel are described in general along with a brief overview of the potential impact on you and others. The elements, as they appear in Concept Lesson 3.4, present a clear progression from one element to the next, but the picture is somewhat misleading. The phases, while they tend to be progressive in nature, have very fluid boundaries, and you may find yourself moving in and out of phases. The depictions also suggest that once the time travel experience begins the progression always ends in a "plosion" of some kind. That is not necessarily the case. In fact you can learn to stop the progress of the time travel experience at any of its stages.

Present Sensations

Time travel can be triggered by a number of variables. The tone of a person's voice or body language can be enough to open the vault to your emotional memories of past life experiences both pleasurable and un-pleasurable. Once your feeling memories are triggered, they begin to seep into your present experience and you are likely to have your perception of present reality altered by your past reality. When this happens you can read someone's body language as being threatening because it reminds you of a physical representation of an encounter in your past that was threatening. The visceral or instinctive reactions you experience will amplify the input you are receiving from your current environment adding further support for your altered perception of reality.

PTSD – like Reactivity

People suffering with Post Traumatic Stress Disorder (PTSD) relive a past traumatic event again and again through nightmares and disturbing memories during the day. They sometimes have flashbacks in which they suddenly lose touch with reality and relive images, sounds, and other sensations from the trauma. Because of their extreme anxiety and distress about the event, they try to avoid anything that reminds them of it. They may seem emotionally numb, detached, irritable, and easily startled. They may feel guilty about surviving a traumatic event where others appear to be more injured than they themselves do. Other symptoms include trouble concentrating, depression, and sleep difficulties. Symptoms of the disorder usually begin shortly after the traumatic event, although some people may not show symptoms for several years or the symptoms may be interpreted as being related to other issues or diagnoses. If left untreated, the disorder can last for years. Additionally, when a previous trauma victim encounters subsequent trauma through reenactment or victimization both accidental and intentional, the symptoms can suddenly re-appear.

A PTSD - like reaction, during time travel, refers to the possibility of experiencing sensations, feelings, and the behavior of others as if we had time traveled to some event in the past when we were exposed to an emotional or physical threat. The reaction can take on many forms. You can begin remembering past hurts as if they were happening in the here and now. The loss of personal autonomy or a diminished capacity to establish and maintain physical and emotional boundaries can generate a sense of emotional threat. Flashbacks can become quite pronounced and the victim can develop increased difficulty accessing their own feelings. People engaged in time travel report confused thinking, diminished trust, and a desire to avoid intimacy or a behavior that might increase vulnerability.

Over – reaction to Present

When we over-react to a situation or a person we are treating the experience as if there were a need to protect ourselves from the environment or the behavior of those around us. Unfortunately, we will not necessarily know that we are over-reacting to the present situation or behavior of others. In fact, we will usually believe our physical and emotional reactions to the perceived threat are justified "given the disturbing behavior" of the other participants or the "dangerousness of the environment." It will take time to train yourself to question the reliability of your perception. It may be helpful in the beginning to remember that your feelings are not facts.

This is especially true when you are trying to heal a painful relationship with loved ones. Additionally, many of our clients have reported a phenomenon that has become quite familiar to us. When attempting to re-engage with people in physically or emotionally intimate ways it is not uncommon to get a visit from a ghost from the distant or recent past. It would appear that intimate moments can leave you feeling quite vulnerable and the sense of vulnerability seems to trigger a trickle or a flood of past traumatic memories. The scenes can quickly move from tender and caring to volatile and combative if those involved are not aware, prepared, and committed.

Implosion/Explosion

The final destination of a time travel experience can be a heightened state of emotional and physical unmanageability or discomfort if it is not stopped. There are a number of variables that will impact what happens next that are too numerous to cover in this text. It is sufficient, in this introduction, to warn that: if the encounter provides a sufficient level of emotional discomfort and the time traveler has a reservoir of unresolved trauma or resentment, there will be a "plosion" of some degree.

This stage in the time travel experience is set off from all the others by the loss of control that occurs during the "plosion". The direction of the "plosion" is determined by the time traveler's past life experiences. If the "plosion" is internal we call it an implosion. When the "plosion" is external we know that as an explosion. The person experiencing an implosion may appear to be detached and unaffected but that is usually far from the case. The imploder is imprisoned by emotions and can see himself or herself as having few options.

The exploder is not generally feeling as powerful as he or she might appear to others. More often than not the rageful exploding individual becomes fearful of his or her loss of emotional control and could prefer that someone else took over.

The following Concept Lesson provides a graphical representation of the course that time travel can follow if not interrupted.

Concept Lesson 3.4 - The Trajectory of Time Travel - Graphic Profile

Again it is important to note that not everyone, when presented with uncomfortable feelings, situations, events, and people will have a PTSD-like reaction, but we have found that addicted people are more likely than the normal population to experience this phenomenon. What is important to highlight about this trajectory is that it appears to render the person increasingly more inadequate to stop the reaction as it progresses through each stage. Therefore, in the next few assignments we will help you to develop an increased awareness of this trajectory so that you will be better able to cease the progression.

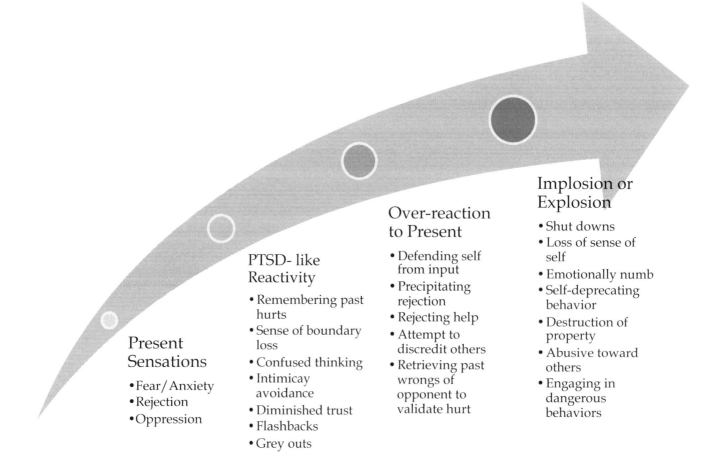

Present Sensations
- Fear/Anxiety
- Rejection
- Oppression

PTSD- like Reactivity
- Remembering past hurts
- Sense of boundary loss
- Confused thinking
- Intimicay avoidance
- Diminished trust
- Flashbacks
- Grey outs

Over-reaction to Present
- Defending self from input
- Precipitating rejection
- Rejecting help
- Attempt to discredit others
- Retrieving past wrongs of opponent to validate hurt

Implosion or Explosion
- Shut downs
- Loss of sense of self
- Emotionally numb
- Self-deprecating behavior
- Destruction of property
- Abusive toward others
- Engaging in dangerous behaviors

Phase 2: Time travel

Course Lesson 3.10 - The Trajectory of Time Travel Recorded

In the next Course Assignment we will be asking you to demonstrate your understanding of how all the segments of a time travel trajectory come together when the process results in either an implosion or an explosion. Please keep in mind that a "plosion" is not inevitable and your work in this course might very well prevent the next one from occurring in your life.

IMPORTANT:

The following descriptions of the various tasks in this lesson are presented to introduce you to the actual written work you will complete in the Course Assignment that follows this lesson. Do not write anything until you reach the assignment.

When you have completed the lesson be sure to share your findings with members of your support system and your therapist if you are working with one.

~ Task 1 ~

Brief description of a recent event when you suspect that you were time traveling:

Describe a recent event when you suspect that you had been time traveling. When describing the event provide only enough detail to inform a prospective support group member about the setting, the environment, or the behavior that would be observable to anyone watching.

~ Task 2 ~

Describe your sensations:

Describe the sensations that you felt at the time. If your memory is unclear about the sensations or you do not know how to describe it, you can guess at what it might have been like based on your clear memories of other instances. If there were any witnesses present whom you trust, you could ask them to describe what you seemed to be feeling or experiencing. Remember you do not need proof that what you were sensing was warranted.

~ Task 3 ~

Describe and PTSD-like reactivity that you experienced:

Describe any PTSD-like reactivity that you experienced. The focus here is on safety or the lack of safety that you felt. While it has been a source of conflict with clients at times, we have held fast to our philosophical position that no adult should dictate to another adult how personal safety should be defined – unless of course the other person is not capable of caring for themselves or where there is a clear and present or imminent threat of harm to self or others, as in the case of a minor or someone suffering from cognitive impairment that would render them less capable of caring for themselves.

Course Lesson 3.10 - The Trajectory of Time Travel Recorded (Continued)

~ Task 4 ~

Describe your over-reaction to the event or situation:

We are not judging whether or not your feelings were real or had a historically warranted basis to them. We are asking you to examine whether or not your reaction to the event or the behavior of another person was tied to a threat to your security in the present moment.

It can sometimes be very difficult to figure out the answer to that question, especially when your body is telling you to run like heck or that you should assume the attack position. We have learned to challenge our perception of reality when we are feeling threatened by a loved one. It can be pretty difficult to pause during a heated exchange and ask one simple question. However, we have often found it revealing and most comforting to really listen for the answer to the following question: It feels like you are trying to attack me – Do I need to protect myself? Neither one of us has ever had our fears confirmed.

This task is asking you to describe how you over-reacted – not what your motivation was or whether or not it was justified. Describe your over-reaction in terms of what you thought, how you felt, what you said, and how you behaved.

~ Task 5 ~

Describe the implosion or explosion that you experienced as a result:

An implosion refers to a profound disconnection or shut down that you may have experienced. It may have manifested itself in an inability to find your voice and speak up for yourself or an inability to hear and recall what was being said. There are far too many examples to offer in the scope of this work. It is important for you to examine and communicate your implosion process with your therapist or support group.

The term explosion refers to a profound loss of emotional control that results in an outward manifestation of your perceived need to protect yourself. An explosion can manifest itself in a stormy retreat from the environment or a physical and verbal assault on self or others. Regardless of the course that your explosion takes, it will cut off communication and can make it more difficult to get perspective especially if those around you begin time traveling and experience "plosions" of their own.

When an implosion or explosion occurs someone is always getting hurt. In an over-reaction it is not necessarily the case that you or someone else has been injured.

Course Assignment 3.10 – The Trajectory of Time Travel Recorded

Identify a time recently when you suspect that you might have been time traveling. Try to recall what you experienced.

IMPORTANT: If you find that you need more space please feel free to continue the writing on a separate piece of paper.

~ Task 1 ~

Brief description of a recent event when you suspect that you were time traveling:

~ Task 2 ~

Describe your sensations:

Course Assignment 3.10 – The Trajectory of Time Travel Recorded (Continued)

~ Task 3 ~

Describe a PTSD–like reactivity that you experienced:

___

___

___

___

___

___

~ Task 4 ~

Describe your over-reaction to the event/situation:

___

___

___

___

___

___

Course Assignment 3.10 – The Trajectory of Time Travel Recorded (Continued)

~ Task 5 ~

Describe the implosion or explosion that you experienced as a result:

Environmental factors play a role in time travel

The environment that you find yourself in can make a considerable contribution to the onset of a time travel experience. Every comfortable or uncomfortable memory that will flow to you in a time travel experience had its origin in an environment (setting) that included a vast amount of data absorbed by your five senses. The term environment is used in this course as a title for everything that is occurring in the scene in which you find yourself being triggered. There are a *plethora* of possibilities in every triggering environment from the raindrops falling on your head to an innocent wrestling match you are engaged in with another person.

The physical characteristics as well as the body language of those present were recorded by your visual sense. Your audio sense received information from the tone of a person's voice and the music playing in the background. Perfumes, body odor, and the salt air were all absorbed by your sense of smell. Your sense of touch felt the cobblestones beneath your feet, while your taste buds were drawing in data from the ice cream you enjoyed.

Every one of your life experiences has held the opportunity to draw in data through your available senses, so it is not unusual to have memories triggered by one or all of your senses. A time travel experience can begin with a baby's cry, the congestion of a crowded elevator, or the stale smell of an early morning bar room.

The authors have found that the memories of both traumatic as well as euphoric experiences seem to be more easily drawn into present awareness by seemingly meaningless environmental triggers. It is important for you to become more aware of the way that your environment influences your recall of memories that can alter your perception of your current reality.

Course Lesson 3.11 – Environmental Factors That Can Play a Role in Triggering Time Travel

In the following assignment you will be asked to examine the environmental factors that may have played a part in the initiation of a time travel experience. As you are examining this and other experiences you are looking to understand triggers and that triggers are not causes. The booming voice of a support group member is not causing the fear you are experiencing. Your sponsor's loud voice tone and agitated intonations are reminding you of a time in your life when you had reason to feel afraid. Your work in this course will help you to distinguish between past experiences and current realities.

IMPORTANT:

The following descriptions of the various tasks in this lesson are presented to introduce you to the actual written work you will complete in the Course Assignment that follows this lesson. Do not write anything until you reach the assignment.

When you have completed the lesson be sure to share your findings with members of your support system and your therapist if you are working with one.

~ Task 1 ~

Describe a recent event when you suspect that you were time traveling:

Describe a recent event in which you suspect that you were experiencing time travel. Briefly identify the people present and what was happening before the time travel began. If possible, it is best to choose a situation or event in which you have recall of what you were experiencing before and after the time travel. Do not select an episode that went on for hours. For example, a good choice would be:

Sam walked into the beach area and was almost immediately flooded by images of women in provocative swimwear. He and his wife have been looking forward to the beach all week and both were disappointed to have to leave before they got their beach chairs set up. The flood of images that Sam experienced brought him back immediately to his *addictive* forays to nude beaches in the past and he was in trouble. He and Mary drove to a park nearby and worked through the reaction over coffee and bagels.

Avoid using events in which the entire experience was a time travel that you did not realize until later. If you are unable to recall an event, solicit input from those you trust to determine if they have observed you time traveling in the past.

~ Task 2 ~

Describe the environment that you were in at the time and what environmental triggers your five senses might have been reacting to:

Describe the sensations you recall having before and during the time travel experience. List significant sights, sounds, smells, tastes, and physical sensations. Do not bother to analyze

Course Lesson 3.11 – Environmental Factors That Can Play a Role in Triggering Time Travel (Continued)

where they were coming from unless you know. If you have insight into the origin of your reactions to your environment, then include them.

~ Task 3 ~

Describe any PTSD – like reactivity that you have experienced and when you can remember having experienced similar reactions prior to the event that you described in Task 1:

If you have not included your PTSD – like reactivity in Task 2 then list them here. Refer to the description of "PTSD – Like Reactivity" presented earlier in this chapter. Once you have done that, explore your past life experiences to see if you can locate other reference points that are similar in type or context to the one used in Task 1 and describe them briefly here.

~ Task 4 ~

If you were to find yourself headed into a scene tomorrow similar to the one that you described in Task 1 what would you want to change about the environment so the experience is less threatening:

This task is asking you to use what you know about a past traumatic event to examine what you might be able to change about an environment in the future in order to reduce the danger that you might feel.

~ Task 5 ~

Describe the outcome that would result from the changes to the environment that you might make:

Describe what would happen if you could change any component of an environment that historically has been threatening to you.

Course Assignment 3.11 – Environmental Factors That Can Play a Role in Triggering Time Travel

Identify a time recently when you suspect that you might have been time traveling. Try to recall what you experienced.

IMPORTANT: If you find that you need more space please feel free to continue the writing on a separate piece of paper.

~ Task 1 ~

Describe a recent event when you suspect that you were time traveling:

_____

_____

_____

_____

_____

_____

_____

~ Task 2 ~

Describe the environment that you were in at the time and what environmental triggers your five senses might have been reacting to:

_____

_____

_____

_____

Course Assignment 3.11 – Environmental Factors That Can Play a Role in Triggering Time Travel (Continued)

~ Task 3 ~

Describe any PTSD – like reactivity that you experienced and when you can remember having experienced similar reactions prior to the event that you described in Task 1:

_____

_____

_____

_____

_____

_____

~ Task 4 ~

If you were to find yourself headed into a scene tomorrow similar to the one that you described in Task 1 what would you want to change about the environment so the experience is less threatening:

_____

_____

_____

_____

_____

_____

Course Assignment 3.11 – Environmental Factors That Can Play a Role in Triggering Time Travel (Continued)

~ Task 5 ~

Describe the outcome that would result from the changes to the environment that you might make:

___

___

___

___

___

___

___

___

___

___

___

___

___

___

Phase 3 - Fragmentation

In the Second Step we are asked to acknowledge that we have become insane as a result of our *addiction*. There have been numerous attempts to qualify this concept since Bill Wilson wrote the Second Step that can be found in both recovery and professional literature. One of the most popular is the recovery motto that describes insanity "as doing the same thing over and over again while expecting different results". Although this certainly could be described as insane behavior it does little to offer insight into the role our insanity plays in our disease's progression or the cycle of chronic relapse that can develop for an addict in recovery. Therefore, we would like to offer a different framework from which to define insanity that might provide more insight into the addicted sufferer who cannot see the role his or her insanity plays in a relapse cycle. We call this framework the Congruency Model and it will serve as the basis for understanding the third phase of the relapse process. The authors propose that it is potentially hazardous to be feeling one way and behaving another or to be speaking differently than what we are thinking.

While we may present ourselves differently to the outside world than we really are because we want to insulate ourselves from hurt or rejection, it is not going to occur without consequence. Even when our charade of being different self's to different people appears to be working there exists great potential for diminishing our *spiritual* well-being not to mention risking depression and alienation from those we care for or need. In this model we will explain the impact that having multiple versions of self can have on our recovery and the role that it plays in the relapse process.

Fragmentation

Fragmentation is a phase in the relapse process that, if not addressed will increase your risk of returning to *addiction*. When the ways that we Think, Feel, Speak, and Act do not match up we are fragmented because we present a distorted picture of who we are and what we are trying to communicate. Fragmentation is like puzzle pieces that do not seem to connect. Prolonged states of Fragmentation can increase your risk of relapse for many reasons.

One reason that fragmentation increases your relapse risk is related to the distance that fragmentation can generate between you and others. Active *addiction* can be a very solitary existence and it will be fueled by isolation. We need other people to remain fully engaged in the recovery process. A fragmented presentation makes it difficult for us to ask for help and extremely difficult for others to hear our cries for help because of the confusing manner in which we are communicating. The people around us might begin to pull away from us to protect themselves from hurt or because they want to devote their time and energy to people who appear to be willing to accept help. When we are fragmented we do not appear to want help. Additionally, fragmentation can progress to the point that we struggle to identify our own feelings or, in advanced stages, become disconnected from our feeling state altogether as in the case of a dissociative experience. Lastly, the fractured sense of self that develops is likely to trigger the desire to return to the addictive behavior that used to make it feel OK when the world did not make sense and when we did not seem to fit in it.

If you have arrived at the point of admitting the need for help to recover from your addictive disorder then you have already accepted that you will need to talk with others about the challenges that you have been facing. You will be exposed to numerous situations in either therapy or self-help meetings in which you will have the opportunity to access and potentially benefit from the experience, strength, and hope of many other recovering addicts who have travelled the road you are on. The level of benefit you derive from these opportunities will largely depend on your ability to communicate your needs to others. When our thoughts, feelings, spoken expression, and actions are not congruent we will have a difficult time communicating our needs to others. People cannot help if they do not know who you really are and what you need. Improving your ability to communicate your needs to others will decrease your risk of relapsing.

When we are fragmented we begin to "spin" inside and outside. Our behavior can become erratic, our thoughts jumbled and obsessive, our communication with others may be argumentative or superficial, and our emotional moods can swing between depression and euphoria.

Fragmentation generates a confusing picture to casual relationships and a potentially threatening one to those with whom we are close. When fragmented we may be feeling fearful of being abandoned by our partner and be thinking that we are "tired of trying to make it work." At the same time our physical presence looms large and our tone is received as dismissive and uncaring. It is no wonder that people claim that they do not understand us and that they do not know how to help.

In the 1970's prolonged patterns of this type might have been referred to as a *dry drunk*. Although a person labeled a *dry drunk* was thought to be in a toxic and somewhat delusional state, little would be done to intervene on the victim beyond labeling the problem and encouraging the person to "get back on track and work their program." A *dry drunk* is a much more dangerous condition than the overly simplistic direction above would imply. We will examine the phenomenon in greater depth later in this course.

Congruency

Congruency, a core communication goal in recovery, is measured by the degree to which what we think and feel and how we speak and act fit together like pieces of a jigsaw puzzle. The ability to get our needs met is largely related to our ability to be one person. If you discuss the challenges of work with your coworkers in a style different than you present the issues with the members of your support group, you are lacking in congruency and are failing to be one true you. We are not suggesting that your level of honesty should be the same in every relationship or every setting. If you are deeply troubled by developments at work, which you only address honestly with your spouse or partner, you are not likely to be able to successfully address the conflict. It is not expected that you will be as vulnerable at work as you are at home or with your support group, but you need to stop pretending that you are not bothered when you are talking with your co-workers or supervisors. Likewise, if you are remaining resentful about the promotion that you were passed over for and do not discuss the true nature of your rejection with your sponsor, you are not likely to get the help you need.

Please remember though that your level of self-disclosure should always match the severity and sensitivity of the situation and/or the nature of your relationship with the person. When your turn comes at the grocery store to check out at the register, it is not appropriate to spill your guts to the store clerk who asks, "how are you doing?" In that setting with a stranger the question, "how are you?" really means "hello" and does not mean "tell me about your Fifth Step".

When we put on other faces to disguise our true emotional state or fail to verbalize or test out the assumptions playing through our mind, we are embracing an alternate reality. In congruency, there can only be one ME without any game playing and as a result I will be afforded the opportunity to be a part of reality. The more we are grounded in reality the more connected, supported, and loved we can be. However, congruency can be a great deal of work. It is easy for us to allow the various roles that we have in our life to create Fragmentation via *compartmentalization*. When we say we have no right to feel angry with a child if we consider ourselves good parents, we are *compartmentalizing*. In order for the jigsaw pieces to stay together we need glue. This glue comes in the form of a sense of safety. Strategies for enhancing your sense of safety will be addressed in detail in Section 5.

Concept Lesson 3.5 – Personal Fragmentation

The depiction of the unconnected puzzle pieces is intended to demonstrate a state of fragmentation. Use the image to trigger your reflection on the types of circumstances, events, and situations involving uncomfortable people where you might present to others as fragmented. In Course Assignment 3.12 examine an example of you being fragmented through the completion of the six tasks.

Course Lesson 3.12 – Personal Fragmentation

Fragmentation is the first phase in the relapse process in which distance is likely to occur between you and the people who might be able to help you. In the following assignment you will be asked to explore a recent situation or event when your communication was fragmented. The six tasks associated with this assignment will help you to focus on the ways in which your overall communication can become distorted or fragmented.

IMPORTANT:

The following descriptions of the various tasks in this lesson are presented to introduce you to the actual written work you will complete in the Course Assignment that follows this lesson. Do not write anything until you reach the assignment.

When you have completed the lesson be sure to share your findings with members of your support system and your therapist if you are working with one.

~ Task 1 ~

Describe a recent situation or event when your communication was fragmented:

Fragmentation refers to a communication profile that is likely to leave those around you confused about what you are trying to communicate or result in them misunderstanding your message entirely. In this task, describe a situation or event in the recent past when you believe that you did not accurately communicate your desired message to others and they were confused by your communication and behavior in a way that tells you that they misunderstood what you were trying to relate.

In this task limit yourself to describing the setting or what the purpose of the event was and who was present. Do not describe the thoughts, feelings, verbal communication, or your actions as they will be covered in the remaining tasks.

~ Task 2 ~

Describe your thinking:

This task asks you to describe what you were thinking in the situation or event you described in the above task. Thoughts usually appear as dialogues between you and the other people involved in the situation or as conversations that you are having with yourself. Unfortunately, those around you do not usually get to hear these thoughts. Do not confuse this task with Task 4, which addresses what you may have communicated verbally. We only want you to write out the thoughts that you were having in the situation. It is likely that your thoughts were very different from how you were behaving or what you were saying – that is what makes it an example of fragmentation.

Course Lesson 3.12 – Personal Fragmentation (Continued)

~ Task 3 ~

Describe your feelings:

Describe the feelings that you were experiencing prior to the situation developing and the feelings that you were aware of during the situation. Again, it is likely that your feelings were different than what you were thinking or how you were behaving. If you need descriptive feeling words to describe your emotional state during the event, consult the list of feeling words we have provided for you in Appendix B.

~ Task 4 ~

Describe how you spoke or what you verbally communicated:

Describe the way that you spoke to the people you were engaged with. It may be particularly helpful if you attempt a verbatim transcript of the back and forth dialogue between you and them. If you are not able to recall the dialogue, then do the best you can to accurately communicate what you said rather than what you meant or what you intended to say. If the situation is an example of being fragmented then it is likely that what you said was different than what you meant or what you had intended to say. Additionally the words we use during times of Fragmentation usually do not match how we are feeling. Most importantly the way we say something can communicate a totally different message than the words we used. How many times have you thought or said, "it was not what someone said but the way that they said it that hurt so much"? The tone of voice that we use can be different than the words we use. "I love you too" can be said in a way that communicates a strong mutual bond or in a way that communicates a frustration and obligation to return the sentiment.

Try to examine the way that you said what you did and include it in your description. Since it is an example of Fragmentation you are likely to remember people reacting in ways that you did not expect them to behave in response to what you said. Perhaps they were "listening" to how you said it and not what you said.

~ Task 5 ~

Describe your behavior or physical mannerisms:

This task is asking you to describe how you behaved and the non-verbal body mannerisms that others involved in the situation might have observed. This level of self-examination can be the most difficult to undertake because we can have more difficulty seeing how we behave or the body or facial posture we wear when communicating with others. If you have developed a keen awareness of your non-verbal communication please provide your detailed description in the space provided. If it is challenging for you to see yourself as others observe you then consider asking other people who were present at the time of the situation what they observed in your behavior and what their reaction to it was. If you can not get access to such people then consult with members of your support group or therapist. Ask them to share their observations of your behavior when they have seen you interact in similar situations or how they suspect you would have been behaving based on their experience with you when you are addressing similar topics in other situations.

~ Task 6 ~

Describe how the people around you responded to your fragmented communication:

Describe how the people around you responded to the way that you were communicating. If the people involved in the situation repeatedly asked you to explain further what you meant then it is likely that your presentation was one of fragmentation. If they withdrew or presented an emotional reaction different than the one you expected or if they seemed emotionally flat then it is possible that your fragmented presentation played a role in their reaction. Describe what you observed in others in the space provided.

Course Assignment 3.12 – Personal Fragmentation

Identify a time recently when you suspect that you might have been fragmented (when what you were thinking, feeling, speaking, and how you were behaving were not well synchronized) and complete the following tasks.

IMPORTANT: If you find that you need more space please feel free to continue the writing on a separate piece of paper.

~ Task 1 ~

Describe a recent situation or event when your communication was fragmented:

___

___

___

___

___

~ Task 2 ~

Describe your thinking:

___

___

___

___

___

Course Assignment 3.12 – Personal Fragmentation (Continued)

~ Task 3 ~

Describe your feelings:

___

~ Task 4 ~

Describe how you spoke or what you verbally communicated:

___

Course Assignment 3.12 – Personal Fragmentation (Continued)

~ Task 5 ~

Describe your behavior or physical mannerisms:

_____
_____
_____
_____
_____
_____
_____

~ Task 6 ~

Describe how the people around you responded to your fragmented communication:

_____
_____
_____
_____
_____
_____
_____

Concept Lesson 3.6 - Personal Congruency

The depiction of the interlocked puzzle pieces is intended to demonstrate a state of congruency. Use the image to trigger your reflection on the types of circumstances, events, and situations involving uncomfortable people where your presentation was congruent. If you have difficulty recalling an instance where you remained congruent while in uncomfortable settings then focus your attention on congruent communication with people whom you are comfortable with. In Course Assignment 3.13 examine an example of you being congruent through the completion of the six tasks.

Congruency represents a significant degree of emotional sobriety. Your therapist could introduce you to several examples of a congruent state of recovery. If you need examples that are personal then discuss the lesson with and solicit input from members of your support group.

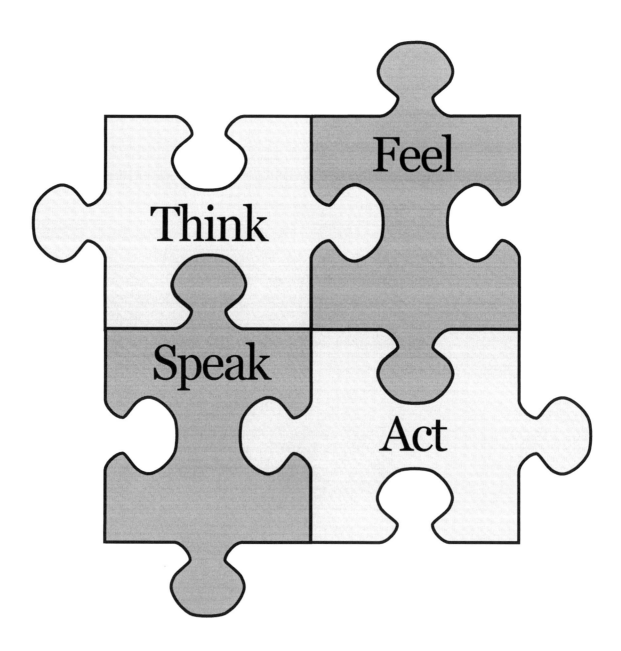

Course Lesson 3.13 - Personal Congruency

Congruency is a core communication goal in the development of your emotional sobriety. As such, a decision on your part to monitor your congruency level will play a vital role in maintaining your Personalized Relapse Prevention Plan.

In the following assignment you will be asked to explore a recent situation or event when your communication is fragmented. The six tasks associated with this assignment will help you to focus on the methods you could use in the future to remain congruent.

IMPORTANT:

The following descriptions of the various tasks in this lesson are presented to introduce you to the actual written work you will complete in the Course Assignment that follows this lesson. Do not write anything until you reach the assignment.

When you have completed the lesson be sure to share your findings with members of your support system and your therapist if you are working with one.

~ Task 1 ~

Describe a recent situation or event when your communication was congruent:

You could use the same situation or event that you described in the last assignment but this time imagine that your communication was congruent (what you were thinking, feeling, speaking, and how you were acting was well synchronized). If you would prefer to portray a different event in which you know that you were congruent than please feel free to select the example that is the best fit for you and allows you to demonstrate your being congruent.

In this task limit yourself to describing the setting or what the purpose of the event was and who was present. Do not describe the thoughts, feelings, verbal communication, or your actions as they will be covered in the remaining tasks.

~ Task 2 ~

Describe your thinking:

This task asks you to describe what you were thinking in the situation or event you described in the above task. Thoughts usually appear as dialogues between you and the other people involved in the situation or as conversations that you are having with yourself. Unfortunately, those around you do not usually get to hear these thoughts. Do not confuse this task with Task 4, which addresses what you may have communicated verbally. We only want you to write out the thoughts that you were having in the situation. It is likely that your thoughts were similar to how you were behaving or what you were saying – that is what makes it an example of congruency.

Course Lesson 3.13 - Personal Congruency (Continued)

~ Task 3 ~

Describe your feelings:

Describe the feelings that you were experiencing prior to the situation developing and the feelings that you were aware of during the situation. It is likely that your feelings were similar to what you were thinking or how you were behaving. If you need descriptive feeling words to describe you emotional state during the event consult the list of feeling words we have provided for you in Appendix B.

~ Task 4 ~

Describe how you spoke or what you verbally communicated:

Describe the way that you spoke to the people you were engaged with. It may be particularly helpful if you attempt a verbatim transcript of the back and forth dialogue between you and them. If you are not able to recall the dialogue, then do the best you can to accurately communicate what you said rather than what you meant or what you intended to say. If the situation is an example of being fragmented then it is likely that what you said was different than what you meant or what you had intended to say. Additionally, the words we use during times of congruency usually match how we are feeling.

Try to examine the way that you said what you did and include it in your description. Since it is an example of congruency you are likely to remember people reacting in ways that you would expect them to behave in response to what you said.

~ Task 5 ~

Describe your behavior or physical mannerisms:

This task is asking you to describe how you behaved and the non-verbal body mannerisms that others involved in the situation might have observed. This level of self-examination can be the most difficult to undertake because we can have more difficulty seeing how we behave or the body or facial posture we wear when communicating with others. If you have developed a keen awareness of your non-verbal communication please provide your detailed description in the space provided. If it is challenging for you to see yourself as others observe you then consider asking other people who were present at the time of the situation what they observed in your behavior and what their reaction to it was. If you can not get access to such people then consult with members of your support group or therapist. Ask them to share their observations of your behavior when they have seen you interact in similar situations or how they suspect you would have been behaving based on their experience with you when you are addressing similar topics in other situations.

Course Lesson 3.13 - Personal Congruency (Continued)

~ Task 6 ~

Describe how the people around you responded to your congruent communication:

Describe how the people around you responded to the way that you were communicating. If the people involved were individuals that you were close to then you are likely to have experienced their reactions as confirming or validating even if they did not agree with what you were saying. In most cases a congruent presentation by you will encourage those around you to be more personally forthcoming about their own experience, strength, and hope. Describe what you observed in others in the space provided.

Course Assignment 3.13 - Personal Congruency

Use the same situation or event that you described in the last assignment but this time imagine that your communication was congruent (what you were thinking, feeling, speaking, and how you were acting was well synchronized). When you have completed the two examples take a moment to reflect on the differences.

IMPORTANT: If you find that you need more space please feel free to continue the writing on a separate piece of paper.

~ Task 1 ~

Describe a recent situation or event when your communication was congruent:

_____

_____

_____

_____

_____

~ Task 2 ~

Describe your thinking:

_____

_____

_____

_____

_____

Course Assignment 3.13 - Personal Congruency (Continued)

~ Task 3 ~

Describe your feelings:

~ Task 4 ~

Describe how you spoke or what you verbally communicated:

Course Assignment 3.13 - Personal Congruency (Continued)

~ Task 5 ~

Describe your behavior or physical mannerisms:

~ Task 6 ~

Describe how the people around you responded to your congruent communication:

Phase 4 - Gathering justification

Gathering Justification is a key phase in the process of making it OK to relapse because we have to find some place to lay the blame. Every relapse has a justification, or so we think, when we have reached the point that we have made it OK to return to our *drug of choice*. The justification to return to active *addiction* flows from a progressive deterioration of our *spiritual* well-being. The process of gathering justification may go largely undetected by all but our most intimate of confidants because most of the conflict is internal to the addicted person. When the addict can no longer contain the unrest it becomes external chaos. This external chaos triggers the Elimination of the Witnesses phase of the relapse process that we will be covering in the next chapter. First, we will examine the internal loss of sanity.

If you have ever experienced emotional sobriety and the *promises* it brings, then you will undoubtedly agree that a decision to relapse, and we do mean a decision, is the result of a growing and progressive insanity. The introduction to the twelve *promises*, as listed on pages 83 and 84 in *Alcoholics Anonymous* is reprinted below for your reference. The *promises* represent the presence of a soundness of mind or if you like, sanity. When you find yourself falling *spiritually* or fear that you could be engaged in a relapse process you can use the *promises* as a set of spiritual markers for you to aim your thoughts and behavior toward. The *promises* read:

> "If we are painstaking about this phase of our development, we will be amazed before we are half way through. We are going to know a new freedom and a new happiness. We will not regret the past nor wish to shut the door on it. We will comprehend the word serenity and we will know peace. No matter how far down the scale we have gone, we will see how our experience can benefit others. That feeling of uselessness and self-pity will disappear. We will lose interest in selfish things and gain interest in our fellows. Self-seeking will slip away. Our whole attitude and outlook upon life will change. Fear of people and of economic insecurity will leave us. We will intuitively know how to handle situations that used to baffle us. We will suddenly realize that God is doing for us what we could not do for ourselves. Are these extravagant promises? We think not. They are being fulfilled among us—sometimes quickly, sometimes slowly. They will always materialize if we work for them."

The material in this chapter will introduce you to the denial process that enables an addict to maintain the delusional thinking and irrational justification for returning to his or her *drug of choice* after a period of recovery. The mode of operation of any particular addict can differ so vastly from other addicts in denial that it is quite impossible to provide every reader with the reference points that each will need to develop the self-awareness necessary to interrupt a relapse process. You are encouraged to work with a therapist on this section if you have difficulty understanding how you have in the past, or might in the future, gather the justification for relapsing.

The chapter begins with a working definition of insanity and progresses to an overview of the role that *defects of character* play in preparing to blame others for the quality of your life and in justifying a relapse into active *addiction*. The Course Assignments included are aimed at helping you to better understand your pattern of "insane" behavior that has or could alienate you from others.

A working definition of insanity

The basic text of the Twelve Step model of recovery, *Alcoholics Anonymous*, uses the terms sanity or insanity 14 times and in each case the reader is referred to either the course that one takes towards relapse (insanity) or the absence of the need to *drink* again (sanity). On page 37 the author of *Alcoholics Anonymous* highlights an early A.A. member's (Jim) decision-making process that preceded his return to *drinking*. The author writes:

> Whatever the precise definition of the word may be, we call this plain insanity. How can such a lack of proportion, of the ability to think straight, be called anything else? You may think this is an extreme case. To us it is not far-fetched, for this kind of thinking has been characteristic of every single one of us. We have sometimes reflected more than Jim did upon the consequences. But there was always the curious mental phenomenon that parallels with our sound reasoning there inevitably ran some insanely trivial excuse for taking the first drink. Our sound reasoning failed to hold us in check. The insane idea won out...

The author is referring here to Jim's rationalization that a jigger of whiskey in a glass of milk after eating several sandwiches could not hurt on a full stomach as an example of insanity. While we agree that a decision to relapse warrants that label of insanity we suggest a closer look at Jim's story, which will reveal that the final decision to *drink* again came at the conclusion of a relapse process punctuated with unresolved resentment. Jim describes:

> "I came to work on Tuesday morning. I remember I felt irritated that I had to be a salesman for a concern I once owned. I had a few words with the boss, but nothing serious" (p.36).

The author does not tell us much about the road that Jim traveled to the point of relapse but one could guess that Jim had probably awakened many other mornings before that Tuesday being resentful that he now worked in a car dealership he had once owned outright following an inheritance. It would be safe to assume that he was coping with those uncomfortable feelings in a way that was inadequate because he drank again. We do not know what Jim did about those feelings but the story tells us that he might have dumped some of them on his boss.

One aspect of the insanity is the seemingly rational process we will undertake to justify the insane decision to relapse. While, as we have said, we agree that it is pure insanity to assume that whiskey diluted in a glass of milk and taken on a full stomach will make it acceptable to *drink* again we believe the core to Jim's insanity lies earlier in the story. The strategies that Jim employed to address the feelings associated with the loss of his business are the epicenter of his insane behavior and not the delusions he created to make his return to his *drug of choice* sound rational.

The delusional thinking that evolved with justifications and rationalizations were dynamics of a numbing dishonesty to obscure, for a time, the pain of living. We know that formula for dishonesty and self-deception to be denial. While denial is an integral part of every relapse back into active *addiction*, it is not where Jim's insanity or relapse began. His relapse began many Tuesday mornings before that fateful lunch at the roadside café.

Jim is not the only one of us that has suffered this type of insanity. This author thought it made perfect sense to drink whiskey with a chaser of liquid antacids. It was reasonable to complain about the after taste of the soda used to cut the grain alcohol he mixed with it. It represented sound thinking to give up driving when his friends feared for his life because of the way he drank when he was going to be driving. These were all absurd self-delusions that were formulated after a decision to *drink* again had been made.

The addicted person's decision to return to the use of an addictive substance or addictive behavior seems to him or her to be a "good thing to do at the time," when the road to relapse leaves you with the perception that you have exhausted all of your options. At the end of the relapse process the addicted person feels there is no other way and can be heard muttering something like: "if you can't beat them join them" or "who would blame me". The same author was once interrupted during a deluded justification for the next *drink* when he was masterfully presenting at a Twelve Step meeting by an old timer who quietly announced, "… and just for the record kid, if you drink, I am blaming you." He was dead on and perhaps I would have been too if I did not heed his warning – dead, that is.

One of the authors, like Jim, was miserably ineffective at coping with the emotional challenges of life. He had exhausted all of the coping strategies he had acquired for handling discomfort in life. These maladaptive coping strategies were leading him straight to the momentary relief of *addiction*. Fortunately he began to address these *defects of character* before relapsing because he understood that they represented the core of his insanity and if they were not challenged he would have surely relapsed. Those *defects of character* represented the way he had learned to cope with life as a child and young man. They may have eased the pain of living for a while but they eventually failed him. If those defects had adequately addressed discomfort then *addiction* would not have taken hold. He came to understand that his *defects of character* represented the person he was. With time he began to support the warning found in the recovery literature that " …*the person I was will relapse again.*" It is vital that you understand the role of *defects of character* in the relapse process because if you continue to use the tools you have always used to cope with the social and emotional challenges in your life your misery will return.

"If you find this new way of life does not suit you, you can return to your old strategies and your misery will be refunded", as the recovery folk-wisdom claims.

The role of character defects in the relapse process

If you have relapsed or you are headed in that direction, the process began innocently enough with an attempt to cope with an uncomfortable emotion. The way that you chose to cope with the emotions was undoubtedly maladaptive or you would not have relapsed or be at risk for relapse. We refer to it as a maladaptive coping strategy because even though history tells us that the strategy has been inadequate for handling the emotional problem in the past, we continued to use it anyway. The unhealthy and unproductive strategies for coping with discomfort represent our *defects of character*.

Developing a comprehensive understanding of these *defects of character* and how to intervene on the behavior associated with them will be a necessity if we are going to know the freedom from the insanity of *addiction* that we are promised. The work you will undertake in your Sixth and Seventh Steps will be vital to your relapse prevention efforts but the tasks associated with the development of comprehensive Sixth Step intervention plans are outside of the scope of this guide.

The employment of a defect in our character to cope with uncomfortable feelings, challenging situations, people, and events was a seemingly natural reaction to the feeling of discomfort. In many cases the discomfort we are attempting to cope with has grown out of our desire to fulfill our natural instincts. The unmet need for love or security can generate a great deal of discomfort. The needs we have are not wrong and neither is the discomfort that we feel when they go unmet. The discomfort that we feel is as God given as the need itself. The problem comes in the way that many of us go about getting our needs met or the methods we use to cope with discomfort. The desire for money, power, sex, and emotional security is not the problem. The problem comes when we repeatedly use strategies for getting our needs met that are unreliable, seldom work the way we think they should, or in some cases cause more problems than we had before we employed the strategy. By way of illustration consider the following profile:

> Consider that you are feeling inadequate or inferior to others because you cannot do something as well as others can or as well as you would like to. The discomfort associated with the feeling of inadequacy is to be expected. It is natural so to speak. If you were to share those feelings with others with similar experiences to yours, you would be less likely to feel stuck or less valuable. You would be more likely to be able to obtain a balanced perspective of your strengths and weaknesses. If, however, you began gossiping about those you view as superior to you or perhaps as more fortunate than yourself, your self-esteem will be temporarily lifted by your criticism of others. The key word in the previous sentence is temporarily. You will not actually know how to play a piano as well as the person you feel inferior to and you are less likely to do something about your desire to play the piano as well as your target of gossip. If that were not bad enough, gossip will always diminish your value with others, create distance between you and the God of your understanding, and if you get sober you will need to make amends to those you have gossiped about. You could take piano lessons and purposefully address the feelings that you have, but you will have to stop gossiping because it will consume the energy you might put into practicing the piano.
>
> Let's reflect on where we have been. When the discomfort of a relapse process began, we sought escape but we had not counted on being launched into time travel. The whirlwind of emotions and collage of hurtful memories that developed made it difficult for us to

remain our true self. We became fragmented and could not get our
emotional needs met. As the discomfort grew we struggled to find
an explanation for our pain and, as usual, looked outside ourselves.

The tendency for addicts to blame others for the quality of their life is one of the hallmark features of an active addictive illness and, as such, the act of blaming others is a real threat to our sobriety. Once inside the relapse process you will find yourself looking for someone to blame and this will generally take no longer than a minute or two.

Gathering Justification is a particularly insane phase in the relapse process because we secretly know that we are in trouble by the time fragmentation begins. We know that we are being none too smart and that there will be a bill to pay when the wild ride is all over. The process of gathering justification identifies who we are going to blame and where we are going to send the emotional bill. The act of gathering justification is the first of two steps required in making the relapse okay. Once the relapse is okay the illusion that an addictive substance or addictive behavior is the solution does not seem like an illusion at all – it just seems like the right thing to do at the time. We look to blame situations, people and events for our pain. The second step in making the relapse okay is the process of eliminating the witnesses.

If we are going to interrupt a relapse process at this stage then we will need to stop blaming situations, people and events for the quality of our life. Many of us have mounted convincing arguments in support of the position that forces outside of our control were responsible for the pain we sought to escape through the use of addictive substances or behaviors. Our resentments were justified and as we prepared to "drink the poison intended for others" you could hear our negative spirit's battle cry:

SOMEBODY MUST PAY FOR THIS!

Gathering justification for a relapse is a process that relies heavily on the development and maintenance of resentments. While a resentment can be defined simply as a "re-feeling," a slightly more in-depth examination of the dynamic development of a resentment and the resources needed for the maintenance of a storehouse for resentments is in order here. First, we will explore how resentments are developed by examining the core of resentment.

All resentments share a common central belief that other people, places, events and/or situations or circumstances are responsible for the way we feel and that they should be held accountable for the diminished quality of our lives. While we do believe that no one can make you feel anything and that *sober living* demands that each of us takes full responsibility for our own feelings, we will save that debate for another time. We will concede that one person's behavior toward another can trigger emotional discomfort because of the reaction the target person has to the behavior and it can create great emotional pain. The decision to harbor that discomfort and continue to blame the "wrong doer" for ongoing anger, mistrust of others, generalized negativity, low self-esteem, depression, and the mistreatment by you of others, etc., involves the process of developing a resentment.

The art of placing the blame outside of yourself

The art of blaming situations, people, and events for the quality of our own lives is a skill that is acquired as a child. Children do not start out lying and blaming others. Children generally begin by blaming themselves for the poor behavior of others. A child learns to lie because it eases the pain of what he or she has done or what he or she is experiencing. Lying is a mood changing behavior and can become quite addictive.

A child will break something and generally feel bad even though they might not look that way when the incident is first discovered. The broken object is now of less value and the child may also feel like he or she are of less personal value as well because he or she had failed to properly care for the object that is now broken. The experience is painful enough without the hurtful consequences often imposed by adults. The toy is no longer the same and the child feels bad that they were unable to take care of it in the way that he or she had imagined they could. It can get worse when the losses are discovered. If someone discovers the broken toy and the child is emotionally shut down or fragmented and fails to take responsibility for the broken object then it is likely that others will want to assign the responsibility to someone. Assigned responsibility usually comes in form of blame and generally is accompanied by shame. You can hear for yourself:

Mom: John, do not run when you are carrying that piggy bank!

John: Thinks to himself - what the heck, I can do it – I can do anything!

Sound: C R A S H

Mom: John!!!! How could you? Your grandmother just brought you that piggy bank. You should be ashamed of yourself. You are going to be the death of me!

John: It dropped. I did not do it. I don't care about some dumb piggy bank anyway. Where is the candy? I am hungry! There is never any food in this house.

A child says, "It broke" and a man, provided he has become a man, says, "I broke it".

When addicts begin to feel the pain of the brokenness that develops in the course of the progression of their illness they will look for something outside of themselves to explain the problems they or others are experiencing. This highly individualized system of rationalizations and alibis will be discussed in greater depth in other works but it is important to note here that it represents the core of every addict's DENIAL. If the addict has had a period of abstinence then they will need to justify a return to their *drug of choice*. A target, irrational or not, must be identified. There must be someone, something, or some event to blame for why we relapse. Relapse, remember, begins with feelings of discomfort that we look to avoid or deaden in some way. Since the tendency to blame other *people, places, and things* for the quality of his or her life is a hallmark feature of an addict's denial, the individual headed for relapse will find a target to blame. The list of possible targets to blame is endless.

When we set out to blame people, situations, and events for the quality of our own lives, we are merely trying to deaden the painful reality of the costs of our *addiction*. In an effort to lessen the pain of our reality anything and anyone is fair game. Course Lesson 3.14 and Course

Assignment 3.14 will introduce you to sample targets and provide an opportunity for you to identify your own.

Identifying a target to blame for how you are feeling or why you intend to misbehave or have misbehaved in the past is really quite easy if you are looking for one. Life is full of people who appear to offend us when they have failed to behave the way we have wanted them to. These offenses and the people we associate with them can be stored in our resentment banks for quite a long time and are quickly retrieved when we are looking outside of ourselves for an explanation for why we are disturbed. Circumstances and events that do not turn out the way we had hoped for or failed to materialize altogether will provide many targets when we are looking for justification for unhappiness in our lives. Unfulfilling careers, dissolved marriages, broken family ties, and many other disappointments can all be blamed on other people, circumstances and events when we are looking for a justification for doing something that we know is wrong.

The tendency to look outside ourselves for the cause of the problem is a character defect that many of us acquired as children when the perceived or real costs for appearing "wrong" were frighteningly high. During those high stakes moments in childhood many of us discovered that lying would ease the pain of what we did and, if accepted as being the truth by others, would wipe our slate clean. The "drug like" behavior of deceiving others and eventually ourselves became a "first addiction" for those of us who would perfect the art of self-justification that at times appeared to be an *addiction* in its own right.

Course Lesson 3.14 - Sample List of Potential Targets for a Relapse Justification

If we are planning to do something that we are going to regret or have done something that is shameful, we look inside ourselves for the pain that would explain the behavior or upcoming relapse. We generally find it filed under harms others have done to us. The pain we have endured supplies many of us with the justification for the wrong that we are about to commit even when we suspect that our behavior is going to generate more pain. The targets we acquire to blame for the quality of our lives must be identified for the scapegoats we have made them out to be. If we are going to "know a new freedom and a new happiness" that sobriety promises we need to know who we blame and STOP IT!

The following Course Assignment is designed to help you to recall the people, circumstances, and events you have used as a justification for your *addictions* or as the target of your justification for a relapse. The list below is intended for you to identify all the targets you have used to justify a relapse so that you can transfer this list to the assignment that follows. Although this list is not intended to be all-inclusive it does contain the most common targets that our clients have reported to us during our clinical work.

IMPORTANT:

The following descriptions of the various tasks in this lesson are presented to introduce you to the actual written work you will complete in the Course Assignment that follows this lesson. Do not write anything until you reach the assignment.

When you have completed the lesson be sure to share your findings with members of your support system and your therapist if you are working with one.

~ Task 1 ~

Naming the target:

In this task you are to examine the potential targets under each of the three group headings: People, Circumstances, and Events. Place a check mark in the box alongside each of the potential targets that you can identify with. The limited number of samples are not meant to be exclusive and you are encouraged to list your own in the spaces provided titled Other. When you are finished proceed to the next Course Lesson where you will be asked to address each of the targets you selected.

Course Assignment 3.14 – Sample List of Potential Targets for a Relapse Justification

Please select those items that are most applicable to you or use the list to help you brainstorm your own list of applicable targets. Check all the items that apply under each of the three headings: people, circumstances, and events. In the space provided add your personal targets that you do not find listed.

It will be important to review this list with your therapist or members of your support system because if you have focused on these targets in the past it is more likely that you might find yourself struggling with them in the future. Add as much additional specificity to the list as is needed to personalize it for you in order to make it easier for your support group to help you stay out of trouble in the future.

IMPORTANT: If you find that you need more space please feel free to continue the writing on a separate piece of paper.

~ Task 1 ~

Naming the target:

People

- ☐ Parents
- ☐ Spouses
- ☐ Lovers
- ☐ Bullies
- ☐ Young People
- ☐ Authority Figures
- ☐ Rich People
- ☐ Rebellious Children
- ☐ Law Enforcement

- ☐ Customer Service Agents
- ☐ Poor Drivers
- ☐ Late Arrivals at Meetings
- ☐ Un-surrendered Sponsees
- ☐ Loud/Obnoxious Neighbors
- ☐ Bosses
- ☐ Clergy/Church Members
- ☐ Entitled Customers
- ☐ Hurtful Friends

- ☐ Underhanded Coworkers
- ☐ Rude Stranger at the Store
- ☐ Abuser
- ☐ Extended Family Member
- ☐ Doctor/Therapist
- ☐ Sibling
- ☐ Other: _____
- ☐ Other: _____
- ☐ Other: _____

Circumstances

- ☐ Cultural Influences
- ☐ Religious Influences
- ☐ Chronic Health Distractions
- ☐ Astrological Forces
- ☐ Economic Insecurity
- ☐ Limitations of Age
- ☐ Mental Health Handicaps
- ☐ Sexual Frustration

- ☐ Educational Deficits
- ☐ Unfulfilling Job/Career
- ☐ Status in Community
- ☐ Lack of Opportunity
- ☐ Long History of Relapse
- ☐ Public Embarrassment
- ☐ Lack of Family Support
- ☐ A Triggering Environment

- ☐ Lack of Appreciation
- ☐ Long History of Betrayal
- ☐ Lack of Positive Role Models
- ☐ Prolonged State of Poverty
- ☐ Physical Disability
- ☐ Other: _____
- ☐ Other: _____
- ☐ Other: _____

Course Assignment 3.14 – Sample List of Potential Targets for a Relapse Justification (Continued)

Events

☐ Political Conflict	☐ Personal Failure	☐ Upcoming Court Date
☐ Family Conflict	☐ Rejection at a 12 Step Meeting	☐ Relocation
☐ Economic Losses	☐ Argument with a Friend	☐ Starting College
☐ Death of a Loved One	☐ Betrayal of a Loved One	☐ Retirement
☐ Parent/Child Conflict	☐ Natural Disaster	☐ Divorce
☐ Birth of a Child	☐ Ruined Vacation	☐ Other: _____
☐ Loss of a Job	☐ Large Promotion	☐ Other: _____
☐ Traumatic Injury	☐ Bad Date	☐ Other: _____

Course Lesson 3.15 - Blaming People, Circumstances, and Events

This Course Assignment is intended to help you to identify, for future reference, the pattern of justifications that might contribute to the denial that would precede a relapse into active *addiction*. In the following four tasks you will have the opportunity to identify the top ranking targets you have used or might use to justify a relapse into active *addiction*. Remember these targets and the behaviors associated with them do not provide real justification for returning to the pain and shame of active *addiction*. These targets are people, circumstances, and events that you have blamed or might blame for a poor quality of life. The people that you choose may have wronged you in many real or perceived ways in the past but no person's actions are ever responsible for our decision to relapse.

IMPORTANT:

The following descriptions of the various tasks in this lesson are presented to introduce you to the actual written work you will complete in the Course Assignment that follows this lesson. Do not write anything until you reach the assignment.

When you have completed the lesson be sure to share your findings with members of your support system and your therapist if you are working with one.

~ Task 1 ~

Naming the target:

In the first box you will identify the target by name or the title you gave it in the above Course Assignment 3.15. You will have the opportunity to identify the top ten people, circumstances, and events that may have or might serve as a target for your justification to return to active *addiction*.

~ Task 2 ~

Ranking the power or frequency of use:

Your ranking of the target is a composite of the frequency with which you target a particular person, set of circumstances or events and the pull that you feel toward using the target you are examining. The simple ranking system of 1 – Low, 2 – Medium, 3 – High is used here.

~ Task 3 ~

How would you justify blaming the target:

Provide a brief description of the self-talk you would experience during the time preceding assigning the blame. If you are writing about an actual exchange between you and a human target, present the accusations you delivered.

Course Lesson 3.15 - Blaming People, Circumstances, and Events (Continued)

~ Task 4 ~

Most recent used:

Indicate the approximate date for the last time you can remember targeting the person, set of circumstances, or an event.

Course Assignment 3.15 - Blaming People, Circumstances, Events

Check each of the examples you have targeted in Course Assignment 3.14 - Sample List of Potential Targets for a Relapse Justification. If you have been fortunate enough to avoid relapse but found yourself in the relapse process in which you are blaming people, circumstances, and events for the way you are feeling, transfer the items you selected in the previous list and describe how they were used or are used to justify your behavior. After you have completed this step, assign a rank value to indicate how strong the use of that particular target and justification was/is for the resulting behavior. Lastly, indicate the last time you used the particular item as a target for justification.

IMPORTANT: If you find that you need more space please feel free to continue the writing on a separate piece of paper.

Task 1: Target	Task 2: Rank	Task 3: How You Would Justify Blaming This Target	Task 4: Most Recent Use

Course Lesson 3.16 - Harboring Resentments

The next Course Assignment is intended to introduce you to the importance and value of understanding the mood-altering role that resentments can play in our lives. The idea that the maintenance of resentment can serve as a mood altering function in your life may be a foreign concept to you. You are not alone. Many of us have struggled with letting go of the child-like tendency toward blaming others for the quality of our own lives. And for others of us who have been haunted for years by resentment towards people who are no longer in our day-to-day lives, the idea that we were purposefully holding on to resentments seemed absurd. The authors have been challenged many times by clients who took exception to the notion that they might be harboring the resentment to avoid having to make changes in their own lives. Your work on the Sixth and Seventh Steps will take you further into the dynamic nature of lingering resentments. For now our focus is on the identification of the role that resentments play in the relapse process.

IMPORTANT:

The following descriptions of the various tasks in this lesson are presented to introduce you to the actual written work you will complete in the Course Assignment that follows this lesson. Do not write anything until you reach the assignment.

When you have completed the lesson be sure to share your findings with members of your support system and your therapist if you are working with one.

~ Task 1 ~

Describe an illogical/irrational resentment that has surfaced in the past 30 - 90 days:

While we could argue that all resentments are illogical and irrational, we are not going to introduce that debate in this course. When you find yourself running the videotape of a hurt in your mind over and over and it is using up valuable time or spoiling your day, it makes no rational sense. When your childhood bullies are living rent free in your head it defies logic and reason.

Describe briefly a resentment you've had surface in the past 30 - 90 days that does not make sense in light of all that you have in your life today.

Describe how you were hurt when the event first happened and what impact that injury is still having on your life today.

~ Task 2 ~

What is the age of this resentment and how many times has it been recycled:

What is your first recollection of the birth of this resentment? Remember that resentment is a re-feeling of a previously endured or perceived harm. Do not list the age of the first offense but the first time you re-felt a previous harm that you perceived or endured. Provide a guess about the number of times that you have re-felt the original real or perceived harm.

Course Lesson 3.16 - Harboring Resentments (Continued)

~ Tasks 3 ~

What has the resentment cost you:

Resentments contribute to or cause depressed moods. The time spent ruminating over old injuries without making changes is time lost forever. The loss of energy and productivity that can result from resentfulness can greatly diminish your gratitude and can create the perception that your recovery efforts are not worth it. We could go on for chapters about the price of untreated resentments but we assure you that harboring resentments will eventually generate a bill that you will not be able to cover. Since there is no safe harbor for our resentments we will need to be rid of them no matter how entitled we feel. Resentment is the ingestion of the poison we intend for others.

In this task, list the costs of harboring resentments. This quick assessment will be valuable to your recovery even if you have not yet begun clearing away the wreckage of your past.

~ Task 4 ~

Describe the last pre-relapse or last known resentment:

If you have suffered a relapse, review the period just prior to active *addiction* to see how you were feeling about the people, circumstances, and events in your life. If you cannot recall the material, question those close to you for input about how they viewed you. If you cannot identify a pre-relapse resentment or have been fortunate to not have endured the pain of relapse, then choose the last time you remember feeling resentful. If you can recall no resentments in your life then perhaps you are not an addicted person – only kidding.

When you identify the focus of your resentment, describe briefly what you experienced, how you handled it, and what the lasting impact was or has been.

Course Assignment 3.16 - Harboring Resentments

Harboring resentments creates a system of rationalizations and justifications that serves as the core of denial. We have learned that neither the battle nor the relapse is necessary. The recovery text *Alcoholics Anonymous* suggests that we stop the blame game in the promise that "we have ceased fighting anything or anyone - even alcohol. For by this time sanity will have returned." It could be argued that there can be no sanity as long as we look for others to blame for the quality of our own lives. There are numerous cautions in the recovery literature against the harboring of resentments so it behooves us to rid ourselves of the burden they impose on our recovery. When we are gathering the justification for our pain we are justifying the insane act of returning to an addictive process.

In the space below, identify one of the most irrational or illogical resentments you have used to explain your own emotional disturbance in the past 30 – 90 days. Identify how old the resentment is and guess how many times you have re-felt it. Tally up what the cost of the resentment has been to you since the events that gave birth to it occurred. Finally, describe the last resentment that preceded your last *acting out episode*.

IMPORTANT: If you find that you need more space please feel free to continue the writing on a separate piece of paper.

~ Task 1 ~

Describe an illogical/irrational resentment that has surfaced in the past 30 - 90 days:

_____

_____

_____

_____

~ Task 2 ~

What is the age of this resentment and how many times has it been recycled:

_____

_____

_____

_____

Course Assignment 3.16 - Harboring Resentments (Continued)

~ Tasks 3 ~

What has the resentment cost you:

_____
_____
_____
_____
_____
_____
_____

~ Task 4 ~

Describe the last pre-relapse or last known resentment:

_____
_____
_____
_____
_____
_____

Phase 5 - Eliminating the witnesses

In the last days of the older author's (John) active alcoholism the atmosphere that was the most inviting to his self destructive night of oblivion was hardly what you would expect from a 19-year old riding on the crest of the era known for sex, drugs and rock 'n' roll. The wild beach parties and riotous drinking games had faded like dusk and left him at Zotto's Bar & Grille. Zotto's served shots and beer to whomever could reach the bar and had the money. Most of the patrons failed to make it to the men's room in time and if they did, you would hear them gasp for air before entering because once inside you did not dare inhale.

The lights were dimmed down and the patrons seldom looked at each other and rarely spoke. No one was ever going to look down their nose at you. You never had to speak to anyone if the bartender knew what you drank. Most importantly the mirrors were frosted over so you always looked better than reality. Zotto's was a perfect place to numb out because there were no witnesses.

Eliminating the witnesses is the second step of insanity found in the process of making the relapse OK. The behaviors associated with this step are aimed at helping to obscure from the addict's perception that he or she is in any danger. If his or her spouse's input might cause him to experience an honest self-appraisal he or she will need to be eliminated. If the addict's support group or children begin to complain about his or her unavailability, the relationships involved will need to be re-defined. If prayer and meditation time or favorite fellowship meetings begin to illuminate the distress the addict is in, then meeting schedules will have to change. All the behaviors found in this stage will seem perfectly legitimate to the addict because he or she will view themselves as only trying to take care of his or her own emotional security. If someone is bringing you bad or unwanted news the easy thing to do is to "kill" off the messenger. NO, we are not trying to say that it is acceptable to exterminate people or cut them out of your life; however, death by character assassination and starving someone emotionally will have nearly the same impact.

The witch in the fairytale asks the mirror who the fairest in all the land is. When she is told that it is someone other than her, she smashes the mirror for telling her the truth. The phase of Eliminating the Witnesses is a lot like the fairytale but with much greater real human costs. The addict has the greatest urgency to silence those he or she has come to depend on the most. When we silence people, whose input, love, attention, and support we need, it serves only to threaten the security we set out to preserve in the first place.

First, we push people away to avoid the pain of seeing ourselves the way that others see us. Before long a sense of isolation develops that threatens our emotional security and increases the attraction that relapse has for us. The vicious cycle is hurling us closer to relapse because a final decision to act out or take an addictive substance is always preceded by a desire to change the way we feel.

In this phase of the relapse process you can do as much damage to the important relationships in your life as was inflicted during the active use of addictive substances or behavior. This is the time when we do whatever is necessary to discredit or dismiss the concerns that our loved ones have for us. Our partners and sponsors can be the first casualties because they are likely to be first to know that we are in trouble. Support group members, co-workers and extended family members are not usually far behind because of the likelihood of them having more frequent contact with us gives them the opportunity to observe our behavior and experience our mood changes.

We push people away because their caring input and fearful concerns open the windows to our soul and the darkness we see growing there reminds us where the relapse process is taking us. We have to eliminate the witnesses to the destructive course we are on or we cannot continue.

The available strategies for eliminating the witnesses are limited only by the imagination and resourcefulness of the addict. The strategies that individual people use in eliminating the witnesses are tied to the *defects of character* that they have developed over the years. We are warned that our *defects of character* will mark the path to relapse but the false sense of security that can develop with abstinence leaves many believing that all will be well once the *addictive* behavior is stopped and regular attendance at Twelve Step meetings is maintained. If all we do to recover is stop using or *acting out*, the change in our personality will be minimal. Remember: *the person I was will relapse again*.

The following Course Lessons and Course Assignments will introduce you to the interactive dynamics of the process of eliminating the witnesses from the vantage point of both the person being rejected as well as the rejecting party.

Course Lesson 3.17 - Eliminating the Witnesses: Being Rejected

A relapse process, like active *addiction* itself, is not a solitary journey. There are usually other people that are negatively impacted in every phase of the relapse process. It may be a particularly lonely journey for the addict but we are seldom the only ones feeling the pain. When we are engaged in behavior aimed at eliminating the witnesses, we are usually aware that we are unhappy with other people but we may not know why and seldom see clearly how we are behaving.

Since it is usually easier to identify the flaws in others, the first Course Assignment in this chapter begins with a recording and analysis of an event in which you found yourself being eliminated by someone you were concerned about.

IMPORTANT:

The following descriptions of the various tasks in this lesson are presented to introduce you to the actual written work you will complete in the Course Assignment that follows this lesson. Do not write anything until you reach the assignment.

When you have completed the lesson be sure to share your findings with members of your support system and your therapist if you are working with one.

~ Task 1 ~

Explain what your input to the person who eliminated you was:

Highlight what the basis for your concern was and how you introduced that concern to the person. Do not bother to include evidence to support the justification for your concern. It will not add any value to this assignment and is likely to distract you from the work you are doing. It is not necessary to disclose the person's identity

~ Task 2 ~

Describe how you were eliminated:

Describe what the other person said or did to push you away and block your attempt to provide them with meaningful input. The elimination would not have required an angry exchange or a personal attack on you but it might have. Provide enough details so that the reader will understand what your experience was like.

Course Lesson 3.17 - Eliminating the Witnesses: Being Rejected (Continued)

~ Task 3 ~

Describe, as best you can, what you imagine the person was thinking and or feeling about themselves and the input you delivered at the time of the event:

We are not suggesting that you can or should try to read anyone's mind. Only describe what appeared to be going on in the other person. You can do this by reflecting on the voice tone you heard or the body language you observed. You might also get some idea of what may have been going on for the other person if you were to imagine what it was like for them to hear the message you were attempting to deliver. How would you have responded to similar input from another person to you?

~ Task 4 ~

Describe the feelings you had during or since the encounter and what you, if anything, learned about yourself from the experience:

Describe the thoughts and feelings that you have had since the encounter where your input was rejected. Did you feel rejected yourself or was it merely your input that was unwanted or rejected? Have you discussed the encounter with others in a way that suggests that you are resentful or still hurting from the rejection? Did you learn anything about yourself from the exchange? Did you have any insights into the way that you respond or react to input when someone is concerned about you?

Course Assignment 3.17 - Eliminating the Witnesses: Being Rejected

Describe the last time that you attempted to share your genuine concern for someone or for his or her recovery and it was not received well.

IMPORTANT: If you find that you need more space please feel free to continue the writing on a separate piece of paper.

~ Task 1 ~

Explain what your input to the person who eliminated you was:

_____

_____

_____

_____

~ Task 2 ~

Describe how you were eliminated:

_____

_____

_____

_____

Course Assignment 3.17 - Eliminating the Witnesses: Being Rejected (Continued)

~ Task 3 ~

Describe, as best you can, what you imagine the person was thinking and/or feeling about themselves and the input you delivered at the time of the event:

_____

_____

_____

_____

_____

_____

~ Task 4 ~

Describe the feelings you had during or since the encounter and what you, if anything, learned about yourself from the experience:

_____

_____

_____

_____

_____

_____

Course Lesson 3.18 – Eliminating the Witnesses: Rejecting Another

In the relapse process it is likely that someone other than us will know that we are in trouble. It is not unusual to hear in the recovery culture that several people had shared a common fear for the stability of another member's sobriety who eventually relapsed. Some will take the risk to share their concerns and others will not. It is common to hear that a relapse has occurred and no one attempted to alert the addict of an impending crash. The communication may not have been direct and confrontational but it is likely that you will be able to recall some reference of concern that others attempted to communicate to you even if they failed to use a 2 X 4 to get your attention.

In the last assignment you had an opportunity to briefly explore what it was like for you to be the one eliminated. In this assignment we are asking you to take what you learned about yourself in Course Assignment 3.18 and use it to more fully examine your experience with eliminating the witnesses in your life. Do not concern yourself with trying to select the perfect example. You could choose to complete as many different assignments as you choose. There are many ways to eliminate the witnesses from verbally attacking them to avoidance. The focus of this assignment is on the setting of a verbal exchange.

IMPORTANT:

The following descriptions of the various tasks in this lesson are presented to introduce you to the actual written work you will complete in the Course Assignment that follows this lesson. Do not write anything until you reach the assignment.

When you have completed the lesson be sure to share your findings with members of your support system and your therapist if you are working with one.

~ Task 1 ~

Briefly explain what you were told by the person who you eliminated:

      This task examines both the message of concern that was delivered and the way that it was framed. It is in your best interest if you select an event that involves a messenger whom you would normally trust and material that the messenger should know something about. We want to help you to understand and be able to identify the action of eliminating the witnesses. We do not want you to get bogged down in whether or not the messenger is trustworthy, as it will distract you from your relapse prevention work.

~ Task 2 ~

Describe, as best you can, how you eliminated the witness (how you reacted to the input of concern that put distance between you and the messenger):

      There are probably an infinite number of ways of eliminating the witnesses in our lives who try to get our attention about the concern that they have for our recovery. Focus on what you were being asked to examine about yourself and the point at which you began to shut him or her out. For some of us the elimination begins when the messenger says, " I'd like to talk with you about something."

Course Lesson 3.18 – Eliminating the Witnesses: Rejecting Another (Continued)

For those of you with hair trigger shut downs to any input: your elimination of the messenger will seem immediate but most of us will get some degree of warning threat that we are about to get "bad news". Before we raise our deflection shields we justify the elimination. It may be as simple as "nobody really cares about me anyway" or "I can never get it right – so why bother".

Others who are more apt to take an actively defensive position or an aggressive position, the elimination begins with the gathering of evidence of the messenger's wrongs in order to discredit him or her and the message being delivered, and ends with a grand exodus or posturing intending to intimidate the messenger and chase him or her off.

Describe in simple detail how you eliminated the witness during or after the event without justifying your behavior.

~ Task 3 ~

Explain the thoughts and/or the feelings that you had that made it difficult for you to receive the input:

This could become a daunting task if a thorough analysis of the event were undertaken because there could be a great number of life experiences that made it difficult for you to accept any input whether it was praise or criticism. Your Fourth and Sixth Step work will help you get a handle on many of the dynamics that drive your reactions or *defects of character*.

List or describe the thoughts or feelings that blocked you from the input and made it necessary to eliminate the witness.

~ Task 4 ~

Describe the outcome:

Every time we eliminate a witness there is an outcome. Some are short-lived while others can become life-long. Describe the immediate and delayed consequence/s to you and how you believe that others were impacted by your eliminating behavior.

Course Assignment 3.18 – Eliminating the Witnesses: Rejecting Another

Describe the last time that someone who cares for you expressed a genuine concern for you or your recovery and you did not receive it well.

IMPORTANT: If you find that you need more space please feel free to continue the writing on a separate piece of paper.

~ Task 1 ~

Briefly explain what you were told by the person who you eliminated:

_____

_____

_____

_____

_____

~ Task 2 ~

Describe, as best you can, how you eliminated the witness (how you reacted to the input of concern that put distance between you and the messenger):

_____

_____

_____

_____

_____

Course Assignment 3.18 – Eliminating the Witnesses: Rejecting Another (Continued)

~ Task 3 ~

Explain the thoughts and/or the feelings that you had that made it difficult for you to receive the input:

_____

_____

_____

_____

_____

_____

~ Task 4 ~

Describe the outcome:

_____

_____

_____

_____

_____

_____

_____

Phase 6 - Dry Drunk

The Dry Drunk phase in the relapse process marks the last jumping off point before a relapse back into active *addiction*. The *dry drunk* phenomenon represents the level of behavioral, emotional, and *spiritual* toxicity that often leaves observers suspecting that the addicted person has already relapsed. This level of toxicity can intensify to the point of rationalizing a return to your *drug of choice* and eventually deteriorate into an actual relapse action. The behaviors associated with a *dry drunk* are extremely addict-specific and therefore quite varied from one person to the next. We will not even attempt an overview of the behaviors associated with a *dry drunk* phenomenon because it is far beyond the scope of this work and will fill several volumes. It will be critical to your Personal Relapse Prevention Plan for you to be able to develop and monitor a profile of what you might look like if you were experiencing a *dry drunk*. Your personalized detail of your *dry drunk* profile can also help others to help you because it might not otherwise be clear to your support group that you are in that degree of trouble.

During a Dry Drunk phase there is generally little doubt, even in the mind of the addicted person, that something has gone very wrong. Sometimes the insanity of a *dry drunk* will frighten the addicted person into making changes in his or her recovery strategies. Those who care about the addicted person will want to help but it will be very difficult unless they have become an intimate member of the addict's support group and are prepared in advance for such a crisis.

The Course Lesson and Course Assignment that follow will help you to identify for you and others what you might look like if you were struggling in a Dry Drunk phase and on the verge of a relapse.

Course Lesson 3.19 - A Personal Definition of a Dry Drunk

A *dry drunk* can and will eventually impact every area of the addicted person's life from career to physical well-being. A dry addict may not look a whole lot different than the average miserably cynical and depressive person in a very bad moment in time or phase of life. The difference between average people and us will become readily apparent if a *dry drunk* leads to an actual relapse. If our *dry drunk* state leads to a relapse we can become miserably cynical and depressed for quite a long time.

The reference to the similarity between the *dry drunk* and the average miserable person is not intended to be comforting so we understand if you found no solace in the comparison. There is a silver lining to this dark cloud. The steps we need to use to establish and maintain abstinence – because we are not average – can help us to avoid the pain or *dry drunk* of the average miserable person.

As a prerequisite to completing the first tasks you will need to undertake a thorough review of your First Step because the powerlessness and unmanageability you first identified will contain examples of toxic thinking and feeling states as well as references to toxic speech and behavior patterns. A return to the material of your First Step will help you determine if you are in trouble now. The correlation will be easy to spot. It is simple: if you were thinking like, feeling like, behaving like, or speaking like you are now, during your active *addiction* – then you are in trouble now. Once you have identified toxic states during your active *addiction* compare them to toxic states that you have or might experience during your recovery that might leave others thinking you have relapsed.

For example, your First Step material might expose to you that there was a great deal of unproductive or negative thinking that became a standard pattern during your active *addiction*. Your review could reveal that your manner of speaking was harsh, degrading, or vulgar when you were active. If so, ask yourself what that would mean if you behaved that way in abstinence. The behavioral patterns of your active *addiction* might reflect isolation, vindictiveness, defensiveness or a variety of other emotionally and *spiritually* debilitating coping strategies.

If you have not completed a written First Step it would be wise to prepare one from memory or with the help of a knowledgeable and caring historian. Your First Step will provide a snap shot of what it was like before you made a decision to develop and maintain a sober life-style. Review the powerlessness and unmanageability that beat you into a state of willingness. Many of the behaviors that contributed to the consequences you identified in your First Step will begin to appear in a *dry drunk*. The following areas represent the typical locations of powerlessness and unmanageability:

- Physical well-being
- Emotional peace of mind
- *Spiritual* grounding
- Romantic/Sexual fulfillment
- Financial security
- Legal/Social propriety

Now that you have thoroughly reviewed and perhaps made addendums to your First Step you are ready to complete Task 1.

Course Lesson 3.19 - A Personal Definition of a Dry Drunk (Continued)

IMPORTANT:

The following descriptions of the various tasks in this lesson are presented to introduce you to the actual written work you will complete in the Course Assignment that follows this lesson. Do not write anything until you reach the assignment.

When you have completed the lesson be sure to share your findings with members of your support system and your therapist if you are working with one.

~ Task 1 ~

List examples of your toxic thoughts, feelings, speech and behavioral patterns from your active addiction:

Describe through example under the four headings of thoughts, feelings, speech and behavioral patterns how you or others might know that you were toxic in the past.

~ Task 2 ~

Describe times of toxicity in recovery when you suspect that you were experiencing a dry drunk:

Examine a time since first entering recovery from your *addiction* that you can identify examples of toxic thinking and have reason to suspect that you were having a *dry drunk* experience. Avoid any desire to explain and or defend your behavior. In this assignment, it does not matter why or how you became toxic – only that you demonstrate that you are able to identify toxic behavior.

~ Task 3 ~

Create a hypothetical scene from the future, based on what you know about your toxicity, that contains signs for those around you to use as the basis of their perception that you are having a dry drunk experience:

Look into the future and focus on circumstances or events in which you could imagine or fear that you might begin to slip in the quality of your program. Describe what is toxic about your thoughts, feelings, speech and behavioral patterns.

Course Lesson 3.19 - A Personal Definition of a Dry Drunk (Continued)

~ Tasks 4 ~

Take any dry drunk scene, real or imagined, and identify what concerns those who care about you might have or what they might do to help you see that you were in trouble.

Pick any real or imagined *dry drunk* scene and briefly describe what is happening that suggests that you are experiencing a *dry drunk*. Once you have given a brief description place each of the important people in your life in the scene with a strategy that they might use to help you see that you are in trouble. Do this in a way that you would be likely to receive the input.

Course Assignment 3.19 – Personal Definition of a Dry Drunk

The following Tasks will help you to be able to articulate clearly to members of your support group or your therapist how they might know that you were experiencing a *dry drunk*.

IMPORTANT: If you find that you need more space please feel free to continue the writing on a separate piece of paper.

~ Task 1 ~

List examples of your toxic thoughts, feeling states, speech and behavioral patterns from your active addiction:

Toxic Thoughts:

_____

_____

_____

_____

_____

Toxic Feeling States:

_____

_____

_____

_____

_____

Course Assignment 3.19 – Personal Definition of a Dry Drunk (Continued)

Toxic Speech Patterns:

Toxic Behavioral Patterns:

~ Task 2 ~

Describe times of toxicity in recovery when you suspect that you were experiencing a dry drunk:

Describe the events:

Course Assignment 3.19 – Personal Definition of a Dry Drunk (Continued)

List the examples of your toxicity from that scene:

~ Task 3 ~

Create a hypothetical scene from the future, based on what you know about your toxicity, that contains signs for those around you to use as the basis of their perception that you are having a dry drunk experience:

Describe the event:

List signs of your toxicity that others might use to identify that you are having a dry drunk experience:

Course Assignment 3.19 – Personal Definition of a Dry Drunk (Continued)

~ Tasks 4 ~

Take any dry drunk scene, real or imagined, and identify what concerns those who care about you might have or what they might do to help you see that you were in trouble.

Describe the event and examples of your toxicity:

_____

_____

_____

_____

_____

_____

_____

List the important people by name and role in your life and how they might have successfully helped you see that you were in trouble:

_____

_____

_____

_____

_____

_____

Phase 7 - Relapse

Relapse or *acting out* will take on many forms. In order to clearly define a personal relapse one must have known something of sobriety. Many old timers and newcomers alike report that in spite of the original discomfort that seemed to engulf them when they decided to get help, the early days of recovery were incredible – almost miraculous. Most marvel at the freedom that they experienced as they rose from the ashes of shame that had blanketed them like the pervasive deposits left by a volcanic eruption. Newcomers speak of true brother/sisterhood, the likes of which many had not known before. The *promises* of recovery referred to at many meetings they had been attending seemed like it could be possible for them. In fact, many changes in home and family life had begun to materialize before their very eyes. For many it was a magical time. In order to fully understand the insanity of relapse one must begin to enjoy the fruits of recovery.

Those who preach that relapse is a part of the recovery process and as such is an example of a low point or setback in recovery have probably never freely climbed out of the wreckage left by an active *addiction*. We who have known the shame, the prevailing sense of indecency, the insanity of the broken promises, and shattered dreams of active *addiction* would never describe relapse as an expected aspect of recovery in the normal course of things. Relapse is not a stage or an aspect of the recovery process – it is the eventual outcome for someone who has languished in the process of relapse without intervening or accepting help. The insanity of relapse is not a part of recovery, so do something when someone tells you that they are concerned about you or your recovery. The decision you have made to engage in this course is a beginning. Stick with it and get any and all the help you might need to complete your commitment to the development and maintenance of a Personalized Relapse Prevention Plan.

This chapter introduces two strategies that may be helpful to you when all other interventions in your Personal Relapse Prevention Plan have failed. If you find yourself teetering on the verge of relapse we encourage you to complete the Course Assignments 3.20 and 3.21. The chapter ends with a Course Assignment that guides you through the completion of a Relapse Recording Journal Entry for you to begin your re-stabilization process should your efforts to avoid a relapse fail.

Course Lesson 3.20 – Thinking the Relapse Through

If you find yourself wrestling with a desire to relapse or struggling to find reasons to remain sober we encourage you to complete the Course Assignment that accompanies this lesson. It is wise, however, to practice completing this now when your thinking is clearer than it is likely to be if you find yourself contemplating a relapse. If you are fortunate to never have thought of relapse then focus your reflections on the days when you knew you were in trouble and continued to return to your *drug of choice* anyway.

A relapse, as we have said previously, is not a predictable and understandable development in the course of recovery from an addictive disorder. As you are learning, relapse is a process that can be interrupted in any phase of the progression, even at the point of a mental obsession to return to your *drug of choice*. This assignment is intended to teach you an intervention strategy to employ when you find yourself alone with a desire to return to your *drug of choice*. The tasks below will guide you in the implementation of this strategy

IMPORTANT:

The following descriptions of the various tasks in this lesson are presented to introduce you to the actual written work you will complete in the Course Assignment that follows this lesson. Do not write anything until you reach the assignment.

When you have completed the lesson be sure to share your findings with members of your support system and your therapist if you are working with one.

~ Task 1 ~

Describe the most recent relapse impulse or desire to return to your drug of choice in the area below. First, illustrate the environment by identifying the individuals who may have been present. Second, describe the physical characteristics of the area, and the physical reaction, if any, that you experienced prior to the desire to relapse:

This task is asking you to recall the last time you had a desire to return to your *drug of choice* and closely examine the environment in which the desire occurred. Once you have described the environment including the identities of the people involved, the physical surroundings (sights, sounds, smells, etc.), and the physical sensations that you had been having, if any, describe the desire that you experienced and what your plan for relapse was, if it developed that far.

~ Task 2 ~

What is your expectation about how the people with whom you share emotional intimacy or a bond of mutual support within your life would react to learning that you had relapsed? Make sure to include everyone who is meaningful to you even though they might not know much about your addiction:

A decision to relapse will frequently include the perception that others would be better served if we were out of their life. The self-delusion associated with this form of denial can deteriorate to the point that suicide appears on the horizon as a solution to the problem. If you

Course Lesson 3.20 – Thinking the Relapse Through (Continued)

have thoughts of taking your life, please seek emergency medical help. The fantasy that suicide brings peace to self or others has powerful numbing qualities to it and even if you do not believe yourself to be capable at the moment that you first consider it, the idea can grow on us. One of the authors carried the "solution" of suicide around in his back pocket for the first three years of recovery as if it were some kind of "get out of jail free card." It became an intoxicating way of soothing the pain of living without his *drug of choice* but in reality it generated more emotional consequences than it avoided and prevented him from fully engaging in recovery and his own life. The quality of his sobriety and ultimately of his life was greatly diminished by the affair-like fascination that he was having with death.

Most addicts are fortunate enough to escape the pains associated with the brand of insanity described above but many try to avoid pain in ways that ultimately bring on greater pain. If you have ever considered that loved ones would be better off without you, then you understand the point we are introducing. When an addicted person justifies relapse by saying to themselves that "it does not matter anyway" and "no one would care" they are deluding themselves into thinking that the *drug of choice* will be a solution to the problem that will not hurt anyone but themselves. We have never – not ever – found that to be the case. In fact, when you have people in your life that you imagine would be better off if you slipped into the darkness of *addiction*, you have people in your life that you care about. If you care about them and they have endured your *addiction* and are still around, then the chances are that you are wrong – imagine that! People who care about you would certainly care if you use them to rationalize a return to the darkness.

This task directs you to imagine the people that you care about as well as those who you suspect care about you have learned of your relapse. When you have created a list of the key people, then describe what you think that they will be feeling about you and about themselves when they learn of your relapse and write it down in the area provided. Again, we are not suggesting that you can or should try to read anyone's mind. Only describe what you suspect he or she would be feeling.

~ Task 3 ~

Picture yourself at your next Twelve Step fellowship meeting announcing that you are "coming back". How do you feel? What are the reactions on the faces of the people around the circle? Identify individual reactions of group members if possible, then a general description of how the group might react:

In this task picture yourself returning to your first Twelve Step meeting with the knowledge that you have to tell the truth about what happened. You are likely to have a wide range of emotions depending on how long it took you to return to the recovery rooms. If you were missing for a while and had to deal with calls you answered or avoided from support group members who were reaching out, you are likely to feel much worse about your re-entry than you did about your relapse.

If you have experienced a relapse and a return to the recovering community, then you know the feelings associated with the realization that you can only be a newcomer once. It is likely that you will be welcomed back but it is less likely that you will FEEL welcomed back for

Course Lesson 3.20 – Thinking the Relapse Through (Continued)

some time. Many addicts who relapse will remain outside the recovery community even if they did not continue relapsing. It can be really difficult to return especially when you do not have a clear understanding of how it all happened or of what you are going to do to prevent the next one. If you have endured numerous relapses, then you have probably known the fear of having hope again because you have lost the ability to trust what you think, say, or feel about recovery anymore.

In the space provided describe how you imagine you would feel as you walk back into your meeting and speculate about the reactions of those you know and what is motivating their reactions.

~ Task 4 ~

What do you expect that the consequences of your relapse will be to you and people who care for you:

There is never a relapse without consequences. Some relapses, because they are short lived, might suggest that it was an accident and the consequences are minimal. There are no accidental relapses. All relapses follow a decision to return to one's *drug of choice*. There are stories of people not being aware of the fact that someone had switched or spiked their drink and other accounts of addicts recovering from sex *addiction* who did not realize that a trip to the movies was going to expose them to sexually-charged material. These situations are accidents and one could argue, as we do, that they are not relapses. However, accidents of this type are only accidents one time and one time only. The next time you get a glass of Coke at a wedding reception – do not put it down and risk that someone might spike it or replace it. The next time you go to a movie, know what you are going to be exposed to and if you are exposed to triggering material, leave the theatre. A relapse occurs because of a decision to return to your *drug of choice* or a decision to not protect yourself from your *drug of choice*.

Relapses that last for one event or one *drink* are still relapses and there will be costs even if you do not get the "bill" right away. If you doubt this, then think back to the early days of your progression into *addiction* when you fancied that you were being none too smart to be doing what you were doing but were relieved that there were no lasting consequences for your actions. An honest First Step will clear that delusion up for you if you examine each and every episode. You will see that the seemingly innocuous times in your *addiction* were anything but harmless. The consequences were accumulating and the bill came due when you hit *bottom*.

In this task focus the microscope of rigorous honesty on the reality that will follow a relapse. Describe what you imagine it will cost you and those who care for you or depend on you.

Phase 7 – Relapse

Course Assignment 3.20 – Thinking the Relapse Through

A desire to relapse, however fleeting, should never be ignored because it will always have a present day trigger and when dismissed is likely to reappear at a later date with more intensity. The following Course Assignment should be practiced pro-actively during your progression through this course regardless of how long ago your last desire to relapse was triggered.

IMPORTANT:

If you find that you need more space please feel free to continue the writing on a separate piece of paper.

~ Task 1 ~

Describe the most recent relapse impulse or desire to return to your drug of choice in the area below. First, illustrate the environment by identifying the individuals who may have been present. Second, describe the physical characteristics of the area, and the physical reaction, if any, that you experienced prior to the desire to relapse:

_____

_____

_____

_____

~ Task 2 ~

What is your expectation about how the people with whom you share emotional intimacy or a bond of mutual support within your life would react to learning that you had relapsed? Make sure to include everyone who is meaningful to you even though they might not know much about your addiction:

_____

_____

_____

_____

Course Assignment 3.20 – Thinking the Relapse Through (Continued)

~ Task 3 ~

Picture yourself at your next Twelve Step fellowship meeting announcing that you are "coming back". How do you feel? What are the reactions on the faces of the people around the circle? Identify individual reactions of group members if possible, then a general description of how the group might react:

_____
_____
_____
_____
_____
_____
_____
_____

~ Task 4 ~

What do you expect that the consequences of your relapse will be to you and people who care for you:

_____
_____
_____
_____
_____
_____
_____

Course Lesson 3.21 - Lessons Learned from Others Journal Entry

The purpose of this journal entry is to record what you have learned from your participation in the analysis of the relapse challenges that your fellow recovery members have endured.

Never include the names of group members or information that could identify anyone but you.

IMPORTANT:

The following descriptions of the various tasks in this lesson are presented to introduce you to the actual written work you will complete in the Course Assignment that follows this lesson. Do not write anything until you reach the assignment.

When you have completed the lesson be sure to share your findings with members of your support system and your therapist if you are working with one.

~ Task 1 ~

List challenging feelings/situations you need to monitor for yourself:

There is a great deal that you can learn from the people, circumstances, events and feelings that others have found to pose challenges to the quality of their recovery. We are not spectators of the troubles that others endure. We are fellow survivors of the same shipwreck and our decision to study and learn from the difficulties that others experience is an obligation that we share to raise the *bottoms* of all who are suffering or will suffer from *addiction*.

In this task you will focus your attention on the relapses of others that you have some knowledge of. Choose at least one of those relapses to describe the feelings that you can identify with that were either reported by the presenting person whose recovery you are trying to be a student of, or others that you know to be valid historians, such as the addict's spouse or sponsor. Examine the sources of discomfort in your informant's life that became the catalyst for the relapse you are studying. Make a list of the sources of discomfort that preceded (not caused) the relapse. Highlight the situations, circumstances, or personalities, if any, that exist in your life that are similar to the challenges identified in the relapse you are examining.

~ Task 2 ~

Describe the impact similar relapses have had on your life:

Describe your identification with the discomfort that you uncover regardless of whether or not you have relapsed. If you have had a relapse that is similar to the one you are studying, describe your identification with the relapse and/or the preceding challenges that were reviewed. Share your insight with your therapist or support group. Additionally, if you identify a personal relapse that you have not developed much insight into, make note of it here and introduce it for analysis at a later time with your therapist or your support group.

Course Lesson 3.21 - Lessons Learned from Others Journal Entry (Continued)

~ Task 3 ~

List actual or hypothetical threats to your security:

Challenges are not problems – they are potential problems. Challenges can quickly become a problem when we do not have a plan. In this course you will develop a specific plan for monitoring the potential threats to your recovery and strategies for intervening before there is a problem. For now, we want you to begin exploring the areas that present as potential challenges in the future. Generate a list of feelings and situations you need to monitor because you suspect they may pose challenges to your recovery.

If you are uncertain about what feelings and situations would be advisable for you to monitor than we encourage you to learn from the mistakes that others have made while coping with uncomfortable feelings, people, circumstances and events. In the space provided describe how your various bases of security, (love relationships, financial stability, social standing, etc.) would have been threatened if you found yourself facing similar challenges.

~ Task 4 ~

List actual or hypothetical consequences of the relapse to your life:

This task focuses on the consequences of the relapse itself, whether your identification is real or hypothetical. In the space provided describe the real or imagined consequences that a relapse of this sort had or would have on your life in terms of the key sources of security (love relationships, financial stability, social standing, etc.).

Course Assignment 3.21 – Lessons Learned from Others Journal Entry

There is a great deal to learn from the struggles that others have overcome in their recovery. We listen every day to stories at the meetings we attend that tell of the gratitude our fellows have experienced as a result of making sober decisions in their lives. If you are a willing student there is just as much to learn from the failures others endure as from their successes.

This assignment provides you with a framework within which you can develop a personal lesson to learn from the failures of others. If you are interviewing the person to obtain the information for this assignment rather than drawing from your first-hand awareness of their failure, make sure you have informed consent. Most people will agree to your probing questions if they know you intend to use it for your own mental and *spiritual* health.

IMPORTANT:

If you find that you need more space please feel free to continue the writing on a separate piece of paper.

~ Task 1 ~

List challenging feelings/situations you need to monitor for yourself:

_____

_____

_____

_____

~ Task 2 ~

Describe the impact similar relapses have had on your life:

_____

_____

_____

_____

Course Assignment 3.21 – Lessons Learned from Others Journal Entry (Continued)

~ Task 3 ~

List actual or hypothetical threats to your security:

_____

_____

_____

_____

_____

_____

~ Task 4 ~

List actual or hypothetical consequences of the relapse to your life:

_____

_____

_____

_____

_____

_____

_____

Course Lesson 3.22 - Relapse Recording Journal

If your intervention efforts failed and you are returning from a relapse, the Course Assignment that accompanies this lesson will help you to prepare for re-entry and a return to *sober living*. If you have never relapsed then you can skip this lesson and assignment. If you would like to do it as a preventative measure, then focus on an attempt you've made to stop your addictive behavior before sobriety.

Some members of the *addiction* recovery culture would have you believe that every one of their relapses was necessary to bring about the *bottom* they needed to develop true sobriety. While we would never challenge any recovering addict's story, we must offer the professional opinion that relapse is never necessary to get "true sobriety." We are even more certain that relapse, in and of itself, will not teach you anything. If you are going to be a student of recovery then you must be committed to learning from relapse whether it belongs to you or someone else. Another common presentation of a relapse sufferer is that of having "lost" his or her sobriety.

Sobriety or abstinence is never lost or misplaced – it is always resigned. The Relapse Recording Journal is offered as a preliminary examination of a relapse and is designed to help you communicate the experience to your sponsor, your spouse/partner, and other members of your support group. Failure to disclose or thoroughly examine a relapse sets the stage for the next relapse. First, because we can never be more sober than our secrets and second, because our failure to learn from our mistakes dooms us to repeat them.

We encourage you to complete a quick examination of every relapse you have suffered and can recall with the Relapse Recording Journal. Then follow that up with a more in-depth understanding through the dissection of each relapse or the relapses of others with whom you are intimate using the Anatomy of a Relapse worksheet available online at www.leademcounseling.com.

The following descriptions highlight what each of the tasks of the Relapse Recording Journal is intended to produce.

IMPORTANT:

The following descriptions of the various tasks in this lesson are presented to introduce you to the actual written work you will complete in the Course Assignment that follows this lesson. Do not write anything until you reach the assignment.

When you have completed the lesson be sure to share your findings with members of your support system and your therapist if you are working with one.

~ Task 1 ~

Identifying challenging or uncomfortable feelings:

In this task identify the challenging or uncomfortable feelings that you were experiencing during the time leading up to your decision to return to your *drug of choice*. Do not concern yourself with getting the perfect words to describe what you were experiencing. Be sure to address physical sensations as well as emotions.

Course Lesson 3.22 - Relapse Recording Journal (Continued)

~ Task 2 ~

Brief description of the situations in which the challenging or uncomfortable feelings occurred:

In this task you are asked to describe the setting, who was there, what was said or done that you found challenging or uncomfortable.

Highlight the situations in which your challenging or uncomfortable emotions developed. If your discomfort came during a "flashback" reminder of an earlier event in your life that you found troubling, then first describe the past event and then the current situation in which the "flashback" occurred. Remember that our feelings never know what time it is. Events that occurred many years ago could be causing you distress today even if there does not appear to be adequate justification for what you are feeling.

~ Task 3 ~

Describe the feelings and outcomes that you expected from the relapse:

In this task you are being asked to describe or list the feelings that you hoped you would experience or the outcome you desired to achieve once you relapsed.

When we relapse it is usually with an expectation that we are going to experience something comfortable or move away from something uncomfortable, which is ostensibly the same thing. Some might argue that they are *acting out* because they prefer the pain of the consequences but under closer examination you will find that the pain of relapse is being brought on to distract the addict from another pain. Sometimes the comfort is found in the ability to choose the type of, or time and place, of the pain. Regardless of what the rationalization is, relapse is expected to move us away from a particular discomfort. This is true even when it appears that the relapse is chosen as part of the celebration of something good.

~ Task 4 ~

List the actual feelings or emotional states that resulted from the relapse:

The feelings or outcome of a relapse can be overwhelming and if not addressed quickly and thoroughly can easily trigger the next impulsive urge or compulsive behavior pattern that leads to the next relapse. You might consider this section a mini First Step update in that you will be describing the powerlessness and unmanageability that has occurred as a result of your decision to resign your sobriety. It is common to hear from well-meaning fellowship members that "relapse is to be expected and that you really have not lost anything ... " and " ... you should quickly pick yourself up, dust yourself off and get back into recovery". While it is true that you should quickly get yourself back into recovery and embrace the warmth and acceptance of the fellowship, it is not true that relapse is to be expected or that all you need is to get back on the

Course Lesson 3.22 - Relapse Recording Journal (Continued)

horse. If you intend to avoid that trap of chronic relapse, then you will need to take a painstaking examination of what went wrong so that you might correct the deficits in your recovery program.

~ Task 5 ~

Describe the cost of the relapse:

In this section you will describe the cost of the relapse in terms of what you lost and what will have to be repaired.

When an addict enters a pattern of chronic relapse the loss of hope can be profound and the person can become fearful of having hope and doubtful of ever being restored to sanity. In many cases the insanity will be accompanied by the loss of ability to connect with the emotional costs of the relapsing behavior. The addict for whom the emotional cost becomes too difficult to identify or articulate may have a vague sense of the pain of relapse as viewed through the eyes and heart of those who care for him or her but even that will start to fade in the scorching reality of chronic relapse. The emotionally empty presentation of the chronic relapsing person should not be assumed to satisfy the description in the "Big Book" of *Alcoholics Anonymous* of the individual who is "… constitutionally incapable of being honest with himself or others" (p. 58). People who are constitutionally incapable of being honest with themselves or others usually do not question whether or not they fit in the category.

~ Task 6 ~

Describe how you are coping or did cope with the costs:

A close examination of the coping strategies you employed for dealing with the outcome will be invaluable to you in your efforts to learn from your relapse. It is not necessary for you to explain why you behaved the way you did when the "bill" for your relapse came due. The input you solicit from others will help you to better understand your maladaptive coping strategies (*defects of character*) or serve to re-enforce the adaptive (sober) strategies that you have put to use.

In this task describe how you behaved as you addressed the consequences of your relapse. Describe the healthy, as well as the unhealthy things you did to cope with the outcome. Who did you discuss your feelings with? How did you treat those who were hurt by your behavior? Who did you reach out to for support? What was the nature of the support you received or are receiving? Describe the mood or the feelings that you are having as you are writing about the events that have taken place.

Course Lesson 3.22 – Relapse Recording Journal (Continued)

~ Task 7 ~

Log the sobriety input you received from members of your support group and important family members:

To be a student of relapse it will be necessary to submit your recovery for review. It can be difficult at times to open oneself to criticism but there is much to learn from others if we can develop the ability to examine ourselves through the eyes of others. We do not have to accept others input as being the truth but we do need to allow the input we receive to challenge our perception of the truth. Remember this is one of the only diseases that employs its victim as its ally. *Addiction* is a disease of self-delusion.

In this task you will enter for further and future consideration the input you receive from your group members, sponsors, spouse, and other members of your support systems about the benefit you might derive from making changes to your recovery plan. You are encouraged to share the input with all who have an interest in your recovery and with whom you have trust.

Course Assignment 3.22 - Relapse Recording Journal

Every relapse that we experience or observe is full of opportunity for us to develop further insight into our particular *addiction* and ways to avoid the perils. Please do not confuse this to mean that we need to relapse to learn how not to relapse.

This journal entry will hopefully be the last time you evaluate a relapse of your own. You do not need to commit the same mistakes others have.

IMPORTANT:

If you find that you need more space please feel free to continue the writing on a separate piece of paper.

~ Task 1 ~

Identifying challenging or uncomfortable feelings:

_____

_____

_____

_____

_____

~ Task 2 ~

Brief description of the situations in which the challenging or uncomfortable feelings occurred:

_____

_____

_____

_____

_____

Course Assignment 3.22 - Relapse Recording Journal (Continued)

~ Task 3 ~

Describe the feelings and outcomes that you expected from the relapse:

_____
_____
_____
_____
_____
_____
_____
_____

~ Task 4 ~

List the actual feelings or emotional states that resulted from the relapse:

_____
_____
_____
_____
_____
_____
_____

Course Assignment 3.22 - Relapse Recording Journal (Continued)

~ Task 5 ~

Describe the cost of the relapse:

_____

_____

_____

_____

_____

_____

~ Task 6 ~

Describe how you are coping or did cope with the costs:

_____

_____

_____

_____

_____

_____

Course Assignment 3.22 - Relapse Recording Journal (Continued)

~ Task 7 ~

Log the sobriety input you received from members of your support group and important family members:

Section 4

Understanding the Symptoms of the Phases of Relapse

Introduction

Each of the phases in the relapse process can manifest themselves in different ways for each of the different addictive disorders. A dry drunk may look different for a person suffering with an eating disorder than someone recovering from a love *addiction*. It is likewise true that the symptoms that one addicted person will identify as belonging to the Fragmentation phase will be seen by another to be a problem identified during time travel. The phases, as we have said, are not clearly distinct from each other and you will identify elements of each of the phases in many of the others. The same is true for the symptoms you identify in each of the phases. For some, a symptom will appear to fit better within the Fragmentation phase where for others that same symptom may seem to belong within the Gathering Justification phase of the relapse process.

Avoid the tendency that many of us have to want a perfect fit between how you will describe a symptom or the phrase and how your therapist or sponsor might describe the same symptom or phrase. What is key in this section is that you learn to identify your own problematic behavioral patterns and communicate them in a way that others will be able to understand.

What to Expect from the Following Chapter:

- provide you with a general description of the symptoms most often associated with a particular phase

- offer a framework within which you can identify your particular symptoms in each of the phases

- direct you to examine the specific challenges that you must overcome to thoroughly address any particular symptom

Recovery – like relapse – is a process

Recovery, much like relapse, is a process and not an event. There may have been an event that caused you to hit *bottom*, acknowledge your problem, and accept the need for help but there never was and never will be a single recovery event. You made a decision to give up the imagined "solution" to life's challenges that you thought you were going to find in pursuit of your *drug of choice*. You, more than likely, made the decision to acknowledge your problem because the system of rationalizations and justifications you had tried to protect yourself with over the years had begun to fail you. Important people in your life may have stopped accepting your excuses, the projected blame for the diminished quality of your life, or the responsibility for getting you to behave differently. You exhausted your reserve of plausible apologies. You no longer experienced relief or comfort by pointing the finger at everyone but yourself. This state of being was best described in the early 70's as being "sick and tired of being sick and tired". Not terribly profound; but you will agree that it describes the condition of most sufferers who make a decision to take the Third Step without reservation.

If recovery were an event you would not be reading this right now. If recovery were an event, like a surgery or a healing, it would have removed the problem. Since there is no cure for what ails us we will need to remain vigilant for indications in our day-to-day experiences that suggest we are experiencing emotional distress. We are promised a "daily reprieve contingent on the maintenance of our *spiritual* condition". No one is immune to relapse.

Whereas, we are all capable of relapse and none of us will relapse with impunity for very long, we must learn to intervene on both the *antecedents* and the triggers to relapse. We must be committed, in fact, to intervene on relapse itself whether we employ strategies to interrupt a relapse process before we resign our sobriety or proactively establish fail safes to minimize the depth of our fall should we relapse. This section of the course will provide you with two resources.

First, you will be introduced to a sample selection of symptoms that have been frequently reported by our clients over the past 40 years. The symptoms offered are intended to help you and your therapist or support group begin the process of identifying the signs that might indicate that your sobriety is being threatened and you are drifting into one of the phases of relapse. The symptoms have been placed in the relapse phase that we have most often found them in our clinical examination of relapse cases. It may not be the best fit for you, and you are encouraged to make changes that best suit your needs. After the Course Lesson, which presents a descriptive overview of the symptoms in each of the phases, you will be guided through a series of brief descriptions of the symptoms. You will be instructed to select those symptoms that make sense for you or work with your therapist or support group to design strategies that work for you.

The symptom list is far from comprehensive and is not intended to be. It is hoped that it will provide you with a place to start identifying your personal symptoms. You are welcome to select some, all, or none of them but you will eventually need to be able to describe how you and others would know that you were in one of the Relapse phases. In the space provided, add symptoms that might fit your experience better. Give each a name and a description.

Course Lesson 4.1 – Identifying Personal Symptoms for Each Phase of the Relapse Process

This Course Lesson and the Course Assignment 4.1 that follows will introduce you to a selection of symptoms we have come to associate with each of the phases in the relapse process. In this Course Assignment there will be one task associated with each phase of the relapse process. Review the symptoms we have identified under each phase in the relapse process and select the ones that fit you by placing an X in the box ☐ alongside of the symptom titles that appear in *italics*.

You may find that the symptom titles and descriptions fit better in a different phase than the one that we have it listed in. Feel free to place them where they make the most sense to you. Additionally, you may find that you have experienced a particular symptom in several different phases. There are no rules about which phase a symptom belongs in or how it should best be described. Change the wording as you see fit. At the end of Course Assignments 4.2 Parts 1 through 6 (the ones that cover problems and challenges) you will have an opportunity to craft your own titles and descriptions under the phases that you would like to place them.

The list is intended to be a small sample of the symptomatic ways in which a particular phase in the relapse process will manifest itself. You do not need to identify with all of the symptoms or the accompanying descriptions. Select the ones that fit for you.

~ Task 1 through Task 6 ~

Identifying the symptoms for each phase of the relapse process:

Each task in the following Course Assignment is dedicated to a phase of the relapse process. Review the symptoms that are found listed under each task and identify the symptoms you believe best describe how you have behaved. As you identify the symptoms you believe you have exhibited place an X in the box to the left of the symptom name.

Course Assignment 4.1 – Identifying Personal Symptoms for Each Phase of the Relapse Process

The symptoms of each of the phases in the relapse process are listed below under their respective headings. Place an X in the box ☐ alongside the names we have given to the symptoms that fit with your history after you have reviewed the description. The symptoms that have been selected for each phase of the relapse process are intended to be a sample to guide you in your work of constructing a comprehensive Personal Relapse Prevention Plan. You will discover many variations of the samples provided. Feel free to alter the sample names to best suit you as well as include personalized symptoms in the upcoming Course Assignments.

IMPORTANT:

If you find that you need more space please feel free to continue the writing on a separate piece of paper.

~ Task 1 ~

Uncomfortable Feelings phase of relapse process – Identifying the symptoms:

☐ *General emotional discomfort*

General emotional discomfort should be chosen as a symptom when you are feeling physically uncomfortable or in pain related to a health problem that is being addressed medically and it generates emotional or *spiritual* discomfort or unrest. This symptom can also be selected when you are emotionally uncomfortable and you do not yet know why.

☐ *Negative self-talk*

Self-talk is the internal dialogue we use to view the world, explain situations and communicate to ourselves. The type of self-talk you use, both negative and positive, can have a great impact on the quality of your sobriety in general and the depth of your intimate relationships in specific. *Negative self-talk* can take many forms from name-calling like "stupid" and "loser" to doomsday messages like "you're never going to find someone to love you" and "people always disappoint you". This symptom should also be considered if you or others see a pattern of:

- self-talk that reflects low self-esteem
- a depressive outlook on life or your ability to cope with it
- a general view of yourself as not being worthy of good things happening to you
- behavior where you find yourself using "name calling" to voice your feelings about others or are the target of name-calling from others

If your *negative self-talk* includes threats to harm yourself or others you should seek emergency medical attention immediately.

☐ *Depressed mood*

A depressed mood is an emotional state that may have its roots in a wide variety of feelings, such as rejection and loss, and be related to an equally diverse collection of life

Course Assignment 4.1 – Identifying Personal Symptoms for Each Phase of the Relapse Process (Continued)

experiences ranging from the death of a loved one to financial instability. There are times when a depressed mood is actually a feature of depression. If you suspect that you are suffering with depression, please consider consulting with a therapist or your family physician. A depressed mood, regardless of its origin, will negatively color the way that we look at life and make it difficult to fully engage in your recovery.

☐ *Anxiety/Worry*

The symptoms of anxiety and worry are featured in the diagnostic literature as elements of a number of psychological problems. If you are concerned about your level of anxiety or worry do not hesitate to consult with a therapist or your family physician. Anxious and worrisome feelings can greatly diminish the quality of your life in general and recovery in specific. This symptom group would be appropriate for you to select if you have been bothered by ongoing worry about upcoming events or fear about events or circumstances you expect might develop in the future. If your anxiety/worry makes it hard for you to take needed action or it limits the life choices you have, it would be appropriate to select this symptom.

☐ *Unrealistic view of problems*

If you misread the true nature of the problems you experience or witness in others, it may be true that your view of what is going on is off or unrealistic. Additionally, if the strategies that you employ to address problems is usually unsuccessful or off track according to the perception of those you trust then you might benefit from selecting this symptom.

The symptom may manifest itself in a variety of ways. On one end of the spectrum you may find yourself asserting that someone's PTSD driven avoidance of crowds and insistence on solitary vacations is the action of a "control freak who always wants his or her own way". The person in question might very well be trying to control the threat level he or she finds in his or her surroundings. And, perhaps the person is a real "freak" (whatever that means), but to go no further than calling the person a control freak is an unrealistic view of the problem.

On the other end of the spectrum you may find that you are over-reacting to problems that do not warrant the attention you are giving them or the amount of time that they are taking up in your life. When you become angry with your child because she is using a fork "the wrong way" than perhaps you should question your perception of the problem as being your daughter's crude table etiquette. Anyways, forks do not come with directions. Perhaps something is really wrong with you.

☐ *Resentment*

There are many differing opinions about the definition or description of resentment but little disagreement about the threat that resentments can generate to the quality of our sobriety. Most relapses are preceded by resentment but, unfortunately, little time is spent addressing what to do with them in Twelve Step recovery circles. We suspect that the lack of attention paid to the "number one offender" is largely attributable to the tendency of many in

Course Assignment 4.1 – Identifying Personal Symptoms for Each Phase of the Relapse Process (Continued)

recovery to avoid working through the most resilient *defects of character* that provide the fuel for us to remain resentful and stuck.

Resentment, in simple terms, is an unproductive and intentional re-feeling of a disturbing past event. We are not suggesting that you are responsible for the original injury. We have known great pain at the hands of others and can empathically support the position that "sticks, stones, and names" and people can really hurt you in ways that you could not defend yourself from. Do not deny the pain that you have suffered. Do not take the blame for or superficially excuse the way that others have treated you and do not harbor or defend your resentments as they ONLY serve to re-injure you. We describe resentment as unproductive because it does not ease the pain of the injuries you endured and it can block your ability to make needed emotional and personality changes and to enjoy *spiritual* fulfillment. The re-feeling of disturbing past events has benefit when undertaking the tasks associated with clearing away the wreckage of your past in the course of your step or therapy work or when used as the basis of identifying with the needs of those you are attempting to be of service to.

The definition includes a sometimes-controversial reference to an intentional re-feeling. We are not suggesting that the painful feeling memories are intentionally drawn into conscious awareness for the purpose of feeling bad. We do not subscribe to the shaming adage that the resentful person is "not happy unless he or she is unhappy". We are suggesting that the avoidance of step work designed to release you of the bondage of your resentfulness is a decision; therefore, the unproductive re-feeling of past harms is intentional. Some of us hold onto our resentments because the harms that they are based in can be used as the rationalization or justification for continued unmanageability in our lives and, if unchallenged, a state of resentfulness can lead right to a relapse. One of the authors, whose identity will be kept strictly confidential, (initials = JVL) was once able to hold a resentment in each hand and still manage to pick up a bottle of beer.

☐ *Guilt*

While many of us would assert that guilt has a very long and useful life span, scientific research has found that it is only of value to recovering people for about 6 seconds (sorry we are just making that part up). When the realization of guilt causes us to identify the need for change, we make a plan for change, and execute a plan for change, then guilt serves a meaningful role in the recovery process. The longer we hold onto guilt without change, the more difficult change will become and the more toxic guilt will become. If we hold onto to it long enough, it will begin to muddy the lens through which we look at life. Then hope will become more challenging to harvest from our recovery work.

Course Assignment 4.1 – Identifying Personal Symptoms for Each Phase of the Relapse Process (Continued)

~ Task 2 ~

Time Travel phase of relapse process – Identifying the symptoms:

☐ *Over-reacting to the behavior of others*

The symptom of over-reacting to the behavior of others or environmental triggers is a fairly common indication that time travel is occurring. This time travel experience is influencing your perception of your environment and negatively impacting your decision-making and therefore the likelihood of reactivity is increased. When we are over-reacting to the situation at hand it is generally clear to others before we become aware of it. Oftentimes our first awareness that we are experiencing this time travel symptom is when others become upset with how we have spoken or behaved.

The over-reaction in question could be coming from the accumulation of challenges that have been recently endured and our current reactivity is a product of our growing intolerance of emotional stressors. This type of reactivity can be damaging to your relationships and destabilizing to your recovery. It deserves your attention and will be addressed in several areas of your Personal Relapse Prevention Plan. The symptom we are concerned with in this phase of the relapse process is specifically associated with a time travel experience. When you find yourself thinking, "she is just like my mother", or using phrases like "always" and "never" and trying to understand why "everyone is always hurting me", then it would be wise to explore the intervention strategies that are offered for interrupting a time travel experience.

☐ *Negative self-talk*

As noted above, *negative self-talk* is a form of internal dialogue we use to view the world, explain situations and communicate to ourselves. It focuses our attention on what we believe to be wrong with us or life. This symptom can develop in most of the phases of the relapse process, but it is particularly powerful when it occurs during a time travel experience where you are interacting with others. Clinical experience suggests that much of the data for *negative self-talk* is acquired during our youth when we are the most impressionable. If you are experiencing time travel and actively engaged in *negative self-talk,* you may begin to relive the painful injunctions and rejections of your childhood and adolescence as if they are actually being delivered by the other people involved in the moment.

☐ *Day mares*

A nightmare is a bad dream that can cause a strong negative emotional response typically in the form of fear. The dream may contain situations of danger, discomfort, psychological or physical terror. A *daymare* is a phrase we have come to use to explain the desire to flee a situation or protect ourselves because we feel we are in danger despite the absence of real evidence to support the perceived threat. *Daymares* can also generate

Course Assignment 4.1 – Identifying Personal Symptoms for Each Phase of the Relapse Process (Continued)

unwanted thoughts or perceptions that, when exposed through closer examination, are found to be untrue. To illustrate, consider the following brief vignette:

> John had barely settled into his seat at his home group meeting shortly after sharing his Fifth Step with his sponsor, when he began to imagine that the other group members were judging him for what he had disclosed during his confidential talk with his sponsor. The feeling of being in a "cellophane bikini" quickly generated feelings of threat and danger that had no basis in reality. No one really knew what he had shared earlier in the day and they could not read his mind. His feeling of threat was related to the intense anger and self-rejection he was experiencing and he was way off base about the "dirty looks" that he "knew" his fellow group members were giving him. This dream-like state, in which perception is altered by PTSD-like reactions, can be quite disturbing and can commonly generate a desire to run from the scene.

☐ *Defending yourself from input*

There are many explanations for defensive behavior and a decision to protect yourself is understandable when you are actually being judged, threatened, or attacked. This particular symptom in the Time Travel phase of relapse is intended to describe a situation that begins with your informed consent to receive input from others, which becomes an argument or creates emotional distance in the transaction between you and the other people involved. If you have ever been in group therapy and presented a problem for peer examination and found yourself getting angry with or becoming frightened of the person or the input being offered, then you may have experienced this symptom. We are not suggesting the input is always delivered in a non-threatening manner. If you feel like you are being attacked and need to defend yourself, consider the following response. "It feels like I need to defend myself. Are you trying to attack me?" The response that you get from the others involved should quickly clear up any confusion.

☐ *Euphoric recall*

The term euphoric recall, as it is used in this symptom, refers to the tendency to remember the positive feeling aspects of a life experience both with and without accurate recall for the events that transpired or consequences as if they are happening in the present reality. It should not be confused with an earlier reference in this work that presented another descriptive reference to a feature of the addicted person's denial system. We are not referring to the phenomenon found in the memory of an addicted person.

☐ *Dysphoric recall*

The term is used to describe the feeling perception that can occur during a time travel experience in which we find ourselves feeling the emotional or physical discomfort from a past life experience that is not supported by the present reality. When we have experienced this symptom, we have not always understood where it originated in our history or that it

Course Assignment 4.1 – Identifying Personal Symptoms for Each Phase of the Relapse Process (Continued)

was even driven by past memories. Often times, dysphoric recall presents itself as if it is the truth about this moment in time.

☐ *Implosion*

This symptom can occur when we find ourselves in an emotionally or physically threatening experience and imagine that there is no way to leave or to take care of ourselves. A mechanical implosion occurs when the difference between internal (lower) and external (higher) pressure is so great that a structure collapses into itself as in the case of a submarine that goes deeper in the ocean than it is designed to tolerate. We humans can experience an implosion, as it is used here, when the perceived environmental threat is greater than we suppose we can safely manage. When we suffer an implosion we seem to lose our ability to speak up for ourselves or assert our own autonomy.

The likelihood of suffering an implosion is increased during a time travel experience because we are or could be drawing on a great many past memories of our inability to advocate for ourselves or to keep ourselves safe when we were young.

☐ *Explosion*

In scientific terms an explosion is a rapid increase in volume and release of energy in an extreme manner. While we humans do not usually explode in a way that leaves those around us splattered with our internal organs, we have been known to erupt in emotional, verbal, and physical ways that are often destructive to ourselves and those around us. When an explosion occurs during a time travel experience it will generally keep people away from us or trigger a reaction to flee. Verbal and physical explosion can result in the needless destruction of property or in worse cases emotional or physical abuse of self or others.

☐ *Avoidance of intimacy*

There are a great many explanations for why we humans will avoid being intimate. The reference to intimacy avoidance used here is intended to describe the way that we will react to the perceived threat of vulnerability that can occur during a time travel experience. Fear of self-exposure and emotional closeness can be triggered by memories of previously threatening experiences from our past with the people in our immediate environment or distant past.

☐ *Retrieving past wrongs of an opponent to validate your emotional pain*

When we have felt hurt or injured in some way by a person, it is common to find our thoughts drifting back in time to situations in the past when we have felt wronged by the same person. This time travel symptom is fairly commonplace and most people are not likely to view it as problematic. When we argue with others about some real or perceived injustice or problem we are likely to draw from our past life experience with that person to justify our "rightness" or to bring further validation to the pain we are experiencing. When we are losing an argument with a romantic partner, for example, it generally will not take long before we are introducing material from the past to substantiate our position. Most illogical or irrational arguments are fueled by memories of wrongs endured in the past and generally

Course Assignment 4.1 – Identifying Personal Symptoms for Each Phase of the Relapse Process (Continued)

accomplish only one thing – they cause more hurt. Many times the angry escalation exacerbated by the time travel experience scares the heck out of one or both of the combatants and the fight ends. All too often the fight ends without resolution and the memories of the hurt the parties inflicted on each other adds material to the next time travel experience.

☐ *Retrieving or reviewing your past wrongs to justify the hurtful things you are doing to yourself or are allowing others to do to you*

This symptom of time travel is similar in some ways to the penchant for retrieving or reviewing the past wrongs of others noted above. It generally occurs during times of perceived personal injury, and the memories create a dysphoric reaction to a current emotional challenge. It is dissimilar and somewhat more dangerous because it can foster intentional self-injury or make the otherwise intolerable treatment by others palatable.

If you find yourself in a situation where you are being mistreated by someone and you are making excuses for his or her wrongs by focusing on your hurtful behavior in the past, then this symptom fits for you.

☐ *Attempts to discredit those you have come to trust*

This symptom could easily fit with the choice of symptoms for the Eliminating the Witnesses phase in the relapse process but it appears to be a more passive method for discounting the value of those you might draw support from. The other symptoms for the phase that eliminates witnesses are more direct and purposeful attempts to put a line through the name of those we fear will expose us. The time travel experience may be triggered by a fear of being vulnerable to someone but the process is more likely to be private and results in a connection to past hurts in a seemingly automatic way.

This symptom is impacting you when you are finding justification for discrediting the input from a member of your support group by focusing in on suspicions of them that you had in the past. This symptom could also become a problem when you are receiving unflattering input and you find yourself drifting off to people in your past that unjustly accused you of some wrong.

~ Task 3 ~

Fragmentation phase of the relapse process – Identifying the symptoms:

☐ *People with whom you are sharing do not appear to understand what you are trying to communicate*

When we are fragmented, most people will have a difficult time fully understanding where we are coming from. If you find yourself saying that, "people really do not understand" you then perhaps you need to examine yourself through the eyes of those you are accusing of being confused. A pattern of feeling misunderstood or moving from one set of opinions to the next in search of the "right" answers is a pretty good indication that you could be suffering in this phase of the relapse process.

Course Assignment 4.1 – Identifying Personal Symptoms for Each Phase of the Relapse Process (Continued)

☐ *Difficulty demonstrating emotions freely and without constraint*

Fragmentation makes it difficult to accurately communicate our thoughts as well as our feelings to others but it can also make it difficult to express our feelings at all. Intellectualization, blaming and resentfulness can block us off from the ability to identify our own feelings or at least to see all that we are feeling. Angry rages seldom communicate all that we are feeling. For example, consider the fearful emotional reactions that can develop when you expected your child home by the ten o'clock curfew time. At 10:30 you find yourself irritable and disappointed in your child's disrespect for your authority. By midnight your disappointment has been replaced by fear as you start your search for your missing child. It is 3:00 AM and your fear has long since been replaced by terror and your calls to the police and emergency rooms bring no comfort. At 3:30 AM your son walks through the front door and your fear quickly evaporates into a firestorm of anger and rage. I am sure that you would argue that the angry reaction is understandable but that would be missing the point. What happened to the fear and all the terrible things that you imagined and what of the prayerful pleadings to God to bring him home safe – no matter what?

The parent in the above vignette is behaving in a fairly congruent manner with the circumstances that were unfolding up until the child arrives. The anger and rage could not be more fragmented a demonstration of what the parent had been thinking and feeling at 3:29 AM.

Fragmentation blocks us off from the full spectrum of emotions that can occur in a given event.

☐ *Inability to make yourself understood*

This symptom is similar to the first one listed in this task, in that we view the problem as being related to the lack of understanding that others seem to have with what we are saying, but it goes further than that. When we are fragmented we are less likely to see that our desire to be heard has become an obsession.

☐ *Struggling to identify your own feelings*

The outward dishonesty and self-deception associated with Fragmentation will eventually create a significant struggle to identify your own feelings even when you want to. We can become shut off from our emotions or at least the cognitive awareness of them if we tell too many lies to others or ourselves. We would respectfully argue that those of us who were deemed to be "constitutionally incapable of being honest with ourselves or others" were not "born that way". We submit that unless a person is neurologically impaired at birth then the inability to be honest with themselves or others is the consequence of having told one too many lies. Fragmentation is the end result of deception of self and of others that will eventually lead to a place where we do not even know our own feelings.

Course Assignment 4.1 – Identifying Personal Symptoms for Each Phase of the Relapse Process (Continued)

☐ *Obsessive thinking*

Obsessive thinking is often an element in a state of Fragmentation as it is very difficult to access our feelings, present them in clear and concise ways, and behave in a way that is congruent with what we are thinking or feeling when we become dominated by our thoughts. Obsessive thinking will often generate impulsive behavior that becomes compulsive and consuming. We are less available to others and have more difficulty communicating our authentic self.

~ Task 4 ~

Gathering Justification phase of the relapse process – Identifying the symptoms:

☐ *Justifiable anger*

While it has been said that "justifiable anger ought to be left to more balanced folk" than we addicts, this symptom of the relapse process is usually ignored until it generates unwanted consequences from our reactive behavior. When we are defending our right to be angry we are defending our right to be miserable, ineffective, hurtful toward others, and sometimes self-destructive. We will resign our sobriety and choose to relapse, and we will need a justification because our time in recovery would have taught us that returning to the "problem" to fix a problem is insane. It is not uncommon to get even with the wrongs of others through acts of self-injury. Many of us learned the coping strategy as children – "I will show them, I'll hurt me".

☐ *Judgmental*

Negative judgmental thoughts will only result in the identification of unacceptable differences between us and other people. These differences can create obstacles between us and important others in our lives. We cannot learn from those we find to be unacceptable and a sober person should be able to find a teacher wherever he or she is. If the folk wisdom that suggests that we are likely to find our own faults in others is accurate, then our judgment of others will eventually lead to isolation from others and alienation from our own selves as we must, by virtue of the identification, reject ourselves.

☐ *Blaming others for the way you feel or behave*

When we are negatively judging people we have decided that they are, in some way, responsible for the diminished quality of our life. We say to ourselves that we would be different or feel different if only they would be different. When we blame others for the diminished quality of our own lives and we mandate that they change, we are usually disappointed. Healthy people will not succumb to such oppression and we are left to feel that we are powerless over our discomfort. When one of the authors found himself feeling powerless over his discomfort because others were unwilling to accept the blame for his

Course Assignment 4.1 – Identifying Personal Symptoms for Each Phase of the Relapse Process (Continued)

misery, his mind usually wandered to fantasies associated with his *drug of choice* – Southern Comfort.

☐ *Disconnect*

When we are disconnecting from those around us, even if we have not eliminated them, we lose the opportunity to benefit from their insights, love, and support. We disconnect as a result of a reliance on our *defects of character* for coping with emotional stressors in our life or in response to a traumatic incident. Our disconnect may take many forms that are discussed in the description of other symptoms of relapse and be precipitated by a number of variables, but it is never a good thing. We need others. When we are disconnected we could end up without a vital link to hope – people.

☐ *Lack of emotional support*

If you find yourself without emotional support, it is probably because you have successfully constructed a justification for your discomfort. If your discomfort has required justification then you are more than likely going to benefit from the discomfort or, worse yet, you are planning to use it to justify a relapse. If you look around and your support system is getting weaker and it is increasingly more difficult for you to find someone to talk to or who you are willing to allow to help you then you are on your way to experiencing this symptom.

☐ *Difficulty empathizing with others*

Empathy, defined as the ability to understand and share the feelings of others, is a critical strategy for embracing the vital sense of fellowship available to us in the recovery community. If we are gathering justification for a relapse into our active *addiction*, we are going to experience difficulty empathizing with others. We will not want to be close to others or know how they feel, as it will make it more difficult to justify that we have no choice but to return to our *drug of choice*.

~ Task 5 ~

Eliminating the Witnesses phase of the relapse process– Identifying the symptoms:

☐ *Gossiping & character assassination*

There are so many ways to eliminate the witnesses in our lives that a partial list could fill a book. Two common ways of eliminating the people from our lives that might cause us to have to examine our thinking, communication, and our behavior are found in the *defects of character* that go by the names of gossip and character assassination. We use these or other strategies for stepping out of the sunlight of the truth; we do so by exposing real, perceived, or manufactured flaws in the targets of our elimination. Many times these *defects of character* masquerade around as "caring and sharing" or as an example of "honestly trying to process feelings about a mean person". You might really care about the person you are gossiping about but if you are not telling him or her then you probably do not care as much as you

Course Assignment 4.1 – Identifying Personal Symptoms for Each Phase of the Relapse Process (Continued)

claim. You are right to believe that there is great benefit to be derived from processing your emotions with trusted friends and support group members because it can relieve potentially dangerous pressure and free you up to get important insights about how to change the "things you can change" – namely you. If your sharing about the character or behavior of others encourages or supports the focusing of attention on the target of your elimination, you are not going to get relief or insights into yourself. If you and the person you are sharing the discomfort with are focused on the other "wrong doer" it is going to be hard for you to see yourself.

☐ *Escapism*

Escapism can take many forms. You can physically isolate yourself and avoid contact with others. You can follow one geographical cure for the perceived problem after another. You can frequently change romantic interests because someone is getting too close. One of the authors used to change girlfriends more often than he changed his socks and it caused more problems than stinky feet but we will not get into that as we need to protect John's identity. Most of us understand the adage that "no matter where you run you are going to find yourself" but most of us do not see that truth when we are on the run.

☐ *Always right!*

If you overheard others saying that you "... never lost an argument but ..." you had "... lost a lot of friends," would you be alarmed? Would you stop and reflect on the implications of what has been said by others and examine your behavior, or would you launch into a defense of your honor? The symptom of being "always right" develops in stages. It does not begin with an angry defense of our position or a personal attack on those who question us. The symptom begins when we find ourselves struggling to remain a student of life and with those around us. If you have any question about whether or not this symptom applies to you, ask your three closest support group members if they are uncomfortable with giving you input or challenging your thinking or behavior.

☐ *Inability to acknowledge your own wrongs*

If you cannot remember when the last time it was that you made a thorough amends to someone, then you are either doing really well or you are in some trouble. If you have never made a thorough amends to those you have harmed, then you could be heading for trouble unless you are working toward the Ninth Step and have not gotten there yet.

If you or others find reason to suspect that you struggle with accepting or refuse to acknowledge your wrongs, you have undoubtedly managed to wall yourself off from the relationships that function as mirrors for you to examine yourself. Every time we eliminate a witness, we are trying to insulate ourselves from the pain of some truth about ourselves.

☐ *Rebuff the concerns of others*

In one sense, the symptom of rebuffing the concerns of others is a more advanced stage of the symptom just highlighted above. The inability to acknowledge our own wrongs can be completely passive and go largely undetected by others for some time. It is dangerous

Course Assignment 4.1 – Identifying Personal Symptoms for Each Phase of the Relapse Process (Continued)

because it prevents us from benefitting from the experience, strength, and hope that the input of others might provide but it is not as volatile a coping strategy as actively pushing those who care about us away.

When we rebuff the concerns that others have for us, we will miss the opportunity to learn from them but we are also likely to perpetrate additional wrongs toward others by our defensive or oppositional behavior. When we hurt others who are trying to be helpful, the result can be an increase in the sense of self-condemnation, isolation, and hopelessness.

☐ *Growing isolation*

The road to relapse, since it always leads downhill, can be quickly traversed. You may not see clearly that you are racing toward the *bottom* but there are warning signs. One symptomatic warning sign that you are headed for a crash landing is the absence of other travelers along the road. If you are experiencing an increased or sustained sense of isolation or if your world is getting smaller and there are fewer meaningful relationships to enjoy, then relapse could be near. We end up alone in *addiction* and in recovery we are united. Look around you on your journey. If you are all alone you may have descended into harm's way. Yell for help!

Avoiding meetings and/or fellowship with your recovery community could be a sign that you are eliminating the witnesses regardless of the logical reasons that you have for doing so. If the people or places you are avoiding were once sources of support and places of welcome and you have not replaced them with equally meaningful relationships and meetings you should be alarmed.

~ Task 6 ~

Dry Drunk phase of the relapse process – Identifying the symptoms:

☐ *Mood swings*

There can be many emotional and physical reasons for the presence of significant mood swings and all avenues should be explored to develop an understanding of what they mean and where they are originating from. Many of us grew up in a generation that explained the dangerous mood swings associated with a *dry drunk* episode with nonsense theories like, "I must have woken up on the wrong side of the bed," or "I am easily moved to anger because of my Irish temper". These and a thousand other foolish interpretations do more harm than good. It may ease your conscience to blame a "full moon" for your agitated emotional spike or a "dreary day" for your depressed mood but the truth is generally more complicated than that. Simple answers to complicated problems generally produce fleeting changes that are frequently reversed by the next mood swing. If you are having mood swings that negatively impact your life or the lives of others, get real explanations.

Course Assignment 4.1 – Identifying Personal Symptoms for Each Phase of the Relapse Process (Continued)

☐ *Extreme difficulty with introspection*

A *dry drunk* is a fairly toxic state of being and in this condition it becomes extremely difficult for us to see ourselves. It is common for us, as addicted people, to look outside of ourselves for an explanation for what is wrong with us. After all, most of us have become quite adept at looking outside of ourselves for the solution to the problems of living that we found in our *drug of choice*. In a Dry Drunk phase we may or may not start out with a desire to relapse. In fact, many people will tell you that a relapse was the furthest thing from their mind until they found themselves obsessed with the idea. During a *dry drunk* there are many obstacles to accurate introspection regardless of whether or not it is wanted. Our self-delusion makes it difficult to look inside. It is more painful to look inside, and we are not looking for more pain. We are looking for less. Our negative outlook on life and ourselves would support the wearing of blindfolds, and we are generally running so fast that the picture is going to be blurred should we find ourselves without our blindfolds of rationalization and justification.

☐ *Grandiosity*

Grandiosity is usually associated with an unrealistic sense of superiority. The unrealistic sense that we are better than others will generate many relationship problems in a wide variety of social settings in our lives. There is little doubt that the self-perception that we are superior to others will eventually be understood by those who we see as inferior. When our grandiosity is discovered, there are generally reprisals and relationships are injured. Grandiosity will also manifest itself in a pattern of thinking and coping strategies that suggest that we should know what we really do not know and should not need help regardless of the nature of the problem.

☐ *Intolerance*

As we progress toward a relapse into active *addiction* the emotional pain that we accumulate along the way will become so intense that it is almost numbing. The more emotional pain that we accept, the more difficult it is to remember what good feels like. If we cannot remember what good feels like, then we are prone to view "bad" as being better than "really bad". As our tolerance for discomfort increases we are likely to experience more pain because we will not know enough to get out of harm's way. Eventually this endurance contest triggers intolerance of other people, places, and events. A *dry drunk* can generate so much hurt that we are not really interested in the needs of others and are less likely to be able to work with the shortcomings of others, no matter how minor.

☐ *Impulsivity*

The pain associated with a Dry Drunk phase will leave most suffers to begin a frantic search for a quick fix to whatever the perceived problem is. This internal spinning will generate or increase a tendency toward impulsive decisions without concern for what the consequences might be. The *dry drunk* sufferer will make quite a few poor choices that will

Course Assignment 4.1 – Identifying Personal Symptoms for Each Phase of the Relapse Process (Continued)

generate additional emotional baggage in a variety of forms that all contribute to extra "on board" weight or emotional burden. The heavier we are, the faster we will sink.

☐ *Romanticizing the benefit of addictive behavior*

The concept of euphoric recall has been discussed in detail earlier in this work and it is a commonly understood symptom of engagement in the relapse process. This symptom of romanticizing the benefit of addictive behavior is somewhat different in that it involves both euphoric recall as well as an inaccurate evaluation of what the long term costs associated with our addicted behavior have been. The cocaine dealer, suffering in recovery with economic challenges, can begin to romance about the good old days of using and dealing cocaine and focus on both the feelings of euphoria as well as the economic security. The longing for economic security can leave the *dry drunk* victim fantasizing or planning just one more drug deal that will clean up all debts once and for all. He or she imagines that it may result in a slip, but that the potential risk will be worth it because he or she knows where to get help when problems arise.

☐ *Withdraw from others*

This symptom of withdrawing includes behaviors that will remove sources of strength that might provide experience we could learn from, strength we might rely on, and hope that would motivate us to come out of the whirlwind that is pulling us to the *bottom*. When we have completely withdrawn from others and the God of our understanding, there is nothing to insulate us from the pain and little reason to change.

☐ *Self-absorption*

A Dry Drunk phase will eventually lead each and every addicted person to a point of self-absorption that was once described as being "sick and tired of being sick and tired". If we have managed to end up all alone in our recovery and unable to get sufficient relief from our *defects of character* then we do what we are left to believe is the next right thing – we relapse.

Course Lesson 4.2 – The Problems and Challenges Associated with Relapse Symptoms

The Course Assignments 4.2 (Part 1) through 4.2 (Part 6) that follow will have one task with four steps, which are described below under Task 1. Each of the Course Assignments, 4.2 (Part 1) through 4.2 (Part 6), target a different phase in the relapse process. Remember in the course title "Course Lesson 4.2, that the number 4 refers to the section we are working in and the number 2 following the "4." refers to the number of the assignment we are working on. Most sections have multiple assignments but in this section there are only two assignments and this assignment has six different focal points. These focal points are separated into Parts where each Part refers to one of the six different phases. For your reference they are as follows:

- 4.2 (Part 1) - The Problems and Challenges Associated with Relapse Symptoms: The Uncomfortable Feelings Phase of the Relapse Process
- 4.2 (Part 2) - The Problems and Challenges Associated with Relapse Symptoms: The Time Travel Phase of the Relapse Process
- 4.2 (Part 3) - The Problems and Challenges Associated with Relapse Symptoms: The Fragmentation Phase of the Relapse Process
- 4.2 (Part 4) - The Problems and Challenges Associated with Relapse Symptoms: The Gathering Justification Phase of Relapse Process
- 4.2 (Part 5) - The Problems and Challenges Associated with Relapse Symptoms: The Eliminating the Witnesses Phase of the Relapse Process
- 4.2 (Part 6) - The Problems and Challenges Associated with Relapse Symptoms: The Dry Drunk Phase of the Relapse Process

Each of the Parts, as the titles above suggest, are designed to aid you in further clarifying the problems that the symptoms of relapse cause you and what challenges you face in overcoming them. It is hoped that this improved insight will aid you in your efforts to develop meaningful and practical interventions for stopping a future relapse from occurring. Each of the assignments will ask you to provide a brief description of the problems that you have encountered when experiencing each of the symptoms you have selected. For example, if you have suffered with *Negative Self-talk* under the Uncomfortable Feelings phase of the relapse process the problems you experienced might be listed as:

1. When I engage in *negative self-talk* I begin to pull away from people who care about me.

2. *Negative self-talk* causes me to lose gratitude for things and people I enjoy in my life.

If necessary to make your point, then use a specific example like: "When I was alone in my room thinking about what a loser I was, I turned down several invitations by family members to join them for some basketball while everyone waited for Thanksgiving dinner to be prepared". You are free to list as many problems as are needed to accurately communicate your struggle to members of your support group or therapist. Use extra sheets if needed.

Additionally the assignments ask that you identify at least two challenges that you experience when you attempt to intervene on or stop a symptom. The identification of the challenges that you experience is really important because you will want to know what steps you will need to take or what resources you might need to adequately address a symptom and stop a relapse from happening. For example, two challenges associated with the example used above regarding *Negative Self-Talk* would be:

1. When I am putting myself down through *negative self-talk* I am ashamed of opening up to others because I can't imagine anyone else thinks like I do.

2. I have lost contact with the people I used to share with in the recovery rooms and I do not know who to call for help to stop bashing myself.

Course Lesson 4.2 – The Problems and Challenges Associated with Relapse Symptoms (Continued)

Lastly, under each group of symptoms for each phase you will find space for you to add your personalized entries. Add as many as you need to communicate a clear picture to others and add extra sheets as you need to. Give your personalized entry any name that fits, describe it and then identify the problems and challenges associated with it. Get help from your therapist or members of your support system where you need it.

IMPORTANT:

The following descriptions of the various tasks in this lesson are presented to introduce you to the actual written work you will complete in the Course Assignment that follows this lesson. Do not write anything until you reach the assignment.

When you have completed the lesson be sure to share your findings with members of your support system and your therapist if you are working with one.

~ Task 1 ~

Identify the problems and challenges you will face for each symptom you select:

The first step is to refer to your selections from Course Assignment 4.1 and place an X in the box ☐ alongside the symptom name. Then, list two or more examples of problems caused by each of the symptoms. The third step is to list two or more challenges you experience when attempting to address each of the symptoms. If you get confused, refer to the examples noted above in Course Lesson 4.2. The fourth step is to add any personalized entries you identify.

Course Assignment 4.2 (Part 1) – The Problems and Challenges Associated with Relapse Symptoms: The Uncomfortable Feelings Phase of the Relapse Process

Refer to your selections from Course Assignment 4.1 and place an X in the box ☐ alongside the symptom name that fits your story. List two to three examples of problems caused by each of the symptoms in the space provided and two to three examples of challenges you experience when you think about addressing the symptom. At the end of this Course Assignment there will space for you to add at least two personalized symptom entries of your own. Give your personalized entry any name that fits, describe it and then identify the problems and challenges associated with it.

IMPORTANT: If you find that you need more space please feel free to continue the writing on a separate piece of paper.

~ Task 1 ~

Identify the problems and challenges you will face for each symptom you select:

☐ *General emotional discomfort*

Problems caused by this symptom:

1. _____

2. _____

3. _____

Challenges to addressing the symptom:

1. _____

2. _____

3. _____

☐ *Negative self-talk*

Problems caused by this symptom:

1. _____

2. _____

3. _____

Course Assignment 4.2 (Part 1) – The Problems and Challenges Associated with Relapse Symptoms: The Uncomfortable Feelings Phase of the Relapse Process (Continued)

Challenges to addressing the symptom:

1. _____

2. _____

3. _____

☐ *Depressed mood*

Problems caused by this symptom:

1. _____

2. _____

3. _____

Challenges to addressing the symptom:

1. _____

2. _____

3. _____

☐ *Anxiety/Worry*

Problems caused by this symptom:

1. _____

2. _____

3. _____

Course Assignment 4.2 (Part 1) – The Problems and Challenges Associated with Relapse Symptoms: The Uncomfortable Feelings Phase of the Relapse Process (Continued)

Challenges to addressing the symptom:

1. _____

2. _____

3. _____

☐ *Unrealistic view of problems*

Problems caused by this symptom:

1. _____

2. _____

3. _____

Challenges to addressing the symptom:

1. _____

2. _____

3. _____

☐ *Resentment*

Problems caused by this symptom:

1. _____

2. _____

3. _____

Course Assignment 4.2 (Part 1) – The Problems and Challenges Associated with Relapse Symptoms: The Uncomfortable Feelings Phase of the Relapse Process (Continued)

Challenges to addressing the symptom:

1. _____

2. _____

3. _____

☐ *Guilt*

Problems caused by this symptom:

1. _____

2. _____

3. _____

Challenges to addressing the symptom:

1. _____

2. _____

3. _____

☐ *Personalized entry:* _____

Symptom description:

_____

_____

Course Assignment 4.2 (Part 1) – The Problems and Challenges Associated with Relapse Symptoms: The Uncomfortable Feelings Phase of the Relapse Process (Continued)

Problems caused by this symptom:

1. _____

2. _____

3. _____

Challenges to addressing the symptom:

1. _____

2. _____

3. _____

☐ *Personalized entry:* _____

Symptom description:

_____

_____

Problems caused by this symptom:

1. _____

2. _____

3. _____

Challenges to addressing the symptom:

1. _____

2. _____

3. _____

Course Assignment 4.2 (Part 2) – The Problems and Challenges Associated with Relapse Symptoms: The Time Travel Phase of the Relapse Process

Refer to your selections from Course Assignment 4.1 and place an X in the box ☐ alongside the symptom name that fits your story. List two to three examples of problems caused by each of the symptoms in the space provided and two to three examples of challenges you experience when you think about addressing the symptom. At the end of this Course Assignment there will space for you to add at least two personalized symptom entries of your own. Give your personalized entry any name that fits, describe it and then identify the problems and challenges associated with it.

IMPORTANT: If you find that you need more space please feel free to continue the writing on a separate piece of paper.

~ Task 1 ~

Identify the problems and challenges you will face for each symptom you select:

☐ *Over-reacting to the behavior of others*

Problems caused by this symptom:

1. _____

2. _____

3. _____

Challenges to addressing the symptom:

1. _____

2. _____

3. _____

☐ *Negative self-talk*

Problems caused by this symptom:

1. _____

2. _____

3. _____

Course Assignment 4.2 (Part 2) – The Problems and Challenges Associated with Relapse Symptoms: The Time Travel Phase of the Relapse Process (Continued)

Challenges to addressing the symptom:

1. _____

2. _____

3. _____

☐ *Day mares*

Problems caused by this symptom:

1. _____

2. _____

3. _____

Challenges to addressing the symptom:

1. _____

2. _____

3. _____

☐ *Defending yourself from input*

Problems caused by this symptom:

1. _____

2. _____

3. _____

Course Assignment 4.2 (Part 2) – The Problems and Challenges Associated with Relapse Symptoms: The Time Travel Phase of the Relapse Process (Continued)

Challenges to addressing the symptom:

1. _____

2. _____

3. _____

☐ *Euphoric recall*

Problems caused by this symptom:

1. _____

2. _____

3. _____

Challenges to addressing the symptom:

1. _____

2. _____

3. _____

☐ *Dysphoric recall*

Problems caused by this symptom:

1. _____

2. _____

3. _____

Course Assignment 4.2 (Part 2) – The Problems and Challenges Associated with Relapse Symptoms: The Time Travel Phase of the Relapse Process (Continued)

Challenges to addressing the symptom:

1. _____

2. _____

3. _____

☐ *Implosion*

Problems caused by this symptom:

1. _____

2. _____

3. _____

Challenges to addressing the symptom:

1. _____

2. _____

3. _____

☐ *Explosion*

Challenges:

Problems caused by this symptom:

1. _____

2. _____

3. _____

Course Assignment 4.2 (Part 2) – The Problems and Challenges Associated with Relapse Symptoms: The Time Travel Phase of the Relapse Process (Continued)

Challenges to addressing the symptom:

1. _____

2. _____

3. _____

☐ *Avoidance of intimacy*

Problems caused by this symptom:

1. _____

2. _____

3. _____

Challenges to addressing the symptom:

1. _____

2. _____

3. _____

☐ *Retrieving past wrongs of an opponent to validate your emotional pain*

Problems caused by this symptom:

1. _____

2. _____

3. _____

Course Assignment 4.2 (Part 2) – The Problems and Challenges Associated with Relapse Symptoms: The Time Travel Phase of the Relapse Process (Continued)

Challenges to addressing the symptom:

1. _____

2. _____

3. _____

☐ *Retrieving or reviewing your past wrongs to justify the hurtful things you are doing to yourself or are allowing others to do to you*

Problems caused by this symptom:

1. _____

2. _____

3. _____

Challenges to addressing the symptom:

1. _____

2. _____

3. _____

☐ *Attempts to discredit those you have come to trust*

Problems caused by this symptom:

1. _____

2. _____

3. _____

Course Assignment 4.2 (Part 2) – The Problems and Challenges Associated with Relapse Symptoms: The Time Travel Phase of the Relapse Process (Continued)

Challenges to addressing the symptom:

1. _____

2. _____

3. _____

☐ *Personalized entry:* _____

Symptom description:

_____

_____

Problems caused by this symptom:

1. _____

2. _____

3. _____

Challenges to addressing the symptom:

1. _____

2. _____

3. _____

Course Assignment 4.2 (Part 2) – The Problems and Challenges Associated with Relapse Symptoms: The Time Travel Phase of the Relapse Process (Continued)

☐ *Personalized entry:* _____

Symptom description:

_____

_____

Problems caused by this symptom:

1. _____

2. _____

3. _____

Challenges to addressing the symptom:

1. _____

2. _____

3. _____

Course Assignment 4.2 (Part 3) – The Problems and Challenges Associated with Relapse Symptoms: The Fragmentation Phase of the Relapse Process

Refer to your selections from Course Assignment 4.1 and place an X in the box ☐ alongside the symptom name that fits your story. List two to three examples of problems caused by each of the symptoms in the space provided and two to three examples of challenges you experience when you think about addressing the symptom. At the end of this Course Assignment there will space for you to add at least two personalized symptom entries of your own. Give your personalized entry any name that fits, describe it and then identify the problems and challenges associated with it.

IMPORTANT: If you find that you need more space please feel free to continue the writing on a separate piece of paper.

~ Task 1 ~

Identify the problems and challenges you will face for each symptom you select:

☐ *People with whom you are sharing do not appear to understand what you are trying to communicate*
Problems caused by this symptom:

1. _____

2. _____

3. _____

Challenges to addressing the symptom:

1. _____

2. _____

3. _____

☐ *Difficulty demonstrating emotions freely and without constraint*
Problems caused by this symptom:

1. _____

2. _____

3. _____

Course Assignment 4.2 (Part 3) – The Problems and Challenges Associated with Relapse Symptoms: The Fragmentation Phase of the Relapse Process (Continued)

Challenges to addressing the symptom:

1. _____

2. _____

3. _____

☐ *Inability to make yourself understood*

Problems caused by this symptom:

1. _____

2. _____

3. _____

Challenges to addressing the symptom:

1. _____

2. _____

3. _____

☐ *Struggling to identify your own feelings*

Problems caused by this symptom:

1. _____

2. _____

3. _____

Course Assignment 4.2 (Part 3) – The Problems and Challenges Associated with Relapse Symptoms: The Fragmentation Phase of the Relapse Process (Continued)

Challenges to addressing the symptom:

1. _____

2. _____

3. _____

☐ *Obsessive thinking*

Problems caused by this symptom:

1. _____

2. _____

3. _____

Challenges to addressing the symptom:

1. _____

2. _____

3. _____

☐ *Personalized entry:* _____

Symptom description:

_____

_____

Course Assignment 4.2 (Part 3) – The Problems and Challenges Associated with Relapse Symptoms: The Fragmentation Phase of the Relapse Process (Continued)

Problems caused by this symptom:

1. _____

2. _____

3. _____

Challenges to addressing the symptom:

1. _____

2. _____

3. _____

☐ *Personalized entry:* _____

Symptom description:

_____

_____

Problems caused by this symptom:

1. _____

2. _____

3. _____

Challenges to addressing the symptom:

1. _____

2. _____

3. _____

Course Assignment 4.2 (Part 4) – The Problems and Challenges Associated with Relapse Symptoms: The Gathering Justification Phase of the Relapse Process

Refer to your selections from Course Assignment 4.1 and place an X in the box ☐ alongside the symptom name that fits your story. List two to three examples of problems caused by each of the symptoms in the space provided and two to three examples of challenges you experience when you think about addressing the symptom. At the end of this Course Assignment there will space for you to add at least two personalized symptom entries of your own. Give your personalized entry any name that fits, describe it and then identify the problems and challenges associated with it.

IMPORTANT: If you find that you need more space please feel free to continue the writing on a separate piece of paper.

~ Task 1 ~

Identify the problems and challenges you will face for each symptom you select:

☐ *Justifiable anger*

Problems caused by this symptom:

1. _____

2. _____

3. _____

Challenges to addressing the symptom:

1. _____

2. _____

3. _____

☐ *Judgmental*

Problems caused by this symptom:

1. _____

2. _____

3. _____

Course Assignment 4.2 (Part 4) – The Problems and Challenges Associated with Relapse Symptoms: The Gathering Justification Phase of the Relapse Process (Continued)

Challenges to addressing the symptom:

1. _____

2. _____

3. _____

☐ *Blaming others for the way you feel or behave*

Problems caused by this symptom:

1. _____

2. _____

3. _____

Challenges to addressing the symptom:

1. _____

2. _____

3. _____

☐ *Disconnect*

Problems caused by this symptom:

1. _____

2. _____

3. _____

Course Assignment 4.2 (Part 4) – The Problems and Challenges Associated with Relapse Symptoms: The Gathering Justification Phase of the Relapse Process (Continued)

Challenges to addressing the symptom:

1. _____

2. _____

3. _____

☐ *Lack of emotional support*

Problems caused by this symptom:

1. _____

2. _____

3. _____

Challenges to addressing the symptom:

1. _____

2. _____

3. _____

☐ *Difficulty empathizing with others*

Problems caused by this symptom:

1. _____

2. _____

3. _____

Course Assignment 4.2 (Part 4) – The Problems and Challenges Associated with Relapse Symptoms: The Gathering Justification Phase of the Relapse Process (Continued)

Challenges to addressing the symptom:

1. _____

2. _____

3. _____

☐ *Personalized entry:* _____

Symptom description:

_____

_____

Problems caused by this symptom:

1. _____

2. _____

3. _____

Challenges to addressing the symptom:

1. _____

2. _____

3. _____

Course Assignment 4.2 (Part 4) – The Problems and Challenges Associated with Relapse Symptoms: The Gathering Justification Phase of the Relapse Process (Continued)

☐ *Personalized entry:* _____

Symptom description:

_____

_____

Problems caused by this symptom:

1. _____

2. _____

3. _____

Challenges to addressing the symptom:

1. _____

2. _____

3. _____

Course Assignment 4.2 (Part 5) – The Problems and Challenges Associated with Relapse Symptoms: The Eliminating the Witnesses Phase of the Relapse Process

Refer to your selections from Course Assignment 4.1 and place an X in the box ☐ alongside the symptom name that fits your story. List two to three examples of problems caused by each of the symptoms in the space provided and two to three examples of challenges you experience when you think about addressing the symptom. At the end of this Course Assignment there will space for you to add at least two personalized symptom entries of your own. Give your personalized entry any name that fits, describe it and then identify the problems and challenges associated with it.

IMPORTANT: If you find that you need more space please feel free to continue the writing on a separate piece of paper.

~ Task 1 ~

Identify the problems and challenges you will face for each symptom you select:

☐ *Gossiping & character assassination*

Problems caused by this symptom:

1. _____

2. _____

3. _____

Challenges to addressing the symptom:

1. _____

2. _____

3. _____

☐ *Escapism*

Problems caused by this symptom:

1. _____

2. _____

3. _____

Course Assignment 4.2 (Part 5) – The Problems and Challenges Associated with Relapse Symptoms: The Eliminating the Witnesses Phase of the Relapse Process (Continued)

Challenges to addressing the symptom:

1. _____

2. _____

3. _____

☐ *Always right!*

Problems caused by this symptom:

1. _____

2. _____

3. _____

Challenges to addressing the symptom:

1. _____

2. _____

3. _____

☐ *Inability to acknowledge your own wrongs*

Problems caused by this symptom:

1. _____

2. _____

3. _____

Course Assignment 4.2 (Part 5) – The Problems and Challenges Associated with Relapse Symptoms: The Eliminating the Witnesses Phase of the Relapse Process (Continued)

Challenges to addressing the symptom:

1. _____

2. _____

3. _____

☐ *Rebuff the concerns of others*

Problems caused by this symptom:

1. _____

2. _____

3. _____

Challenges to addressing the symptom:

1. _____

2. _____

3. _____

☐ *Growing isolation*

Problems caused by this symptom:

1. _____

2. _____

3. _____

Course Assignment 4.2 (Part 5) – The Problems and Challenges Associated with Relapse Symptoms: The Eliminating the Witnesses Phase of the Relapse Process (Continued)

Challenges to addressing the symptom:

1. _____

2. _____

3. _____

☐ *Personalized entry:* _____

Symptom description:

_____

_____

Problems caused by this symptom:

1. _____

2. _____

3. _____

Challenges to addressing the symptom:

1. _____

2. _____

3. _____

Course Assignment 4.2 (Part 5) – The Problems and Challenges Associated with Relapse Symptoms: The Eliminating the Witnesses Phase of the Relapse Process (Continued)

☐ *Personalized entry:* _____

Symptom description:

_____

_____

Problems caused by this symptom:

1. _____

2. _____

3. _____

Challenges to addressing the symptom:

1. _____

2. _____

3. _____

Course Assignment 4.2 (Part 6) – The Problems and Challenges Associated with Relapse Symptoms: The Dry Drunk Phase of the Relapse Process

Refer to your selections from Course Assignment 4.1 and place an X in the box ☐ alongside the symptom name that fits your story. List two to three examples of problems caused by each of the symptoms in the space provided and two to three examples of challenges you experience when you think about addressing the symptom. At the end of this Course Assignment there will space for you to add at least two personalized symptom entries of your own. Give your personalized entry any name that fits, describe it and then identify the problems and challenges associated with it.

IMPORTANT: If you find that you need more space please feel free to continue the writing on a separate piece of paper.

~ Task 1 ~

Identify the problems and challenges you will face for each symptom you select:

☐ *Mood swings*

Problems caused by this symptom:

1. _____

2. _____

3. _____

Challenges to addressing the symptom:

1. _____

2. _____

3. _____

☐ *Extreme difficulty with introspection*

Problems caused by this symptom:

1. _____

2. _____

3. _____

Course Assignment 4.2 (Part 6) – The Problems and Challenges Associated with Relapse Symptoms: The Dry Drunk Phase of the Relapse Process (Continued)

Challenges to addressing the symptom:

1. _____

2. _____

3. _____

☐ *Grandiosity*

Problems caused by this symptom:

1. _____

2. _____

3. _____

Challenges to addressing the symptom:

1. _____

2. _____

3. _____

☐ *Intolerance*

Problems caused by this symptom:

1. _____

2. _____

3. _____

Course Assignment 4.2 (Part 6) – The Problems and Challenges Associated with Relapse Symptoms: The Dry Drunk Phase of the Relapse Process (Continued)

Challenges to addressing the symptom:

1. _____

2. _____

3. _____

☐ *Impulsivity*

Problems caused by this symptom:

1. _____

2. _____

3. _____

Challenges to addressing the symptom:

1. _____

2. _____

3. _____

☐ *Romanticizing the benefit of addictive behavior*

Problems caused by this symptom:

1. _____

2. _____

3. _____

Course Assignment 4.2 (Part 6) – The Problems and Challenges Associated with Relapse Symptoms: The Dry Drunk Phase of the Relapse Process (Continued)

Challenges to addressing the symptom:

1. _____

2. _____

3. _____

☐ *Withdraw from others*

Problems caused by this symptom:

1. _____

2. _____

3. _____

Challenges to addressing the symptom:

1. _____

2. _____

3. _____

☐ *Self-absorption*

Problems caused by this symptom:

1. _____

2. _____

3. _____

Course Assignment 4.2 (Part 6) – The Problems and Challenges Associated with Relapse Symptoms: The Dry Drunk Phase of the Relapse Process (Continued)

Challenges to addressing the symptom:

1. _____

2. _____

3. _____

☐ *Personalized entry:* _____

Symptom description:

_____

_____

Problems caused by this symptom:

1. _____

2. _____

3. _____

Challenges to addressing the symptom:

1. _____

2. _____

3. _____

☐ *Personalized entry:* _____

Symptom description:

_____

_____

Course Assignment 4.2 (Part 6) – The Problems and Challenges Associated with Relapse Symptoms: The Dry Drunk Phase of the Relapse Process (Continued)

Problems caused by this symptom:

1. _____

2. _____

3. _____

Challenges to addressing the symptom:

1. _____

2. _____

3. _____

Section 5

Strategies for Interrupting the Relapse Process

Introduction

In this section of the course you will be asked to review each of the phases of relapse again with the intent of selecting intervention strategies that will address the symptoms you identified in each corresponding phase of relapse.

The process of identifying and implementing strategies for intervening on a relapse process will be critical to your success in maintaining sustained abstinence and achieving emotional sobriety. Remember though, that it is a process. Your ability to develop effective strategies for addressing your individual symptoms will grow with time.

The self-examination that you have undertaken thus far in the course has been impressive and undoubtedly has already begun to benefit you but it has only just begun. In the months and years to come new self-awareness will generate the ability to spot additional personal symptoms for you to address. Likewise your day-to-day recovery experience will introduce you to new strategies for addressing recovery challenges as you learn from mistakes and the experiences of others.

This section of the course will introduce you to a selection of intervention strategies that have been designed to aid you in the interruption of a relapse process. When you are creating strategies look into your past for those that may have worked for you or others. Additionally, imagine what strategies you might need to address challenges that you can foresee arising in the near future. These strategies are designed to be observable and measureable in that you and others will be able to assess whether or not you are utilizing the strategies in order to increase your level of accountability and ultimately your safety.

We have attempted to make this selection process less stressful by listing each of the symptoms under the phase they relate to. The corresponding strategies are listed just below the symptoms. The symptoms each person may experience in any given phase in the relapse process will be unique to the individual's recovery history and overall life experience. The interventions offered represent only a brief sample of the strategies that could be employed to stop you from progressing in a particular phase and ultimately help to avert a relapse into active *addiction*.

As mentioned earlier, the interventions presented in one section may have valuable applications in the other phases as well but will not be routinely included as an option in every phase. You are encouraged to explore how interventions can be helpful in phases other than the ones they were assigned to. Additionally, each assignment will give you the opportunity to include strategies that you have historically found effective in addressing the symptom under evaluation.

In Section 6 of this course you will be asked to prepare a Personal Relapse Prevention Plan. The plan you develop should be highly personalized and should include your personal contribution of the troubling symptoms you have experienced and individualized interventions that you can prepare with the help of your support system or a therapist

What to Expect from the Following Chapter:

- provide you with general intervention strategies for each of the phases in the relapse process
- identify specific strategies that may be particularly helpful in addressing specific symptoms in each of the phases of relapse
- provide space for you to include strategies that will help to individualize your plan

Relapse is a process that can and should be stopped

The strategies that will work for you are the ones that most closely match your symptoms and complement your intellectual, emotional, and *spiritual* assets. You are likely to find, as we have, that some strategies that used to work for you are no longer effective. Additionally, our clients frequently report that a particular strategy that they selected for symptoms in one phase is equally as effective in several different phases.

The strategies that you select for intervening on a symptom have to make sense to you. Relapse into active *addiction* is unnecessary as is the discomfort associated with remaining stuck in a symptom. Do not assume that a particular symptom will pass with time. It may not pass on its own. In fact it may be a stepping-stone to more harmful symptoms. Get as much help as you need to develop an effective strategy because it is not healthy for life to be an endurance contest.

The general strategies that are included in the Course Assignment are intended to be a guide for you and only scratch the surface of the potential interventions that you will find helpful. Do not feel limited by the suggestions offered and solicit as much input as you need to come up with meaningful ways to intervene on a difficult symptom or interrupt a phase in the process of relapse. There will always be a strategy that will help to take you out of the spiral that you find yourself in as long as you are willing to go to any lengths to get the help you need.

As we have noted earlier, if relapse were an event rather than a process, which involves progressive phases, you would not be able to do much to stop it once it began. We know that an alcoholic's relapse does not begin with the spontaneous thought to drink today upon awakening from a night's sleep. We may not have a defense against the invasion of a thought to drink but we certainly have a great deal we can do to prevent a thought of drinking to become an act of drinking. The following assignment begins to make that very clear.

Course Lesson 5.1 - Selecting Intervention Strategies to Interrupt the Relapse Process

The following Course Assignments will introduce you to sample intervention strategies that may be helpful to you when trying to interrupt a relapse in each of the six phases of the process. The strategies represent a very small sample of the interventions that have and could be used to interrupt an addict's free-fall into relapse. While a comprehensive list of strategies is outside of the scope of this work, you will soon be able to download a wide variety of strategies and other recovery tools to supplement this text at our corporate website: www.leademcounseling.com.

Each of the following Course Assignments, 5.1 (Part 1) through 5.1 (Part 6), target a different phase in the relapse process. Remember in the course title "Course Lesson 5.1, that the number 5 refers to the section we are working in and the number 1 following the "5." refers to the number of the assignment we are working on. Most sections have multiple assignments but in this section there is only one assignment with six different focal points. These focal points are separated into Parts where each Part refers to one of the six different phases. For your reference they are as follows:

- 5.1(Part 1) - Selecting Intervention Strategies to Interrupt the Relapse Process: The Uncomfortable Feelings Phase of the Relapse Process
- 5.1(Part 2) - Selecting Intervention Strategies to Interrupt the Relapse Process: The Time Travel Phase of the Relapse Process
- 5.1(Part 3) - Selecting Intervention Strategies to Interrupt the Relapse Process: The Fragmentation Phase of the Relapse Process
- 5.1(Part 4) - Selecting Intervention Strategies to Interrupt the Relapse Process: The Gathering Justification Phase of Relapse Process
- 5.1(Part 5) - Selecting Intervention Strategies to Interrupt the Relapse Process: The Eliminating the Witnesses Phase of the Relapse Process
- 5.1(Part 6) - Selecting Intervention Strategies to Interrupt the Relapse Process: The Dry Drunk Phase of the Relapse Process

As you read through each of the Course assignments you will see that each of the assignments like 5.1 (Part 1) - Selecting Intervention Strategies to Interrupt the Relapse Process: The Uncomfortable Feelings Phase of the Relapse Process are repeated several times. Each time one is repeated it is addressing a different symptom within that phase. For example, the first symptom to appear under Course Assignment 5.1 (Part 1) is General Emotional Discomfort. Each symptom in each phase has been formatted to have its own page for easier reference when you are completing your work.

For every symptom you will be given a list of sample *Generalized Interventions* designed to target the problems and challenges associated with that symptom. As you review the sample therapeutic intervention strategies please select those interventions that you and your support system feel will help you to cope with the problems and challenges you identified for each symptom in Section 4. If none of the sample intervention strategies resonate with you and you and your support system discover that additional intervention strategies are needed please add them in the space provided under the heading entitled *Specialized/Individualized Interventions*. If you and your support system added additional symptoms in Course Assignment 4.1 please add them to the Course Assignment in the section that corresponds with the appropriate phase of relapse and then add your own personalized intervention strategies to address the symptom you have added.

IMPORTANT:

Please note that unlike the Course Lessons and Course Assignments found in Sections 2, 3, and 4 the Course Lesson and Course Assignments in Section 5 do not have tasks.

Course Assignment 5.1 (Part 1) - Selecting Intervention Strategies to Interrupt the Relapse Process: The Uncomfortable Feelings Phase of the Relapse Process

Symptom Addressed: **General Emotional Discomfort**

IMPORTANT: If you find that you need more space please feel free to continue the writing on a separate piece of paper.

Generalized Interventions:

- ☐ Journal about what you are feeling with a description of the physical sensations you are having, times when you have felt that way before, what resources you have available to you to help to process or reduce the discomfort.
- ☐ Introduce the feelings that you are having at a meeting and ask members how they cope with them
- ☐ Consult with your sponsor, spouse/partner to obtain examples of their experience, strength, and hope that relate to what you are experiencing.
- ☐ Consult with your therapist/*spiritual* advisor about the feelings you are experiencing and solicit coping strategies.
- ☐ Read recovery literature or inspirational material to help you better focus your energy on understanding what is precipitating your discomfort.
- ☐ Consult with someone with whom you have an emotionally intimate relationship to obtain input about what might be disturbing you.
- ☐ Review your daily journal entrees for the past few weeks or months as it might help you to identify the source/sources of the discomfort.
- ☐ Explore your gratitude list and allow yourself to remember the feelings that you had at the time when you made the entries that are, today, the most meaningful to you.

Specialized/Individualized Interventions:

- ☐ _____
- ☐ _____
- ☐ _____
- ☐ _____
- ☐ _____
- ☐ _____

Course Assignment 5.1 (Part 1) - Selecting Intervention Strategies to Interrupt the Relapse Process: The Uncomfortable Feelings Phase of the Relapse Process (Continued)

Symptom Addressed: **Negative Self-talk**

IMPORTANT: If you find that you need more space please feel free to continue the writing on a separate piece of paper.

Generalized Interventions:

- ☐ Make a list of the things that you say about yourself when no one is listening and share those judgments with a trusted member of your support group to get a more objective perspective and to challenge your self-perception.
- ☐ Ask a member of your support system to give you input about the qualities that they have observed in you with event specific examples.
- ☐ Make a detailed list of your accomplishments in recovery and share them with a member of your support group.
- ☐ Spend 5-10 minutes reading *spiritual* material.
- ☐ Complete a *What's Your Proof?* (You will find this and many other exercises by going to our website: www.leademcounseling.com and clicking on the tab on the left entitled Sober Tools).
- ☐ Review your journal entries for the past two weeks in an effort to understand the basis for your *negative self-talk*.

Specialized/Individualized Interventions:

- ☐ _____
- ☐ _____
- ☐ _____
- ☐ _____
- ☐ _____
- ☐ _____
- ☐ _____
- ☐ _____

Course Assignment 5.1 (Part 1) - Selecting Intervention Strategies to Interrupt the Relapse Process: The Uncomfortable Feelings Phase of the Relapse Process (Continued)

Symptom Addressed: **Depressed Mood**

IMPORTANT: If you find that you need more space please feel free to continue the writing on a separate piece of paper.

Generalized Interventions:

- ☐ Consult with your MD regarding your symptoms and consider the introduction of safe medications.
- ☐ Confide in support group members that you are struggling emotionally and elicit their experience, strength and hope rather than advice about how to "fix" your perceived problem/s.
- ☐ Force yourself to participate in sober activities that may make you feel better.
- ☐ Try to be with other people; it is usually better than being alone.
- ☐ Identify someone for you to be of service to on a daily basis.
- ☐ Cultivate and enhance the depth of your support group relationships.
- ☐ Turn your attention towards working with others so that your mind gets engaged in that work as it will re-route the energy you are investing in your depressed mood and service to others will generally elevate your mood.
- ☐ Do not make major life decisions, such as changing jobs, getting married or divorced, without consulting others who know you well and who have a more objective view of your situation. In any case, it is advisable to postpone important decisions until your depressed mood has lifted.
- ☐ Decide that you are going to fight back and undertake activities that will starve your depressed mood such as exercise, going to a meeting, playing music, reviewing your gratitude list, etc. Do not resign yourself to being depressed.
- ☐ Do something that will put you in touch with the beauty in life via music, nature and art.
- ☐ Examine a previously troubling depressed period that you recovered from with the help of a therapist or sponsor to determine what circumstances or intervention behaviors helped to move you out of the darkness.

Specialized/Individualized Interventions:

- ☐ _____

- ☐ _____

- ☐ _____

- ☐ _____

- ☐ _____

Course Assignment 5.1 (Part 1) - Selecting Intervention Strategies to Interrupt the Relapse Process: The Uncomfortable Feelings Phase of the Relapse Process (Continued)

Symptom Addressed: **Anxiety/Worry**

IMPORTANT: If you find that you need more space please feel free to continue the writing on a separate piece of paper.

Generalized Interventions:

- ☐ Write out your fears and share them with a member of your support group.
- ☐ When a feeling of *panic* hits you make sure you are physically and emotionally safe.
- ☐ Spend time twice a day in prayer & meditation and maintaining a feelings journal.
- ☐ Review your fears in great depth with a therapist to get assistance in determining if you have any clear and present threats to your physical and/or emotional safety.
- ☐ Examine your relationships with someone you trust to identify sources of current oppression in your life because continual exposure to an emotional or physical threat may generate anxiety that you aren't aware of.
- ☐ Construct a gratitude list that specifically identifies times in the past when you were anxious or worried and the anticipated outcome did not materialize as you had feared.

Specialized/Individualized Interventions:

- ☐ _____
- ☐ _____
- ☐ _____
- ☐ _____
- ☐ _____
- ☐ _____
- ☐ _____
- ☐ _____
- ☐ _____

Course Assignment 5.1 (Part 1) - Selecting Intervention Strategies to Interrupt the Relapse Process: The Uncomfortable Feelings Phase of the Relapse Process (Continued)

Symptom Addressed: **Unrealistic View of Problems**

IMPORTANT: If you find that you need more space please feel free to continue the writing on a separate piece of paper.

Generalized Interventions:

- ☐ On a blank piece of paper create three columns. In the first column, make a list of two or three of the problems that you find challenging. In the second column, briefly explain what you think the origin of each problem is. In the third column, write down what interventions you have used to address each of the three problems that were unsuccessful. Review your work with a therapist, trusted support group member, or close friend to get other perceptions of the origins of the problem and what strategies others have used to address them.
- ☐ Describe one reoccurring problem in your life or the life of someone you care for. Under the problem write all the possible explanations for why that problem is reoccurring and compare your findings to those of others whose input you trust.
- ☐ Make a list of all the people that you currently feel over critical or judgmental towards. Write down what your judgment of each person on the list is and what you believe motivates each person's behavior. Interview someone, whose input you trust, and ask him or her to come up with plausible explanations for what motivates the person's behavior. Do not share your analysis of what motivates the behavior of the annoying people with the person you are interviewing. When you are done writing down what the other person's perceptions of the motivations for the annoying person's behavior, share your perceptions and talk about the differences.
- ☐ Complete a *Resentment Analyzer Profile* and share the results with a member of your support group. (You will find this and many other exercises by going to our website: www.leademcounseling.com and clicking on the tab on the left entitled Sober Tools).

Specialized/Individualized Interventions:

- ☐ _____

- ☐ _____

- ☐ _____

- ☐ _____

- ☐ _____

Course Assignment 5.1 (Part 1) - Selecting Intervention Strategies to Interrupt the Relapse Process: The Uncomfortable Feelings Phase of the Relapse Process (Continued)

Symptom Addressed: **Resentment**

IMPORTANT: If you find that you need more space please feel free to continue the writing on a separate piece of paper.

Generalized Interventions:

- ☐ Complete a *Resentment Analyzer Profile* (You will find this and many other exercises by going to our website: www.leademcounseling.com and clicking on the tab on the left entitled Sober Tools).
- ☐ Complete a *Focused Fourth Step Inventory* in which you thoroughly examine at people, places, and events that are at the core of the resentments that you are experiencing.
- ☐ Pray first for your healing and then for the good fortune of those you are resenting.
- ☐ Consult with your MD to evaluate the potential trigger/s for depressed mood or anxiety that could be found in your dietary habits, sleep patterns, and use of prescribed and over the counter medications as well as your general health.
- ☐ Examine the *defects of character* identified in your Sixth Step for insights into the basis for the enduring strength of your resentment/s.
- ☐ Analyze the material that you prepared for Component 2 of you Fourth Step inventory using *Clearing Away the Wreckage of the Past: A Task Oriented Guide to Completing Steps 4 through 7*, (Leadem & Leadem 2011).

Specialized/Individualized Interventions:

- ☐ _____
- ☐ _____
- ☐ _____
- ☐ _____
- ☐ _____
- ☐ _____
- ☐ _____

Course Assignment 5.1 (Part 1) - Selecting Intervention Strategies to Interrupt the Relapse Process: The Uncomfortable Feelings Phase of the Relapse Process (Continued)

Symptom Addressed: **Guilt**

IMPORTANT: If you find that you need more space please feel free to continue the writing on a separate piece of paper.

Generalized Interventions:

- ☐ Complete a *Spot Check Inventory* to identify any wrongs that you could easily correct with a timely amends (You will find this and many other exercises by going to our website: www.leademcounseling.com and clicking on the tab on the left entitled Sober Tools).
- ☐ Share your darker secrets with a trusted confidant regardless of whether or not you have finished Steps Four and Five.
- ☐ Examine your current behavior towards people that you have harmed in the past to determine if your behavior toward them has deteriorated.
- ☐ Complete a thorough Fourth Step examining all wrongs you have perpetrated as well as the harms you have endured.
- ☐ Examine your level of acceptance of the Second and Third Steps as guilt can sometimes be a symptom of a progressive return to "insanity".

Specialized/Individualized Interventions:

- ☐ _____
- ☐ _____
- ☐ _____
- ☐ _____
- ☐ _____
- ☐ _____
- ☐ _____
- ☐ _____

Course Assignment 5.1 (Part 1) - Selecting Intervention Strategies to Interrupt the Relapse Process: The Uncomfortable Feelings Phase of the Relapse Process (Continued)

Symptom Addressed: _____ **(Add Personal Symptoms Here)**

Specialized/Individualized Interventions:

- ☐ _____
- ☐ _____
- ☐ _____
- ☐ _____
- ☐ _____
- ☐ _____
- ☐ _____
- ☐ _____
- ☐ _____
- ☐ _____
- ☐ _____
- ☐ _____
- ☐ _____

Relapse is a process that can and should be stopped

Course Assignment 5.1 (Part 1) - Selecting Intervention Strategies to Interrupt the Relapse Process: The Uncomfortable Feelings Phase of the Relapse Process (Continued)

Symptom Addressed: _____ (Add Personal Symptoms Here)

Specialized/Individualized Interventions:

- ☐ _____
- ☐ _____
- ☐ _____
- ☐ _____
- ☐ _____
- ☐ _____
- ☐ _____
- ☐ _____
- ☐ _____
- ☐ _____
- ☐ _____
- ☐ _____
- ☐ _____

Course Assignment 5.1 (Part 1) - Selecting Intervention Strategies to Interrupt the Relapse Process: The Uncomfortable Feelings Phase of the Relapse Process (Continued)

Symptom Addressed: _____ **(Add Personal Symptoms Here)**

Specialized/Individualized Interventions:

☐ _____

☐ _____

☐ _____

☐ _____

☐ _____

☐ _____

☐ _____

☐ _____

☐ _____

☐ _____

☐ _____

☐ _____

☐ _____

Course Assignment 5.1 (Part 2) - Selecting Intervention Strategies to Interrupt the Relapse Process: The Time Travel Phase of the Relapse Process

Symptom Addressed: **Over-reacting to the Behavior of Others**

IMPORTANT: If you find that you need more space please feel free to continue the writing on a separate piece of paper.

Generalized Interventions:

- ☐ Write out your perception of what is happening and allow people you trust to challenge your perception.
- ☐ Ask yourself if the motive you are ascribing to the behavior of others matches what you know about them.
- ☐ Write out your reactions to the behavior of others by describing exactly what they did and said. Evaluate the material with the help of a therapist or support group member to determine whether or not your reaction or planned action matches what was done by the other person.
- ☐ Write a paragraph in which you pretend to have committed the same offense that you believe yourself to be harmed by. When you have finished the pretend confession, write what you would prescribe as the punishment or consequence if the tables were turned and you were the offender.

Specialized/Individualized Interventions:

- ☐ _____

- ☐ _____

- ☐ _____

- ☐ _____

- ☐ _____

- ☐ _____

- ☐ _____

- ☐ _____

- ☐ _____

Course Assignment 5.1 (Part 2) - Selecting Intervention Strategies to Interrupt the Relapse Process: The Time Travel Phase of the Relapse Process (Continued)

Symptom Addressed: **Negative Self-talk**

IMPORTANT: If you find that you need more space please feel free to continue the writing on a separate piece of paper.

Generalized Interventions:

- ☐ Thought Stopping: As you notice yourself saying something negative in your mind, you can stop your thought mid-stream by saying, "Stop". Saying this aloud will be more powerful, and having to say it aloud will make you more aware of how many times you are stopping negative thoughts, and where there are occurring.
- ☐ Complete a *What's Your Proof? Profile* (You will find this and many other exercises by going to our website: www.leademcounseling.com and clicking on the tab on the left entitled Sober Tools).
- ☐ If the *negative self-talk* is about you, write out what you are saying in your head until you are unable to write anymore. Take your entries to someone you feel cares for you and read it to them. You are likely to feel more tolerant and gentle towards yourself. As the discussion develops take notes about what input the other person/s give you about their perception of you and refer to it throughout episodes of *negative self-talk.*
- ☐ If your *negative self-talk* is focused on who you are going to be or what is going to happen to you at some point in the future, prepare a three-column log. In the first column write out the messages that you are receiving, in the second column an explanation of what you believe will happen to bring those prophetic messages to life, and in the third column what you and your support group have determined you could do to prevent those developments from occurring.

Specialized/Individualized Interventions:

- ☐ _____
- ☐ _____
- ☐ _____
- ☐ _____
- ☐ _____
- ☐ _____

Course Assignment 5.1 (Part 2) - Selecting Intervention Strategies to Interrupt the Relapse Process: The Time Travel Phase of the Relapse Process (Continued)

Symptom Addressed: **Day Mares**

IMPORTANT: If you find that you need more space please feel free to continue the writing on a separate piece of paper.

Generalized Interventions:

- ☐ If you have ever experienced flashbacks to traumatic life experiences refer back to the non-addictive strategies that you found helpful to cope with the fear or anger that accompanied the memories.
- ☐ If the material that you are recalling had been addressed in a previous Fifth Step, return to the recipient of that Fifth Step to revisit the material in a purposeful way within the safety of that relationship.
- ☐ Make a decision to share the event in its entirety with members of your support group. The confidential exposure can help to decrease the sense of being alone and vulnerable.
- ☐ Establish an in-depth journal entry of the event that you can use to process with your sponsor, *spiritual* advisor, therapist or other intimate friend.
- ☐ When a feeling of *panic* hits you, make sure you are physically and emotionally safe.
- ☐ Keep track of the emotional and physical environments that you are exposed to in order to identify potential triggers to your *day mares*.
- ☐ If you are not working with a therapist familiar with trauma, it would be wise to secure additional consultation.
- ☐ Get help to examine the people, circumstances, and re-occurring events in your life that are triggering the memories of your past fears and prepare a plan for getting safe in those environments. Share your findings and plans with members of your support group and therapist if you have one.

Specialized/Individualized Interventions:

- ☐ _____
- ☐ _____
- ☐ _____
- ☐ _____
- ☐ _____
- ☐ _____

Course Assignment 5.1 (Part 2) - Selecting Intervention Strategies to Interrupt the Relapse Process: The Time Travel Phase of the Relapse Process (Continued)

Symptom Addressed: **Defending Yourself from Input**

IMPORTANT: If you find that you need more space please feel free to continue the writing on a separate piece of paper.

Generalized Interventions:

- ☐ Journal about the input you are receiving from others without debate or dialogue and put it aside until you have had a period of peaceful prayer and meditation to review the validity of the input and share your journal with members of your support group.
- ☐ Relate the "unwanted" input you are defending yourself from to a trusted member of your support system or your therapist and request input about how they view you. Do not allow the conversation to become focused on the messenger of the "unwanted" input.
- ☐ Review your Fourth Step material to determine if the undesirable input you are receiving is triggering defensiveness because of injuries you have endured or perpetrated in the past.

Specialized/Individualized Interventions:

- ☐ _____
- ☐ _____
- ☐ _____
- ☐ _____
- ☐ _____
- ☐ _____
- ☐ _____
- ☐ _____
- ☐ _____

Course Assignment 5.1 (Part 2) - Selecting Intervention Strategies to Interrupt the Relapse Process: The Time Travel Phase of the Relapse Process (Continued)

Symptom Addressed: **Euphoric Recall**

IMPORTANT: If you find that you need more space please feel free to continue the writing on a separate piece of paper.

Generalized Interventions:

- ☐ Confide in support group members the seemingly positive memories that you are having about your addictive substance or behavior.
- ☐ Create a journal entry of the euphoric experience with your *drug of choice* and look around at your life at the time you are experiencing euphoric recall to see if you can identify emotional discomfort. Describe the basis for any emotional discomfort that you recall that your *drug of choice* at the time would have numbed or altered in any way.
- ☐ Complete a *Think the Drug of Choice Through Profile* (You will find this and many other exercises by going to our website: www.leademcounseling.com and clicking on the tab on the left entitled Sober Tools).
- ☐ Complete an *Exploding the Fantasy Profile* (You will find this and many other exercises by going to our website: www.leademcounseling.com and clicking on the tab on the left entitled Sober Tools).

Specialized/Individualized Interventions:

- ☐ _____
- ☐ _____
- ☐ _____
- ☐ _____
- ☐ _____
- ☐ _____
- ☐ _____
- ☐ _____

Course Assignment 5.1 (Part 2) - Selecting Intervention Strategies to Interrupt the Relapse Process: The Time Travel Phase of the Relapse Process (Continued)

Symptom Addressed: Dysphoric Recall

IMPORTANT: If you find that you need more space please feel free to continue the writing on a separate piece of paper.

Generalized Interventions:

- ☐ Tell someone about the painful memories you are experiencing in the moment or journal about them so you can discuss it in detail as soon as possible.
- ☐ Secure the assistance of a therapist or support group member to examine your current relationships and life circumstances to determine what the current life trigger is for the uncomfortable recall.
- ☐ Recall times in the past when you have had such memories, journal about how you handled them, what the outcome was, and share the journal entry with a support group member to obtain additional strategies.
- ☐ Take measures to create emotional and physical security to interrupt or diminish the power of the memories.

Specialized/Individualized Interventions:

- ☐ _____
- ☐ _____
- ☐ _____
- ☐ _____
- ☐ _____
- ☐ _____
- ☐ _____
- ☐ _____
- ☐ _____

Course Assignment 5.1 (Part 2) - Selecting Intervention Strategies to Interrupt the Relapse Process: The Time Travel Phase of the Relapse Process (Continued)

Symptom Addressed: **Implosion**

IMPORTANT: If you find that you need more space please feel free to continue the writing on a separate piece of paper.

Generalized Interventions:

- ☐ Pull away from the present stress, if possible, to a safe environment to lessen the fear that you will be harmed by others.
- ☐ Elicit input from support group members about what they imagine you are feeling or what they would be feeling in a similar situation to minimize the risk of an emotional disconnect.
- ☐ Use written communication or artwork to relate to trusted others the experiences that you are having and the discomfort you are feeling.
- ☐ Explore with a trusted support group member or therapist the personal critique that you have about your implosion.

Specialized/Individualized Interventions:

- ☐ _____
- ☐ _____
- ☐ _____
- ☐ _____
- ☐ _____
- ☐ _____
- ☐ _____
- ☐ _____
- ☐ _____

Course Assignment 5.1 (Part 2) - Selecting Intervention Strategies to Interrupt the Relapse Process: The Time Travel Phase of the Relapse Process (Continued)

Symptom Addressed: **Explosion**

IMPORTANT: If you find that you need more space please feel free to continue the writing on a separate piece of paper.

Generalized Interventions:

- ☐ Remove yourself from others who might become a target of your emotionality.
- ☐ Share the thoughts and feelings you are experiencing with a member of your support system and avoid receiving input about the object of your volatility.
- ☐ Use written communication or artwork to relate to trusted others the experiences that you are having and the discomfort you are feeling.
- ☐ Explore with a trusted support group member or therapist the personal critique that you have about your explosion.

Specialized/Individualized Interventions:

- ☐ _____
- ☐ _____
- ☐ _____
- ☐ _____
- ☐ _____
- ☐ _____
- ☐ _____
- ☐ _____
- ☐ _____

Course Assignment 5.1 (Part 2) - Selecting Intervention Strategies to Interrupt the Relapse Process: The Time Travel Phase of the Relapse Process (Continued)

Symptom Addressed: **Avoidance of Intimacy**

IMPORTANT: If you find that you need more space please feel free to continue the writing on a separate piece of paper.

Generalized Interventions:

- ☐ Journal about the fear of intimacy you are experiencing and share it with members of your support system.
- ☐ Examine the past to determine if there were times when your emotional vulnerability seemed to result in greater emotional pain because of rejection or mistreatment by others.
- ☐ Work with a therapist to develop an understanding of *co-occurring event* vs. *cause/effect relationships*.
- ☐ Explore ways of being more intimate with the people you trust the most in order to safely introduce experiences that have historically or recently triggered the fear-based avoidance.
- ☐ Describe what you believe will occur if you become emotionally intimate or vulnerable with each person that you fear exposing yourself to. Look for the common themes that develop and where you might find similar themes in your past.
- ☐ Conduct a thorough examination of the coping strategies that you employ to avoid becoming intimate or vulnerable as there may be defects in your character that are contributing to your fear.

Specialized/Individualized Interventions:

- ☐ _____
- ☐ _____
- ☐ _____
- ☐ _____
- ☐ _____
- ☐ _____
- ☐ _____
- ☐ _____

Course Assignment 5.1 (Part 2) - Selecting Intervention Strategies to Interrupt the Relapse Process: The Time Travel Phase of the Relapse Process (Continued)

Symptom Addressed: **Retrieving Past Wrongs of an Opponent to Validate Your Emotional Pain**

IMPORTANT: If you find that you need more space please feel free to continue the writing on a separate piece of paper.

Generalized Interventions:

- ☐ Avoid digging for proof from your opponent's past behavior to substantiate your current feelings of mistrust or resentment.
- ☐ Ask a member of your support system to help you identify qualities in your opponent that you have admired or enjoyed in the past.
- ☐ Review your gratitude list to see if your opponent shows up there, if not then perhaps he or she should.
- ☐ Deprive yourself of any verbal communication of your thoughts or feelings that use the words "always" and "never" to prevent accessing past material to support your current feeling reaction.

Specialized/Individualized Interventions:

- ☐ _____
- ☐ _____
- ☐ _____
- ☐ _____
- ☐ _____
- ☐ _____
- ☐ _____
- ☐ _____
- ☐ _____

Course Assignment 5.1 (Part 2) - Selecting Intervention Strategies to Interrupt the Relapse Process: The Time Travel Phase of the Relapse Process (Continued)

Symptom Addressed: **Retrieving or Reviewing Your Past Wrongs to Justify the Hurtful Things You Are Doing to Yourself or Are Allowing Others to Do to You**

IMPORTANT: If you find that you need more space please feel free to continue the writing on a separate piece of paper.

Generalized Interventions:

- ☐ If you are having difficulty caring for yourself, find yourself behaving in a self-destructive manner, or allowing others to continually mistreat you, do not look for your wrongs as you might be using the information to justify your own mistreatment.
- ☐ Discuss the circumstances with your therapist or trusted support group member to challenge the perspective that your past wrongs justify your current mistreatment by others or self.
- ☐ Review your Fourth Step material to determine if you had been thorough in the examination of your wrongs as well as the injuries that you have endured at the hands of others. If you find that you need to write more about your wrong doings and that you need to complete an updated Fifth Step, please do so.
- ☐ If you a struggling to set boundaries in your relationships, review Component 2 of your Fourth Step Inventory using the model proposed in *Clearing Away the Wreckage of the Past: A Task Oriented Guide to Completing Steps 4 through 7*, (Leadem & Leadem, 2011).

Specialized/Individualized Interventions:

- ☐ _____
- ☐ _____
- ☐ _____
- ☐ _____
- ☐ _____
- ☐ _____
- ☐ _____

Course Assignment 5.1 (Part 2) - Selecting Intervention Strategies to Interrupt the Relapse Process: The Time Travel Phase of the Relapse Process (Continued)

Symptom Addressed: **Attempts to Discredit Those You Have Come to Trust**

IMPORTANT: If you find that you need more space please feel free to continue the writing on a separate piece of paper.

Generalized Interventions:

- ☐ Attempts to discredit someone you recently or historically trusted is likely to be coming from experiences with others in your past that this experience or person is reminding you of. Make a list of the people your opponent reminds you of and describe the similarity between the two and the ways in which you were hurt in the historical material.
- ☐ Make a list of all the reasons that you might have to discredit the person you have targeted with dates and specifics surrounding the events that you are using to justify your decision. Make a list of all the benefits you have derived from your relationship with the person you have targeted for the discrediting and conduct a careful analysis of the two lists with a member of your support system.

Specialized/Individualized Interventions:

- ☐ _____
- ☐ _____
- ☐ _____
- ☐ _____
- ☐ _____
- ☐ _____
- ☐ _____
- ☐ _____
- ☐ _____

Course Assignment 5.1 (Part 2) - Selecting Intervention Strategies to Interrupt the Relapse Process: The Time Travel Phase of the Relapse Process (Continued)

Symptom Addressed: _____ **(Add Personal Symptoms Here)**

Specialized/Individualized Interventions:

- ☐ _____
- ☐ _____
- ☐ _____
- ☐ _____
- ☐ _____
- ☐ _____
- ☐ _____
- ☐ _____
- ☐ _____
- ☐ _____
- ☐ _____
- ☐ _____
- ☐ _____

Course Assignment 5.1 (Part 2) - Selecting Intervention Strategies to Interrupt the Relapse Process: The Time Travel Phase of the Relapse Process (Continued)

Symptom Addressed: _____ **(Add Personal Symptoms Here)**

Specialized/Individualized Interventions:

- ☐ _____
- ☐ _____
- ☐ _____
- ☐ _____
- ☐ _____
- ☐ _____
- ☐ _____
- ☐ _____
- ☐ _____
- ☐ _____
- ☐ _____
- ☐ _____

Course Assignment 5.1 (Part 2) - Selecting Intervention Strategies to Interrupt the Relapse Process: The Time Travel Phase of the Relapse Process (Continued)

Symptom Addressed: _____ **(Add Personal Symptoms Here)**

Specialized/Individualized Interventions:

☐ _____

☐ _____

☐ _____

☐ _____

☐ _____

☐ _____

☐ _____

☐ _____

☐ _____

☐ _____

☐ _____

☐ _____

☐ _____

Course Assignment 5.1 (Part 3) - Selecting Intervention Strategies to Interrupt the Relapse Process: The Fragmentation Phase of the Relapse Process

Symptom Addressed: **People with Whom You Are Sharing Do not Appear to Understand What You Are Trying to Communicate**

IMPORTANT: If you find that you need more space please feel free to continue the writing on a separate piece of paper.

Generalized Interventions:

- ☐ Try closing your eyes for a moment while you are talking to them to prevent you from seeing their reaction because it could help you verbally present what you are feeling without a scowl or smile on your face that does not match what you are talking about.
- ☐ Complete a *Congruency Profile* and share it with the person you are attempting to communicate with (You will find this and many other exercises by going to our website: www.leademcounseling.com and clicking on the tab on the left entitled Sober Tools).
- ☐ Ask the people involved in the dialogue to relate their identification with what they believe you are attempting to communicate.

Specialized/Individualized Interventions:

- ☐ _____
- ☐ _____
- ☐ _____
- ☐ _____
- ☐ _____
- ☐ _____
- ☐ _____
- ☐ _____

Course Assignment 5.1 (Part 3) - Selecting Intervention Strategies to Interrupt the Relapse Process: The Fragmentation Phase of the Relapse Process (Continued)

Symptom Addressed: **Difficulty Demonstrating Emotions Freely and Without Constraint**

IMPORTANT: If you find that you need more space please feel free to continue the writing on a separate piece of paper.

Generalized Interventions:

- ☐ Write out what you would like to express about your feelings.
- ☐ Draw a picture of what you would like to express about your feelings.
- ☐ Discuss the situations or events in which you find yourself unable to identify your feelings with your therapist or members of your support system and elicit from others what they might be feeling if they were you, as it may help if you are introduced to the feeling labels that others might use to describe their emotions.

Specialized/Individualized Interventions:

- ☐ _____
- ☐ _____
- ☐ _____
- ☐ _____
- ☐ _____
- ☐ _____
- ☐ _____
- ☐ _____
- ☐ _____
- ☐ _____

Course Assignment 5.1 (Part 3) - Selecting Intervention Strategies to Interrupt the Relapse Process: The Fragmentation Phase of the Relapse Process (Continued)

Symptom Addressed: **Inability to Make Self Understood**

IMPORTANT: If you find that you need more space please feel free to continue the writing on a separate piece of paper.

Generalized Interventions:

- ☐ Share what you are thinking or feeling with a safe person before attempting it with a "risky" person.
- ☐ When you find yourself feeling misunderstood take a break from the conversation to write out what you are saying and what message you hope that the other person will get from it. Share your writing with a support group member for input before returning to the conversation.
- ☐ If you suspect that others are not getting your intended meaning write down what you are intending to communicate and what, within you, could be confusing or complicating your intended message.

Specialized/Individualized Interventions:

☐ _____

☐ _____

☐ _____

☐ _____

☐ _____

☐ _____

☐ _____

☐ _____

☐ _____

Course Assignment 5.1 (Part 3) - Selecting Intervention Strategies to Interrupt the Relapse Process: The Fragmentation Phase of the Relapse Process (Continued)

Symptom Addressed: **Struggling to Identify Your Own Feelings**

IMPORTANT: If you find that you need more space please feel free to continue the writing on a separate piece of paper.

Generalized Interventions:

- ☐ Look in the mirror while you are examining your emotions.
- ☐ Begin with the communication that you are feeling comfortable or uncomfortable rather than searching for the perfect label for what you are experiencing.

Specialized/Individualized Interventions:

- ☐ _____
- ☐ _____
- ☐ _____
- ☐ _____
- ☐ _____
- ☐ _____
- ☐ _____
- ☐ _____
- ☐ _____
- ☐ _____
- ☐ _____

Course Assignment 5.1 (Part 3) - Selecting Intervention Strategies to Interrupt the Relapse Process: The Fragmentation Phase of the Relapse Process (Continued)

Symptom Addressed: **Obsessive Thinking**

IMPORTANT: If you find that you need more space please feel free to continue the writing on a separate piece of paper.

Generalized Interventions:

- ☐ Complete a *Spot Check Inventory* to log all of your obsessive thoughts to share with a member of your support group to obtain a more objective perspective (You will find this and many other exercises by going to our website: www.leademcounseling.com and clicking on the tab on the left entitled Sober Tools).
- ☐ Create a list of everything that you believe to be true or that you believe needs to be done and obtain a second opinion about the validity of the list items from a trusted source of support to you.
- ☐ Channel your obsessiveness into a task that can be completed in a short period of time (1-2 hours). In the completion of the task you are encouraged to be as obsessive in your thinking about the task and compulsive in your completion of the elements of the task as you wish. Tasks like organizing your sock drawer or a small closet are ideal for the object of safely funneling your obsession.

Specialized/Individualized Interventions:

- ☐ _____
- ☐ _____
- ☐ _____
- ☐ _____
- ☐ _____
- ☐ _____
- ☐ _____
- ☐ _____

Relapse is a process that can and should be stopped

Course Assignment 5.1 (Part 3) - Selecting Intervention Strategies to Interrupt the Relapse Process: The Fragmentation Phase of the Relapse Process (Continued)

Symptom Addressed: _____ **(Add Personal Symptoms Here)**

Specialized/Individualized Interventions:

☐ _____

☐ _____

☐ _____

☐ _____

☐ _____

☐ _____

☐ _____

☐ _____

☐ _____

☐ _____

☐ _____

☐ _____

Course Assignment 5.1 (Part 3) - Selecting Intervention Strategies to Interrupt the Relapse Process: The Fragmentation Phase of the Relapse Process (Continued)

Symptom Addressed: _____ **(Add Personal Symptoms Here)**

Specialized/Individualized Interventions:

- ☐ _____
- ☐ _____
- ☐ _____
- ☐ _____
- ☐ _____
- ☐ _____
- ☐ _____
- ☐ _____
- ☐ _____
- ☐ _____
- ☐ _____
- ☐ _____

Course Assignment 5.1 (Part 3) - Selecting Intervention Strategies to Interrupt the Relapse Process: The Fragmentation Phase of the Relapse Process (Continued)

Symptom Addressed: _____ **(Add Personal Symptoms Here)**

Specialized/Individualized Interventions:

- ☐ _____
- ☐ _____
- ☐ _____
- ☐ _____
- ☐ _____
- ☐ _____
- ☐ _____
- ☐ _____
- ☐ _____
- ☐ _____
- ☐ _____
- ☐ _____

Course Assignment 5.1 (Part 4) – Selecting Intervention Strategies to Interrupt the Relapse Process: The Gathering Justification Phase of Relapse Process

Symptom Addressed: **Justifiable Anger**

IMPORTANT: If you find that you need more space please feel free to continue the writing on a separate piece of paper.

Generalized Interventions:

- ☐ Read page 90 in the *Twelve Steps & Twelve Traditions* publication by A.A. World Service on the *spiritual* axiom.
- ☐ Review your Fourth Step material, especially Components 1 & 2 found in *Clearing Away the Wreckage of the Past: A Task Oriented Guide to Completing Steps 4 through 7*, to determine if you are reacting from past hurts that others have done to you rather than the current situation or person. Anger does not need to be justified! (Leadem & Leadem, 2011).
- ☐ Examine your Sixth Step material, especially Task 4 to see what your payoff is for remaining angry because sustained anger will hurt you.

Specialized/Individualized Interventions:

- ☐ _____
- ☐ _____
- ☐ _____
- ☐ _____
- ☐ _____
- ☐ _____
- ☐ _____
- ☐ _____
- ☐ _____

Course Assignment 5.1 (Part 4) – Selecting Intervention Strategies to Interrupt the Relapse Process: The Gathering Justification Phase of Relapse Process (Continued)

Symptom Addressed: **Judgmental**

IMPORTANT: If you find that you need more space please feel free to continue the writing on a separate piece of paper.

Generalized Interventions:

- ☐ Make a list of the faults you have identified in people you remain or recently have become uncomfortable with and examine if any part of the problem could be you.
- ☐ Complete Sixth Step using the *Clearing Away the Wreckage of the Past: A Task Oriented Guide to Completing Steps 4 through 7*, (Leadem & Leadem, 2011).
- ☐ Complete a spot check inventory to explore the times when you have felt judged by others and what you imagined at the time motivated their behavior. By developing theories about why others were judging you, you might be able to gain insight into why you have become judgmental and what you might be able to do about yourself.

Specialized/Individualized Interventions:

☐ _____

☐ _____

☐ _____

☐ _____

☐ _____

☐ _____

☐ _____

☐ _____

☐ _____

Course Assignment 5.1 (Part 4) – Selecting Intervention Strategies to Interrupt the Relapse Process: The Gathering Justification Phase of Relapse Process (Continued)

Symptom Addressed: **Blaming Others for the Way You Feel or Behave**

IMPORTANT: If you find that you need more space please feel free to continue the writing on a separate piece of paper.

Generalized Interventions:

- ☐ Write out what you blame others for in one column and what you identify with in that trait in the second column, then share your results with a support group member.
- ☐ Write out what would happen if you took responsibility for your own feelings.
- ☐ Make a list of everyone that you can ever remember blaming for some event or feeling in your life. Review the material with a trusted support group member or your therapist through your eyes and experience of today in recovery. Does the view that you had of their "wrongness" hold true as you examine it with the wisdom you have today?
- ☐ Make a list of what others have blamed you for and review your perception of the validity of their perception with your therapist or support group member.

Specialized/Individualized Interventions:

- ☐ _____
- ☐ _____
- ☐ _____
- ☐ _____
- ☐ _____
- ☐ _____
- ☐ _____
- ☐ _____

Course Assignment 5.1 (Part 4) – Selecting Intervention Strategies to Interrupt the Relapse Process: The Gathering Justification Phase of Relapse Process (Continued)

Symptom Addressed: **Disconnect**

IMPORTANT: If you find that you need more space please feel free to continue the writing on a separate piece of paper.

Generalized Interventions:

- ☐ Write out what you do to make yourself unavailable to others and tell them.
- ☐ Draw a picture that depicts you disconnected from another person and have the portrayal tell the story of how this disconnect has come to be.
- ☐ Examine the people in your life who appear to have experienced an emotional freeze or disconnect. Describe how they behaved during the event and review the points that preceded the disconnect to practice identifying the signs that might indicate that someone is about to shut down.
- ☐ Review scenes or events in which others report you to have disconnected. With the help of trusted historians, examine the *antecedents* to the shutdown.

Specialized/Individualized Interventions:

- ☐ _____
- ☐ _____
- ☐ _____
- ☐ _____
- ☐ _____
- ☐ _____
- ☐ _____
- ☐ _____
- ☐ _____

Course Assignment 5.1 (Part 4) – Selecting Intervention Strategies to Interrupt the Relapse Process: The Gathering Justification Phase of Relapse Process (Continued)

Symptom Addressed: **Lack of Emotional Support**

IMPORTANT: If you find that you need more space please feel free to continue the writing on a separate piece of paper.

Generalized Interventions:

- ☐ Review your relationship with support group members as well as significant others and compare it to the past to help you identify if you are beginning to isolate.
- ☐ Examine the relationships you have with support group members to determine if you are getting your needs met. If not, develop a plan with your sponsor or therapist to redefine those relationships or identify additional sources of support you could rely on.
- ☐ Review your plan for maintaining *spiritual* well-being with your therapist or support group to determine if you are getting your needs met.
- ☐ Obtain help to examine the relationships you maintain with non-support group members to determine if you are being too drained by your support of them.

Specialized/Individualized Interventions:

- ☐ _____
- ☐ _____
- ☐ _____
- ☐ _____
- ☐ _____
- ☐ _____
- ☐ _____
- ☐ _____

Course Assignment 5.1 (Part 4) – Selecting Intervention Strategies to Interrupt the Relapse Process: The Gathering Justification Phase of Relapse Process (Continued)

Symptom Addressed: **Difficulty Empathizing with Others**

IMPORTANT: If you find that you need more space please feel free to continue the writing on a separate piece of paper.

Generalized Interventions:

- ☐ Examine your life to find similar stories in your own life and share those accounts with people you struggle to empathize with.
- ☐ Observe people that seem to have an easy time empathizing with others and question them about how they accomplish the task.
- ☐ Complete a *Spot Check Inventory* on any relationship that you are struggling to experience empathy in and complete a *Fragmentation Profile*. Discuss your findings with your therapist or support group member in order to get help in identifying the obstacles you are experiencing. (You will find these and many other exercises by going to our website: www.leademcounseling.com and clicking on the tab on the left entitled Sober Tools).

Specialized/Individualized Interventions:

- ☐ _____
- ☐ _____
- ☐ _____
- ☐ _____
- ☐ _____
- ☐ _____
- ☐ _____
- ☐ _____

Course Assignment 5.1 (Part 4) – Selecting Intervention Strategies to Interrupt the Relapse Process: The Gathering Justification Phase of Relapse Process (Continued)

Symptom Addressed: _____ **(Add Personal Symptoms Here)**

Specialized/Individualized Interventions:

- ☐ _____

- ☐ _____

- ☐ _____

- ☐ _____

- ☐ _____

- ☐ _____

- ☐ _____

- ☐ _____

- ☐ _____

- ☐ _____

- ☐ _____

- ☐ _____

- ☐ _____

Course Assignment 5.1 (Part 4) – Selecting Intervention Strategies to Interrupt the Relapse Process: The Gathering Justification Phase of Relapse Process (Continued)

Symptom Addressed: _____ **(Add Personal Symptoms Here)**

Specialized/Individualized Interventions:

☐ _____

☐ _____

☐ _____

☐ _____

☐ _____

☐ _____

☐ _____

☐ _____

☐ _____

☐ _____

☐ _____

☐ _____

☐ _____

Course Assignment 5.1 (Part 4) – Selecting Intervention Strategies to Interrupt the Relapse Process: The Gathering Justification Phase of Relapse Process (Continued)

Symptom Addressed: _____ **(Add Personal Symptoms Here)**

Specialized/Individualized Interventions:

- ☐ _____
- ☐ _____
- ☐ _____
- ☐ _____
- ☐ _____
- ☐ _____
- ☐ _____
- ☐ _____
- ☐ _____
- ☐ _____
- ☐ _____
- ☐ _____
- ☐ _____

Course Assignment 5.1 (Part 5) – Selecting Intervention Strategies to Interrupt the Relapse Process: The Eliminating the Witnesses Phase of the Relapse Process

Symptom Addressed: **Gossiping & Character Assassination**

IMPORTANT: If you find that you need more space please feel free to continue the writing on a separate piece of paper.

Generalized Interventions:

- ☐ Complete a historical gratitude list for each of the people that you are considering "getting rid of".
- ☐ Examine, with the help of key support group members, whether or not this behavior is symptomatic of a defect of your character.
- ☐ Let everyone close to you know that you are having a problem with being a gossip and encourage them to confront you when you are.

Specialized/Individualized Interventions:

- ☐ _____
- ☐ _____
- ☐ _____
- ☐ _____
- ☐ _____
- ☐ _____
- ☐ _____
- ☐ _____
- ☐ _____
- ☐ _____

Course Assignment 5.1 (Part 5) – Selecting Intervention Strategies to Interrupt the Relapse Process: The Eliminating the Witnesses Phase of the Relapse Process (Continued)

Symptom Addressed: **Escapism**

IMPORTANT: If you find that you need more space please feel free to continue the writing on a separate piece of paper.

Generalized Interventions:

- ☐ Plan time in your daily schedule of recovery activities to connect with support group members in a meaningful way.
- ☐ Examine, with the help of key support group members, whether or not this behavior is symptomatic of a defect of your character.
- ☐ Describe in writing the ways and means that you have for escape and share them with members of your support system with the intent of having them intervene on you when they see you headed for isolation
- ☐ Prepare a list of interventions that others might use successfully on you for each escape pattern or place that you have identified.
- ☐ Ask members of your support system to provide you with the insights they have regarding their perception of your escape tactics.

Specialized/Individualized Interventions:

- ☐ _____
- ☐ _____
- ☐ _____
- ☐ _____
- ☐ _____
- ☐ _____
- ☐ _____
- ☐ _____

Course Assignment 5.1 (Part 5) – Selecting Intervention Strategies to Interrupt the Relapse Process: The Eliminating the Witnesses Phase of the Relapse Process (Continued)

Symptom Addressed: **Always Right!**

IMPORTANT: If you find that you need more space please feel free to continue the writing on a separate piece of paper.

Generalized Interventions:

- ☐ Examine, with the help of key support group members, whether or not this behavior is symptomatic of a defect of your character.
- ☐ Examine the material from your Fourth Step to examine whether or not this coping strategy is reflective of how you were hurt by others or hurtful behavior that you wronged others with in the past.
- ☐ Write out what you believe that you are "right" about and give all the supporting evidence that you can think of. When you are done complete the same task but this time write the position of your opposition and all the evidence you can identify to support why he or she is right.
- ☐ Complete Sixth Step using *Clearing Away the Wreckage of the Past: A Task Oriented Guide to Completing Steps 4 through 7*, (Leadem & Leadem, 2011).

Specialized/Individualized Interventions:

- ☐ _____
- ☐ _____
- ☐ _____
- ☐ _____
- ☐ _____
- ☐ _____
- ☐ _____
- ☐ _____

Course Assignment 5.1 (Part 5) – Selecting Intervention Strategies to Interrupt the Relapse Process: The Eliminating the Witnesses Phase of the Relapse Process (Continued)

Symptom Addressed: **Inability to Acknowledge Your Own Wrongs**

IMPORTANT: If you find that you need more space please feel free to continue the writing on a separate piece of paper.

Generalized Interventions:

- ☐ Conduct a *Spot Check Inventory* to identify the last time you recall acknowledging that you were wrong about something and how it made you feel. (You will find this and many other exercises by going to our website: www.leademcounseling.com and clicking on the tab on the left entitled Sober Tools).
- ☐ Examine, with the help of key support group members, whether or not this behavior is symptomatic of a defect of your character.
- ☐ Review your Fourth Step material with your therapist or support group to develop an understanding of your past wrongs in an effort to determine if your current behavior is a continuation of your coping patterns from the past.
- ☐ Review the factual points that others have made with you about their perception of your wrongs with your therapist or support group members to get more objective input about your behavior from people that you do not feel a need to defend yourself with.

Specialized/Individualized Interventions:

- ☐ _____
- ☐ _____
- ☐ _____
- ☐ _____
- ☐ _____
- ☐ _____
- ☐ _____
- ☐ _____

Course Assignment 5.1 (Part 5) – Selecting Intervention Strategies to Interrupt the Relapse Process: The Eliminating the Witnesses Phase of the Relapse Process (Continued)

Symptom Addressed: **Rebuff the Concerns of Others**

IMPORTANT: If you find that you need more space please feel free to continue the writing on a separate piece of paper.

Generalized Interventions:

- ☐ Complete Steps Six and Seven and review them with members of your support group to enable them to know when you are attempting to eliminate the witnesses.
- ☐ Describe in writing the various methods you employ when you want to rebuff the concerns that others have for you.
- ☐ Describe at least three times when you have brought your concerns about someone else to the foreground and have been rebuffed in some way. Describe how you felt and what you believe was motivating the other person's behavior.

Specialized/Individualized Interventions:

- ☐ _____
- ☐ _____
- ☐ _____
- ☐ _____
- ☐ _____
- ☐ _____
- ☐ _____
- ☐ _____
- ☐ _____

Course Assignment 5.1 (Part 5) – Selecting Intervention Strategies to Interrupt the Relapse Process: The Eliminating the Witnesses Phase of the Relapse Process (Continued)

Symptom Addressed: **Growing Isolation**

IMPORTANT: If you find that you need more space please feel free to continue the writing on a separate piece of paper.

Generalized Interventions:

- ☐ Make a list of the times during the past 90 days in which someone has shared a concern with you about your being unavailable to them in some way.
- ☐ Make a detailed list of the relationships that you would historically be of service to in some behavioral, emotional, or *spiritual* way. After you have described the ways that you would normally have been of service to each of them describe how you have served them in the past 90 days.
- ☐ Make a detailed list of the relationships that you would have historically been supported by. After you have described the ways that you would normally have been supported in these relationships describe how you have actually allowed them to be of service to you in the past 90 days.
- ☐ Make an effort to secure the opportunity to be of service to a newcomer.
- ☐ Volunteer for some service work within the meetings that your attend.
- ☐ Examine, with the help of your support group, your explanation or justification for avoiding certain meetings or members of the recovering community to help you identify if there is an unhealthy motive to your choices.
- ☐ Solicit help from members of your support system to ride with them to meetings or offer rides to fellowship members who do not have transportation.
- ☐ Complete an inventory of what is lost by eliminating sources of support by examining the cost for each of the sources of support that is eliminated.

Specialized/Individualized Interventions:

- ☐ _____

- ☐ _____

- ☐ _____

- ☐ _____

- ☐ _____

- ☐ _____

Course Assignment 5.1 (Part 5) – Selecting Intervention Strategies to Interrupt the Relapse Process: The Eliminating the Witnesses Phase of the Relapse Process (Continued)

Symptom Addressed: _____ **(Add Personal Symptoms Here)**

Specialized/Individualized Interventions:

☐ _____

☐ _____

☐ _____

☐ _____

☐ _____

☐ _____

☐ _____

☐ _____

☐ _____

☐ _____

☐ _____

☐ _____

☐ _____

Course Assignment 5.1 (Part 5) – Selecting Intervention Strategies to Interrupt the Relapse Process: The Eliminating the Witnesses Phase of the Relapse Process (Continued)

Symptom Addressed: _____ **(Add Personal Symptoms Here)**

Specialized/Individualized Interventions:

- ☐ _____
- ☐ _____
- ☐ _____
- ☐ _____
- ☐ _____
- ☐ _____
- ☐ _____
- ☐ _____
- ☐ _____
- ☐ _____
- ☐ _____
- ☐ _____
- ☐ _____

Course Assignment 5.1 (Part 5) – Selecting Intervention Strategies to Interrupt the Relapse Process: The Eliminating the Witnesses Phase of the Relapse Process (Continued)

Symptom Addressed: _____ **(Add Personal Symptoms Here)**

Specialized/Individualized Interventions:

☐ _____

☐ _____

☐ _____

☐ _____

☐ _____

☐ _____

☐ _____

☐ _____

☐ _____

☐ _____

☐ _____

☐ _____

☐ _____

Course Assignment 5.1 (Part 6) -- Selecting Intervention Strategies to Interrupt the Relapse Process: The Dry Drunk Phase of the Relapse Process

Symptom Addressed: **Mood Swings**

IMPORTANT: If you find that you need more space please feel free to continue the writing on a separate piece of paper.

Generalized Interventions:

- ☐ If you are concerned that your mood swings are related to a medical problem or the medications you are taking, consult your physician.
- ☐ Review your Relapse Recording Journal (p. 190) entries for the past month to look for the presence of unresolved emotional conflict.
- ☐ Evaluate your eating habits as the food you eat or the way you eat might be generating mood instability.

Specialized/Individualized Interventions:

- ☐ _____
- ☐ _____
- ☐ _____
- ☐ _____
- ☐ _____
- ☐ _____
- ☐ _____
- ☐ _____
- ☐ _____
- ☐ _____

Course Assignment 5.1 (Part 6) -- Selecting Intervention Strategies to Interrupt the Relapse Process: The Dry Drunk Phase of the Relapse Process (Continued)

Symptom Addressed: **Extreme Difficulty with Introspection**

IMPORTANT: If you find that you need more space please feel free to continue the writing on a separate piece of paper.

Generalized Interventions:

- ☐ Request that concerned others that you trust meet with you as a group to share their concerns for your emotional/behavioral state and make recommendations to you for emotional/behavioral containment.
- ☐ Review your journal entries for the past 30 days to determine if there has been a pattern to the reduction in your ability to be introspective and *antecedents* that you could intervene on.

Specialized/Individualized Interventions:

- ☐ _____
- ☐ _____
- ☐ _____
- ☐ _____
- ☐ _____
- ☐ _____
- ☐ _____
- ☐ _____
- ☐ _____
- ☐ _____
- ☐ _____

Course Assignment 5.1 (Part 6) -- Selecting Intervention Strategies to Interrupt the Relapse Process: The Dry Drunk Phase of the Relapse Process (Continued)

Symptom Addressed: **Grandiosity**

IMPORTANT: If you find that you need more space please feel free to continue the writing on a separate piece of paper.

Generalized Interventions:

- ☐ Conduct a *Spot Check Inventory* to identify what fears you might be unaware of that are generating a perception that you need to handle life on your own. (You will find this and many other exercises by going to our website: www.leademcounseling.com and clicking on the tab on the left entitled Sober Tools).
- ☐ Make a list of the ways that you are like the people that you are feeling superior to so you can get "right-sized".
- ☐ When your grandiosity is masquerading as perfectionism write a description of what would need to happen, in a given event or situation that you are obsessing over, to make the outcome perfect. When you have done that add at least one more thing that might make it better. Explain why the first "perfect" was not perfect when it is a state that is defined as: "having all the required or desirable elements or qualities".

Specialized/Individualized Interventions:

- ☐ _____
- ☐ _____
- ☐ _____
- ☐ _____
- ☐ _____
- ☐ _____
- ☐ _____
- ☐ _____

Course Assignment 5.1 (Part 6) -- Selecting Intervention Strategies to Interrupt the Relapse Process: The Dry Drunk Phase of the Relapse Process (Continued)

Symptom Addressed: **Intolerance**

IMPORTANT: If you find that you need more space please feel free to continue the writing on a separate piece of paper.

Generalized Interventions:

- ☐ Write yourself a letter as if you were an 'old timer' explaining the benefits of exercising patience towards self and others.
- ☐ Describe a situation in which a person is behaving intolerably on one side of the paper. On the flip side of the page write a story, completely fictional if necessary, explaining why he or she is behaving that way, which is totally different from your original thought. When you are finished, reassess the behavior of the person and clarify whether the person was intolerable or misunderstood.

Specialized/Individualized Interventions:

- ☐ _____
- ☐ _____
- ☐ _____
- ☐ _____
- ☐ _____
- ☐ _____
- ☐ _____
- ☐ _____
- ☐ _____

Course Assignment 5.1 (Part 6) -- Selecting Intervention Strategies to Interrupt the Relapse Process: The Dry Drunk Phase of the Relapse Process (Continued)

Symptom Addressed: **Impulsivity**

IMPORTANT: If you find that you need more space please feel free to continue the writing on a separate piece of paper.

Generalized Interventions:

- ☐ Do not take action on thoughts or feelings unless you have received counsel from significant others and members of your support group until the unstable mood passes.
- ☐ Make a list of your impulsive acts that have caused you problems or generated the outcomes you had expected.
- ☐ Write a letter to the God of your understanding in which you explain why it is that you are about to take the impulsive action.
- ☐ Write a letter from the God of your understanding to you in response to your first letter justifying the impulsive action.

Specialized/Individualized Interventions:

☐ _____

☐ _____

☐ _____

☐ _____

☐ _____

☐ _____

☐ _____

☐ _____

Relapse is a process that can and should be stopped

Course Assignment 5.1 (Part 6) -- Selecting Intervention Strategies to Interrupt the Relapse Process: The Dry Drunk Phase of the Relapse Process (Continued)

Symptom Addressed: **Romanticizing the Benefit of Addictive Behavior**

IMPORTANT: If you find that you need more space please feel free to continue the writing on a separate piece of paper.

Generalized Interventions:

- ☐ Review your First Step with a sponsor or support group member.
- ☐ Complete a *Thinking the Drink Through Profile* (You will find this and many other exercises by going to our website: www.leademcounseling.com and clicking on the tab on the left entitled Sober Tools).
- ☐ Review your Fourth Step material to see what history says about your relationship with your *drug of choice* and what will happen if you return to it.

Specialized/Individualized Interventions:

- ☐ _____
- ☐ _____
- ☐ _____
- ☐ _____
- ☐ _____
- ☐ _____
- ☐ _____
- ☐ _____
- ☐ _____
- ☐ _____

Course Assignment 5.1 (Part 6) -- Selecting Intervention Strategies to Interrupt the Relapse Process: The Dry Drunk Phase of the Relapse Process (Continued)

Symptom Addressed: **Withdraw from Others**

IMPORTANT: If you find that you need more space please feel free to continue the writing on a separate piece of paper.

Generalized Interventions:

- ☐ Intensify your efforts to make contact with those individuals in your life for whom you have been the most grateful.
- ☐ Ask family or support group members to help you make efforts to be more social.
- ☐ Increase the amount or intensity of the professional support you have available to you.

Specialized/Individualized Interventions:

- ☐ _____
- ☐ _____
- ☐ _____
- ☐ _____
- ☐ _____
- ☐ _____
- ☐ _____
- ☐ _____
- ☐ _____
- ☐ _____

Course Assignment 5.1 (Part 6) -- Selecting Intervention Strategies to Interrupt the Relapse Process: The Dry Drunk Phase of the Relapse Process (Continued)

Symptom Addressed: **Self-absorption**

IMPORTANT: If you find that you need more space please feel free to continue the writing on a separate piece of paper.

Generalized Interventions:

- ☐ Attend "beginners meetings".
- ☐ Ask group members to help you identify "newcomers" for you to be of service to.
- ☐ Complete tasks around the home that have routinely been the responsibility of others.
- ☐ Conduct random acts of kindness.

Specialized/Individualized Interventions:

- ☐ _____
- ☐ _____
- ☐ _____
- ☐ _____
- ☐ _____
- ☐ _____
- ☐ _____
- ☐ _____
- ☐ _____
- ☐ _____
- ☐ _____

Relapse is a process that can and should be stopped

Course Assignment 5.1 (Part 6) -- Selecting Intervention Strategies to Interrupt the Relapse Process: The Dry Drunk Phase of the Relapse Process (Continued)

Symptom Addressed: _____ **(Add Personal Symptoms Here)**

Specialized/Individualized Interventions:

☐ _____

☐ _____

☐ _____

☐ _____

☐ _____

☐ _____

☐ _____

☐ _____

☐ _____

☐ _____

☐ _____

☐ _____

☐ _____

Course Assignment 5.1 (Part 6) -- Selecting Intervention Strategies to Interrupt the Relapse Process: The Dry Drunk Phase of the Relapse Process (Continued)

Symptom Addressed: _____ **(Add Personal Symptoms Here)**

Specialized/Individualized Interventions:

- ☐ _____
- ☐ _____
- ☐ _____
- ☐ _____
- ☐ _____
- ☐ _____
- ☐ _____
- ☐ _____
- ☐ _____
- ☐ _____
- ☐ _____
- ☐ _____
- ☐ _____

Course Assignment 5.1 (Part 6) -- Selecting Intervention Strategies to Interrupt the Relapse Process: The Dry Drunk Phase of the Relapse Process (Continued)

Symptom Addressed: _____ **(Add Personal Symptoms Here)**

Specialized/Individualized Interventions:

- ☐ _____
- ☐ _____
- ☐ _____
- ☐ _____
- ☐ _____
- ☐ _____
- ☐ _____
- ☐ _____
- ☐ _____
- ☐ _____
- ☐ _____
- ☐ _____

Section 6

Personal Relapse Prevention Plan

Introduction

The time and energy that you have expended in the development of a heightened awareness of the dynamics of relapse and how you can personally stop an emotional slip from becoming a physical relapse has been impressive. We hope that you now understand that relapse is not an event but a process and hope that you will share the message of hope with others.

Our commitment at LCCS to your continued recovery does not end with the development of your plan. You will find an ever expanding list of therapeutic assignments and strategies for intervening on relapse as well as tools for monitoring your progress available on our website, www.leademcounseling.com.

What to Expect from the Following Chapter:

- guide you through the completion of the tasks associated with your Personal Relapse Prevention Plan that were not covered in the other sections such as forming your personal definition of abstinence, outlining your recovery goals, identifying resources to support your ongoing recovery, scheduling your Twelve Step meetings and recovery activities, and identifying the recovery challenges you might face in the next 90 days

- provide a framework for recording the challenges and interventions you have identified for each of the phases and associated symptoms in the relapse process as they relate to your story and insights

Relapse prevention planning intensifies recovery

In the early 1970's recovery wisdom would invite the newcomer to the Twelve Step process of recovery from *addiction* with the following warranty: "… give the program 90 days and if you are not satisfied you can return to your *addiction* and your misery will be refunded." Many of us would recoil from what seemed like biting sarcasm and the air of superiority with which the warranty was offered. Some years later, when we managed to get our *brains out of hock* it became clear to us that the warranty was neither sarcastic nor judgmental. It was a truth about the First Step without the candy coating. The bitterness of the message was found in the painful reality that many different forms of personal misery had driven most of us to the recovery rooms, and if we could have managed with our *drug of choice* and without help, we would not be where we found ourselves. We had not gotten there because we had eaten too many green beans and were certainly not *nipping the problem in the bud* the way that some of us initially thought.

The first 90 days was a pink cloud for some and a life sentence to boredom and joylessness for others. Some of us thought 90 days was far more time than we would need to be cured of the problem because we were wiser than most. We were wrong about that too. Three months can seem like an eternity when you are in withdrawal or returning from a relapse, but it actually occurs in the blink of an eye when you consider the road that some of us took to get here or the years of happiness and peace that we have been blessed with since recovery began. A great deal can happen in 90 days to challenge the foundation of recovery, whether you are new to the process or returning from a relapse. The commitment we are asking you to make during the 90 day process of implementing your Personal Relapse Prevention Plan will seem like an intense endurance contest at the beginning but it will, in reality, be quite easy to maintain once you have begun the monitoring process.

Your hard work, honesty, and openness are to be applauded. In the following Course Lesson we walk you through the completion of each of the tasks that are required to properly record your plan so as to promote optimal communication between you and your support group, therapist, and others of your choosing. Before you begin, it is time for some really good news – this is your last assignment.

Course Lesson 6.1 – 90 Day Personal Relapse Prevention Plan

You are near the end of the process and will now complete your final plan for review with your therapist, members of your support system, and/or trusted confidant. The following assignment may seem redundant and like busy work but we have found that our clients really begin to feel the importance of all the work they have done and the power of the plan that they have developed. Your plan will not leave you as a potential victim to your "inner addict", even if there were such a separate force. Furthermore, the knowledge that others will gain from studying your plan will aid them in their efforts to be of optimal service to you in your recovery.

IMPORTANT:

The following descriptions of the various tasks in this lesson are presented to introduce you to the actual written work you will complete in the Course Assignment that follows this lesson. Do not write anything until you reach the assignment.

When you have completed the lesson be sure to share your findings with members of your support system and your therapist if you are working with one.

~ Task 1 ~

Define personal abstinence:

Here we ask that you clearly and simply define your abstinence in terms that are observable and measureable. The Twelve Step program you are involved in may suggest a model for defining abstinence or it may not. You need to be clear about how you will measure your progress in treatment. There are some schools of thought that suggest that progress can be measured in terms that measure dynamics, like harm reduction or lowered levels of unmanageability. We do not support such a model. Recovery begins after abstinence and not before it and it stops when there is a relapse.

We are not suggesting, as some do, that all progress up to the time of a relapse is lost when a person returns to their *drug of choice*. A relapse stops forward progress and does not eliminate previous progress. However, we do not believe that you can measure progress until there is a starting point. That starting point - abstinence – occurs prior to taking the First Step or during the course of completing the First Step.

The model you use to define abstinence in your recovery is your responsibility to construct, but you are encouraged to seek counsel in your framing of the model. We hope that you will follow two simple principles: abstinence should be clearly measureable and observable, and should never become less restrictive over time.

~ Task 2 ~

Recovery goals:

This task asks you to record your top two recovery goals. If you have had the opportunity to work with a professional therapist then it is likely that you already have a list of goals that you

Course Lesson 6.1 – 90 Day Personal Relapse Prevention Plan (Continued)

have established for your recovery. If so, review them with your therapist, and record the top two choices in your plan. Keep in mind that your plan is going to be shared with members of your support group.

If you have not had the time to find professional resources to help you construct clear goals for yourself, then you can have a discussion with your support group about what the costs of your relapse or *addiction* have been and what you would like to recover. It is fine to think in terms of material or financial goals but you would be wise not to limit yourself to such a narrow field of choices. The emotional, relational, and *spiritual* costs are most likely what drove you into recovery; therefore it would be wise to construct at least one goal from that material.

It is important that the goals that you choose are obtainable, measureable, and observable. Obtainable goals, for the purpose of this plan, are goals that you could reasonably expect to reach during the next 90 days. Goals that cannot be measured, as in: "I want to be a better father," can generate considerable frustration. If you are focused on your desire to be a better parent that is great, but describe what that would look like. For example, "I want to be a better father and spend at least an hour a day with my children doing something that is interactive", would be a measurable goal; being a better father is not. Observable goals are clear to people who experience you in the course of your daily life and are not restricted to just your most trusted friends. The people in your life are likely to take notice of the fact that you are spending more time with your children if you select the above parenting goals, even though they are were not a part of your planning.

~ Task 3 ~

Resources for support:

It is important to have a clearly defined support system and a record of the resources that you have available to aid you in your recovery efforts. The left-hand column is broken down into two sub-columns titled people and opportunities. Under the people sub-column do not hesitate to select people that you derive support from even if they are not directly involved in your recovery circles such as a grandparent or trusted colleague. The opportunities sub-column can include a variety of resources that can take many forms and will more than likely include specific elements of your gratitude list. For instance, you may want to recognize that you have financial resources or a reliable source of income needed to cover your expenses for the next 90 days. You will undoubtedly want to include the availability of Twelve Step meetings, quality therapeutic services, and a growing faith in your Higher Power or the process of recovery.

The right hand column of this task provides space for you to describe the specific value you expect to derive from the personal relationships or resources you have identified.

Course Lesson 6.1 – 90 Day Personal Relapse Prevention Plan (Continued)

~ Task 4 ~

Schedule weekly meetings and recovery activities:

The specific recovery activities that you plan for the next 90 days should be structured into weekly segments as your meeting plans might change from one week to the next. If you suspect this will be the case, then make twelve copies of the table for Task 4 so you can make changes that better suit your needs and changes that may need to be made to adjust to your life schedule demands. During the first 90 days of recovery or return from a relapse, it would be wise to have a fixed plan of the specific meetings that you are going to attend in order to promote a feeling of being at or coming home. The choice of a home group is also important because it is your "address" in your Twelve Step fellowship and as you get to know the members they will miss you when you are not there. When we see the same faces week in and week out, we begin to look forward to reconnecting to people. It will serve as additional insulation against a relapse if you have people that matter to you and who look for you when you are not there.

Place your meeting choices with location and time in the appropriate day of the week. It is generally understood that the practice of making a meeting a day for the first 90 days in recovery or in your return from a relapse is most valuable. On the days that your schedule prohibits a meeting or unexpected events develop, the recovery activities you have planned will help to fill the void in your meeting schedule. Recovery activities can be anything from a phone or internet-based meeting to a prescribed period of time every day or several days a week that you have set aside to do Twelve Step work or service work with or for other members of your recovery culture. It is not wise to routinely substitute recovery activities for face-to-face meetings. The recovery activities should be thought of as the dessert and it is not healthy for your diet to consist solely of desserts.

~ Task 5 ~

Therapy plan:

If you are fortunate enough to be engaged in professional therapy, log your plan in the space provided for this Task. Do not restrict yourself to traditional talk therapy. Consider movement therapies, resources found in the healthcare industry such as chiropractic care and yoga. There is a huge selection of services to choose from. Be mindful to select those resources and philosophical approaches that are in harmony with your core plan for recovery from *addiction*.

Course Lesson 6.1 – 90 Day Personal Relapse Prevention Plan (Continued)

~ Task 6 ~

Biblio-therapy plan:

This task is intended to help you focus your thoughts on the development of a specific plan to engage in purposeful therapeutic reading. Your therapist, sponsor, and support group members will undoubtedly have many wonderful resources that they can suggest. There are daily standards like the main recovery text of your particular Twelve Step fellowship, guides for developing or improving your meditation efforts, and philosophical and *spiritual* essays galore. If you prepare a plan for augmenting your recovery efforts through the use of print, audio, or visual material you will be more likely to have biblio - therapy become an integral part of your recovery process.

A small section is available for you to note why others have suggested a particular title to you and how you hope to benefit from the title.

~ Task 7 ~

Prospectively challenging feelings in the next 90 days:

This task is comprised of two parts. In the first part of the task, titled **Challenge,** you will have space for you to log your expectation of the kinds of challenging feelings you are likely to experience during the first 90 days. It will help for you to return to Section 3 - The Anatomy of Relapse and review the material with specific attention to the work that you completed in Course Assignment 3.4 as well as the symptoms and strategies you selected in Section 5.

We are not asking you to anticipate each and every feeling you are likely to experience during the next three months. The goal of this task is to guide you through the development of the feelings you expect to have that you have historically felt challenged by. This anticipation is not intended to promote a projected and unnecessary experiencing of the event or circumstance in advance.

In the second part of the task, titled **Plan,** you will create preparedness plans for addressing the feeling should it come as you expect. Use all the resources you have available to you to think about how you might handle a particularly uncomfortable feeling in a way that is different than you have in the past with the idea being one of improving your ability to function under duress.

~ Task 8 ~

Prospectively challenging situations in the next 90 days:

This task is comprised of two parts. In the first part of the task, titled **Challenge**, you will have space to log the prospectively challenging situations that might occur during the next 90 days. Again you are not being asked to plan the outcome – just identify what you plan to do if faced with a challenging situation. If you are new to the recovery process it would be helpful to

Course Lesson 6.1 – 90 Day Personal Relapse Prevention Plan (Continued)

confer with your therapist, sponsor, support group members, and other family members to review the potential circumstances that could develop during the first 90 days of recovery. If you are returning from a relapse or looking to prevent the first one, examine the uncomfortable or challenging situations or circumstances that you have struggled with thus far and determine if you need a different plan to address a similarly occurring situation.

It may be helpful to review the material in Course Lessons 3.5 and 3.6 and the work that you completed in Course Assignments 3.5 and 3.6 before you begin planning for the future.

In the second part of the task, titled **Plan,** you will create preparedness plans for addressing the challenging situations should they come as you expect. Use all the resources you have available to you to think about how you might handle a particularly uncomfortable situation in a way that is different than you have in the past with the idea being one of improving your ability to function under duress.

~ Task 9 ~

Prospectively challenging events in the next 90 days:

This task is comprised of two parts. In the first part of the task, titled **Challenge**, you will have space to log the events that are on the calendar or that you would be likely to participate in during the next 90 days are critical for you to review well ahead of the target date. Review the material previously presented in Course Lessons 3.7 and 3.8 as well as the assignments you completed in Course Assignments 3.7 and 3.8.

There is a great deal of preparation that you can do for a scheduled event, beginning with whether or not it is wise for you to attend. While recovery wisdom suggests that we can go anywhere that normal people go if we have a good reason for being there, the qualifying question is more important than simply whether or not we have a good reason for being there. We can go anywhere because of our newfound freedom and we should not adopt a blanket policy of isolation simply because something could go wrong at the Christmas party or the retirement dinner. You should not rely solely on your judgment when addressing the qualification that you are *spiritually* fit to be going into a particular place or event. If you are recovering from an addictive process such as love and sex addiction or gambling, then additional consideration should be given to identifying certain locations as being counter therapeutic, such as strip clubs for sex addicts and casinos for compulsive gamblers. Avoidance of those locations should be included on your plan for abstinence. If you are new to recovery or returning from a troubling relapse it is not wise to subject yourself to tests of emotional endurance simply because you have an obligation to be there. Our first obligation is to remain sober at all costs.

If you are uncertain about your safety, then do not go, however, if you decide to go make sure that you have a very clear exit strategy. A clear exit strategy includes a previously developed profile of what your Fragmentation might look like in such an event. Refer back to material included with Concept Lessons 3.5 and 3.6, the Course Lessons 3.12 and 3.13, and the Course Assignments 3.12 and 3.13.

Course Lesson 6.1 – 90 Day Personal Relapse Prevention Plan (Continued)

In the second part of the task, titled **Plan,** you will create preparedness plans for addressing the challenging events should they come as you expect. Use all the resources you have available to you to think about how you might handle a particularly uncomfortable event in a way that is different than you have in the past with the idea being one of improving your ability to function under duress.

~ Task 10 ~

Prospectively challenging people that you are likely to encounter in the next 90 days:

This task is comprised of two parts. In the first part of the task, titled **Challenge,** you will have space for you to log the specific people or personality types that you are likely to encounter during the next 90 days that you suspect you will find particularly uncomfortable to be around. In the second part of the task, titled **Plan**, you will have space to create preparedness plans for addressing how you plan to cope with these people should you become uncomfortable.

We are not looking for a long, all encompassing list, but a short list of the really problematic people. Name the person or personality type and establish a well thought out plan for how you will cope with the encounter and consider fully whether or not the encounter should be avoided altogether until the prospect of an encounter does not threaten you. Thoroughly review the material associated with Course Lesson 3.9 and Course Assignment 3.9.

~ Task 11 through Task 16 ~

Review and record the symptoms, challenges, and interventions that you have personally associated with each of the phases in the relapse process:

Tasks 11 through 16 provide space for you to log the symptoms, challenges, and interventions that you have prepared for in your coursework so you can communicate them to your support group and as a reference for ongoing monitoring of your recovery needs. A detailed review of the work you completed in Sections 4 and 5 is suggested.

Make sure you get additional help if needed to prepare a personalized set of interventions to use should you find yourself in the middle of a relapse process.

Course Assignment 6.1 - 90 Day Personal Relapse Prevention Plan

Task 1 - Personal Abstinence

Task 2 - List the Top 2 Dated Recovery Goals
1.
2.

Task 3 - Identify Resources for Support

People	Reasons for Selection & Value to be Derived from Relationship
1.	1.
2.	2.
3.	3.

Opportunities	Reason for Selection & Value to be Derived from Resource
1.	
2.	
3.	
4.	

Course Assignment 6.1 - 90 Day Personal Relapse Prevention Plan (Continued)

Task 4 – Scheduled Weekly Meeting Commitment or Recovery Activities		
Day	*Meeting*	*Recovery Activity*
Monday		
Tuesday		
Wednesday		
Thursday		
Friday		
Saturday		
Sunday		

Course Assignment 6.1 - 90 Day Personal Relapse Prevention Plan (Continued)

Task 5 – Plan for Therapy

Schedule

Monday	Tuesday	Wednesday	Thursday	Friday	Saturday	Sunday

Therapy Goals

1.

2.

3.

Task 6 - Biblio-therapy Plan

Date	Title	Notes to Self – What Do I Hope to Gain from It
1.		
2.		
3.		
4.		
5.		

Course Assignment 6.1 - 90 Day Personal Relapse Prevention Plan (Continued)

Task 7 — Prospectively Challenging Feelings in the Next 90 Days
Challenge
1.
2.
3.
4.
5.
Plan
1.
2.
3.
4.
5.

Course Assignment 6.1 - 90 Day Personal Relapse Prevention Plan (Continued)

Task 8 — Prospectively Challenging Situations in the Next 90 Days
Challenge
1.
2.
3.
4.
5.
Plan
1.
2.
3.
4.
5.

Course Assignment 6.1 - 90 Day Personal Relapse Prevention Plan (Continued)

Task 9 — Prospectively Challenging Events in the Next 90 Days
Challenge
1.
2.
3.
4.
5.
Plan
1.
2.
3.
4.
5.

Course Assignment 6.1 - 90 Day Personal Relapse Prevention Plan (Continued)

Task 10 — Prospectively Challenging People that You Are Likely to Encounter in the Next 90 Days

Challenge

1.

2.

3.

4.

5.

Plan

1.

2.

3.

4.

5.

Course Assignment 6.1 - 90 Day Personal Relapse Prevention Plan (Continued)

Task 11 – Uncomfortable Feelings Phase	
Symptoms:	
1.	2.
3.	4.
Challenges:	
1.	
2.	
3.	
4.	
Interventions:	
1.	
2.	
3.	
4.	
5.	

Course Assignment 6.1 - 90 Day Personal Relapse Prevention Plan (Continued)

Task 12 – Time Travel Phase

Symptoms:

1.	2.
3.	4.

Challenges:

1.

2.

3.

4.

Interventions:

1.

2.

3.

4.

5.

Course Assignment 6.1 - 90 Day Personal Relapse Prevention Plan (Continued)

Task 13 – Fragmentation Phase	
Symptoms:	
1.	2.
3.	4.
Challenges:	
1.	
2.	
3.	
4.	
Interventions:	
1.	
2.	
3.	
4.	
5.	

Course Assignment 6.1 - 90 Day Personal Relapse Prevention Plan (Continued)

Task 14 – Gathering Justification Phase

Symptoms:

1.	2.
3.	4.

Challenges:

1.

2.

3.

4.

Interventions:

1.

2.

3.

4.

5.

Course Assignment 6.1 - 90 Day Personal Relapse Prevention Plan (Continued)

Task 15 – Eliminating the Witnesses Phase	
Symptoms:	
1.	2.
3.	4.
Challenges:	
1.	
2.	
3.	
4.	
Interventions:	
1.	
2.	
3.	
4.	
5.	

Course Assignment 6.1 - 90 Day Personal Relapse Prevention Plan (Continued)

Task 16 – Dry Drunk Phase

Symptoms:

1.	2.
3.	4.

Challenges:

1.

2.

3.

4.

Interventions:

1.

2.

3.

4.

5.

Farewell

We are thrilled that you have completed the course. We hope that the insights that you have gained have helped you craft a Personalized Relapse Prevention Plan that will serve as a solid foundation for your sober life. The clinical field study that served as the foundation for this course has spanned the past 42 years and involved us in the lives of thousands of addicts and their families. We will be forever grateful to the clients who have allowed us to gain intimate access to some of the very darkest days of their lives as they struggled to emerge from the maelstrom of relapse.

Relapse had diminished the self-esteem and social status of every relapsing addict we studied. Many lost financial security or suffered career losses. Most who had managed to retain their families were going to spend months regaining lost trust and helping loved ones to heal from the betrayal that often accompanies relapse. Every single case was heaping with lessons for us to examine. We studied what each of the addicts had failed to do. First, we studied them for our own welfare because we really wanted to learn what we needed to do to avoid the pitfalls that had claimed them. Secondly, we wanted to create a recovery culture in the clinical arenas in which we practiced that understood that relapse was a process and not an event.

Our close work with relapse victims, as they had come to be called, taught us that they were not victims at all but active participants in a process that could be clearly identified and intervened on before lives were reduced to the rubble usually associated with a relapse.

We are committed to learning from the challenges that we have been privileged to help our clients cope with. We are interested in anything you can teach us about relapse or its prevention. If you have developed strategies that might help others whose sobriety is being threatened please contact us. We will be adding relapse intervention strategies to our web site in a section of the site called Sober Tool Kit as a free resource to the recovering community and would welcome to the opportunity to get your anonymous stories of success into the hands of your fellow addicts in need.

If you would like more personal help please contact us at one of our offices and let us know how we can be of service to you. If you are interested in attending one of our relapse prevention workshops or intensives please contact us for more information or check our website on a regular basis. If we have not met you yet it would be our pleasure to talk with a fellow traveler on the path to joyful *sober living*. You never have to recover alone.

Sincerely,

John & Shawn Leadem

Endnotes

1. Clearing Away the Wreckage of the Past: A Task Oriented Guide for Completing Steps 4 through 7 Leadem & Leadem, 2010.

2. The First and Fourth Steps of all Twelve Step programs are the only steps that are different according to what addictive illness is being addressed. The First Step of all 12 Step groups begins with "We admitted we were powerless over…" and ends with "…that our lives had become unmanageable." In this course book we have added "our addictive process" after "powerless over" so you are free to add your own specific drug of choice.

3. Alcoholics Anonymous (3rd ed.). (1953). New York, NY: A.A. World Services, Inc. (A.A.W.S.). The Twelve Steps are reprinted with permission of A.A.W.S., Inc. Permission to reprint the Twelve Steps does not mean that A.A.W.S. necessarily agrees with the views expressed herein. A.A. is a program of recovery from alcoholism only - use of the Twelve Steps in connection with programs and activities which are patterned after A.A., but which address other problems, or in any other non – A.A. context, does not imply otherwise. The references made by page number in this text correspond to pages in 1953 edition of Alcoholics Anonymous with permission of A.A.W.S. The Twelve Steps have been reprinted in their entirety for your ease of reference.

Glossary of Terms

Acting Out

The phrase acting out is a psychological term, which has historically referred to a failure of an individual to exercise adequate self-control and is tied to the language used to discuss ego defense mechanisms. The action done is usually anti-social and may take the form of acting on the impulses of an addiction (eg. *drinking*, *drug* taking or shoplifting) or is a means designed (often unconsciously or semi-consciously) to garner attention (eg. throwing a tantrum or behaving promiscuously).

In general usage, the action performed is destructive to self or others and may inhibit the development of more constructive responses to the feelings. The term is used in this way in sexual addiction treatment, psychotherapy, criminology and parenting.

In this course the phrase will be used to describe any behavior associated with the use of or engagement in one's drug of choice.

Addict Within/Addictive Force

These two phrases and many others like them are used by some in recovery to refer to some force within an addict which is believed to have a mind and a power of its own which the addict must do battle with in recovery. We do not believe that there is a force within us as addicts who want us dead, as the saying goes, but would settle for us relapsing. We believe the idea of being powerless over our drug of choice has gotten construed to mean that we are powerless over addiction. If we were powerless over addiction and not the addictive substance or addictive behavior we would be hopeless and we ARE NOT HOPELESS.

Addiction

The phrases addiction or addictive illness are used throughout the guide to refer to the manifestation of an addictive process that may include substances as in the case of alcoholism or behavior patterns such as sex addiction as well as co-addictive disorders. The co-addicted others in the addicted person's life suffer many of the same symptoms of the illness because of the coping strategies that are developed for living in community with the addicted person.

Antecedents

In this course you will frequently be encouraged to examine the antecedents to the patterns of behavior that you find troubling in others or yourself. When used in this book, it is intended for you to think about the events or life experiences that preceded the behavior that concerns you. We are not suggesting that the people involved in those antecedent events are the cause of your current behavior or the behavior of those you find troubling. The exploration is needed if you intend to develop an understanding of how behavioral coping strategies develop in order to make the changes in yourself or your environment that you need to make to stay sober.

Anon

The term anon is a general reference to the various 12 Step support groups that have formed to provide mutual support and recovery direction to the co-addicted partners or significant others in the addict's life such as Al-Anon aims to support the recovery efforts of the significant others in the alcoholic's life.

Binge

A binge is any behavior indulged to excess. It can refer to: drinking large amounts of alcohol over a short period of time; ingesting large amounts of drugs over a short period of time; eating large amounts of food over a short period of time; gambling sprees and the pursuit of love or sex that involves hours viewing pornography or cruising for prostitutes to name but a few examples.

Bottom

The term bottom refers to the subjective point at which the addicted person realizes that he or she can no longer spring back from an addictive episode or is no longer able/willing to accept the consequences of not getting treatment for the addictive illness.

Brains Out of Hock

Recovery wisdom offers that the early days of recovery can be quite challenging because of the self-deluded state of our thinking and inadequate level of emotional preparedness for coping with the day to day challenges of life. Our pursuit of euphoria led us to pawn our judgment, our values, our integrity and perhaps our ability to think rationally. Newcomers were cautioned to avoid making major decisions during the first year of recovery from addiction because it takes about that long to get one's brains out of hock and to start thinking clearly and behaving rationally.

Clean House

The phrase has two intended meanings: (1) the process of competing Steps Four through Nine in the Twelve Step process because they clear away the wreckage of the past, (2) a place to live which has the potential access to one's drug of choice removed.

Compartmentalizing

Compartmentalizing is an unconscious psychological defense mechanism used to avoid the mental discomfort and anxiety caused by a person having conflicting values, cognitions, emotions, beliefs, etc. within themselves. Compartmentalization allows these conflicting ideas to co-exist by inhibiting direct or explicit acknowledgement and interaction between separate compartmentalized self-states.

Co-occurring vs. Cause-effect

A cause-effect relationship is one in which an action or event will produce a certain response to the action in the form of another event. A co-occurring event is one in which two events or experiences are occurring at the same time. The distinction is important in this course for understanding an individual's reaction to a traumatic event. It is not uncommon to hear from adults who were sexually molested as a child that they have erroneously drawn a connection between their emotional need for attention and/or affection and the sexual molestation by a predator who has taken advantage of the child's vulnerability. There is no cause-effect between the child's need and the victimization that they endured but many adults are hard pressed to view the events as co-occurring. One event is not caused by another. The child does not play a role in any abuse because of his or her emotional neediness or for any other reason.

Cork in the Jug

A phrase used in recovery culture when referring to the inadequacy of merely abstaining from the drug of choice. If the alcoholic attempts to recover by merely "putting the cork in the jug" he will soon discover that there is a great deal more involved in sustaining sobriety. Jug is used as a metaphor for an addict's drug of choice. The sex addict who claims that the treatment for his or her sex addiction is to stop the use of pornography and nothing more – is putting the cork in the jug, because there is a great deal more involved in the treatment of sex addiction.

Cravings

A powerful desire for the use of or engagement in a drug of choice that can occur normally during early recovery as a feature of withdrawal or in response to a desire to flee from emotional discomfort.

Day Mare

Day mares are an experiential phenomenon in which the individual is confused by the seeming unconnected thoughts or feelings in a mild PTSD-like reaction.

Defects of Character

Our defects of character are essential behavioral strategies for living, learned at an early age for coping with uncomfortable emotional situations (at least for a while). Long before any of us ever consumed an addictive substance or initiated any addictive behaviors, we experimented with behavior strategies for changing our moods. Those behavior strategies, as described above, became ways of coping with uncomfortable feelings associated with uncomfortable situations. These coping strategies would fail from time to time to relieve our emotional discomfort and we would bolster their pain-dulling power by using addictive substances or addictive behaviors. Once an addictive dependency set in, our defects of character would seem to be forever linked with our addictive cycles. It seems that they are imprinted on an emotional template for how to cope with people and situations. They seemed to strengthen each other like combining addictive substances or addictive mood changing behaviors. The result was devastating.

Drink/Drinking/Drug

When the terms drink or drug appear they refer to any mood altering addictive substance or behavior that is used or intended to move one from an uncomfortable emotional mood toward euphoria. For some people, the drug is food. For others, it may be the emotional numbing that occurs from controlling others. The consideration is equally true for the person who "celebrates" with an addictive substance or behavior. We do not really need a glass of champagne to celebrate our wedding day.

Drug of Choice

The idea that drinking alcoholic beverages in general and liquor in specific was only a symptom of the alcoholic's underlying spiritual problem was a critical feature of the Twelve Step model. All the steps but the First Step focus the sufferer's attention on the spiritual changes that will be required to ensure sustained freedom from addiction. You only need to replace the word "drinking" with the phrase *return to a state of active addiction*.

Your drug of choice is a phrase intended to portray the object of an addictive obsession. The alcoholic might think about drinking, the food addict about over or under-eating, the gambler about placing a bet, etc.

Drunk

A state of being in which the addict's judgment is temporarily impaired by the toxic use of his or her drug of choice.

Dry Drunk

The dry drunk phenomenon occurs as a result of an untreated relapse process that does not necessarily end in acting out but it certainly could. The fact that we can endure a dry drunk and return to sanity without picking up an addictive substance or engaging in an addictive behavior is a mystery, perhaps the grace of God. Eventually "dry drunks" will get you wet!

Dry/Dryness

Dry or dryness refers to an emotional state in which the addicted or person is no longer using addictive substances or engaging in the more dangerous impulsive/compulsive behaviors but is not necessarily making the emotional and spiritual changes that are required for long term recovery.

Intoxication

A person's indulgence in his or her drug of choice that results in a lost of control of their inherent mental or physical power or behavior.

Negative Self-talk

Negative self-talk is usually a mixture of judgmental messages from oppressive people in your past or present relationships, half-truths, the mistaken belief that our personalities are fixed and we can not change, faulty reasoning, an unbalanced focus on a problem, and the presence of personal secrets that we are sure others would find repulsive. It often occurs when in emotional turmoil, or when we are going through stress or a personal transition.

Nipping the Problem in the Bud

This phrase generally refers to actions taken to put an end to something before it develops into something larger. Many addicts will use the phrase prior to a declaration of powerlessness over and unmanageability from their drug of choice. Many of us would like to think that we are getting our addiction under control (nipping the problem in the bud) before things really get out of hand when we have actually accumulated far many more consequences than we are able to see at the time. By the time that most of us take the first three steps of the Twelve Step recovery process, we have been having problems and accumulating consequences for some time.

Panic

Panic refers to feelings of terror that strike suddenly and repeatedly with no warning. Other symptoms of a panic attack include sweating, chest pain, palpitations (irregular heartbeats), and a feeling of choking, which may make the person feel like he or she is having a heart attack or "going crazy."

People, Places, and Things

The newcomer to addiction recovery will often hear a warning about "avoiding people, places, and things", that they might have come to associate with the use of his or her drug of choice. This warning is generally offered as a kind of insurance against being triggered or tempted to return to a drug of choice because it is believed that less contact with using environments or triggers will decrease the likelihood of relapse.

Plethora

The word usually refers to an excess of something. In this work it is used solely because the authors loved when El Guapo mocks Jefe for not knowing what "a plethora" of piñatas means in the movie *The Three Amigos* and ever since the first time the authors watched this movie they committed to adding the word to every essay, paper, and book they wrote.

Promises

There are many rewards promised for those who are painstaking about the practice of the Twelve Steps in all their affairs. Some students of recovery have identified over 150 promises in the book *Alcoholics Anonymous* within the first 164 pages alone. The promises as they are identified in this text refer to the twelve that are highlighted on page 83-84 in *Alcoholics Anonymous* as introduced after the presentation of the Ninth Step. They have been reprinted here for your reference:

> "If we are painstaking about this phase of our development, we will be amazed before we are half way through. We are going to know a new freedom and a new happiness. We will not regret the past nor wish to shut the door on it. We will comprehend the word serenity and we will know peace. No matter how far down the scale we have gone, we will see how our experience can benefit others. That feeling of uselessness and self-pity will disappear. We will lose interest in selfish things and gain interest in our fellows. Self-seeking will slip away. Our whole attitude and outlook upon life will change. Fear of people and of economic insecurity will leave us. We will intuitively know how to handle situations, which used to baffle us. We will suddenly realize that God is doing for us what we could not do for ourselves".

Rapacious Creditor

The author of the "12 Steps and 12 Traditions" published by *Alcoholics Anonymous* refers to alcohol as a "rapacious creditor". There are two meanings to be inferred by his use of this term. Rapacious is an adjective used to describe greedy or grasping and a creditor is someone or some institution to whom a debt is owed. In this course the term rapacious creditor refers to the aggressive nature of an addictive illness process that can leave the addict with the idea that there is a force "addiction" that is always on the lookout for a way to claim his or her sobriety, security, and sanity.

Safe House

The phrase refers to a living environment that is free of potential drugs of choice and historically powerful triggers for acting out.

Sober Living

The term sober is used throughout this guide with broad reference to mean the life we are building in recovery once abstinence from our addictive substance or behavior has been established.

Spiritual or Spirituality

The terms spiritual or spirituality are often thought to be associated with religion. This course uses the terms when referring to the pursuit of an inner path that can enable a person to discover the essence of his or her being; or the deepest values and principles by which one chooses to live life. Spiritual practices, including meditation, prayer and contemplation, are intended to develop an individual's inner life; spiritual experience includes that of connectedness with a larger reality, yielding a more comprehensive self and ultimately greater personal fulfillment.

Put somewhat differently, spiritual and spirituality are used in reference to the degree to which the addict is comfortable being other rather than self-centered. The individual who struggles to rely on others or a power greater than himself or herself is thought to be suffering spiritually. The person who is comfortable with the development of a healthy reliance on others or a power greater than himself or herself is thought to be spiritually secure.

Surrender Process

The Twelve Steps involve a six-part surrender process:

- In the First Step the addict/co-addict is giving up or surrendering his or her drug of choice.
- The Third Step signals the point at which the addict/co-addict surrenders doing it alone.
- The Fifth Step brings the addict/co-addict out of the shadows as the secrets are surrendered to another human being
- The Seventh Step provides the addict/co-addict with the opportunity to surrender maladaptive coping strategies for healthy ways of coping with his or her emotions and to develop productive interpersonal relationships
- The Ninth Step surrenders the shadows as the addict/co-addict faces those who have been harmed
- The Twelfth Step encourages the addict/co-addict to apply and practice the previous 11 Steps in all areas of his or her life, surrendering the notion that all will be fine once the drug of choice is surrendered

Teasing the Addiction

The phrase refers to the practice of engaging in behaviors that, while they do not breach abstinence or violate the addict's "bottom line," are sexually and romantically titillating for the sex addict. The practice of *teasing* one's addiction has a wide variety of manifestations that are usually associated with the object of one's addictive illness. The alcoholic who continues to "party" with her friends and the co-addicted partner who sneaks peaks at his partner's recovery journal are both *teasing* their addiction. The eventual cost for *teasing* your addiction could be relapse. *Teasing* your addiction can be a form of harassing your spirit. So remember what you were taught in kindergarten: "play fair and don't tease others".

The Person I Was Will Relapse Again

While the phrase was developed in the fellowships supporting recovering alcoholics and drug addicts, it readily applies to the greater universe of people recovering from all addictive disorders. The person I was will relapse again directs that recovery students to be aware that the values and coping strategies that drove the behavior in addiction will need to change. It will not be enough to merely stop the use of one's drug of choice.

Traumatic Experiences

A traumatic event involves a single experience, or an enduring or repeating event or events, that completely overwhelm the individual's ability to cope or integrate the ideas and emotions involved with that experience. The sense of being overwhelmed can be delayed by weeks, years or even decades, as the person struggles to cope with the immediate circumstances. Psychological trauma can lead to serious long-term negative consequences that are often overlooked even by mental health professionals.

After a traumatic experience, a person may re-experience the trauma mentally and physically, hence avoiding trauma reminders, also called triggers, as this can be uncomfortable and even painful. They may turn to psychoactive substances including alcohol to try to escape the feelings. Re-experiencing symptoms are a sign that the body and mind are actively struggling to cope with the traumatic experience.

Twelve Step Widow/Widower

The significant other, who once felt abandoned by his or her actively addicted partner, may feel like the partner's pursuit of recovery has left him or her alone again. The bereaved significant other may be mourning the loss of the partner they had thought was found when abstinence was established because his or her partner now seems consumed with attending meetings and fellowship opportunities. The significant other who fully engages in their own 12 Step recovery process is less likely to feel like the widow or widower to their partner's recovery process but there is usually more involved than can be addressed by joining in the recovery process.

Many romantic partners have longed for the return of their addicted loved one from the throes of active addiction and quite often feel betrayed again in recovery when the addict in his or her life pays more attention to his or her new recovery friends than to the romantic partnership. There are many good reasons for the newly recovering addict to submerge himself or herself in the recovery culture but there is no reason that a marriage to his or her respective 12 Step fellowship needs to result in a divorce from his or her romantic relationship. Far too many newcomers hide in recovery rooms and avoid facing the challenges of rebuilding his or her love relationships. While we would never encourage anything but submersion in recovery, it does not have to be at the expense of a romance or a marriage.

Using Episode

Refers to a period of time in which an individual is actively using his or her drug of choice.

Wet Drunk

The phrase is used to denote behavior associated with someone who has actually returned to the use of his or her drug of choice.

Appendix A: Alcoholics Anonymous - The Twelve Steps

1. We admitted we were powerless over alcohol, that our lives had become unmanageable.
2. Came to believe that a Power greater than ourselves could restore us to sanity.
3. Made a decision to turn our will and our lives over to the care of God, as we understood Him.
4. Made a searching and fearless moral inventory of ourselves.
5. Admitted to God, to ourselves, and to another human being the exact nature of our wrongs.
6. Were entirely ready to have God remove all of these defects of character.
7. Humbly asked Him to remove our shortcomings.
8. Made a list of all persons we had harmed, and became willing to make amends to them all.
9. Made direct amends to such people wherever possible, except when to do so would injure them or others.
10. Continued to take personal inventory and when we were wrong, promptly admitted it.
11. Sought through prayer and meditation to improve our conscious contact with God as we understood Him, praying only for knowledge of His will for us and the power to carry that out.
12. Having had a spiritual awakening as the result of these steps, we tried to carry this message to alcoholics, and to practice these principles in all our affairs.

Appendix B: Feelings Words

abandoned
absent-minded
abused
accepted
accused
admired
adored
adrift
affectionate
afraid
aggravated
aggressive
agitated
alarmed
alert
alienate
alive
alone
aloof
alluring
amazed
ambushed
amused
angry
antagonistic
anxious
apathetic
appalled
apologetic
appreciated
appreciative
apprehensive
aroused
ashamed
astonished
attacked
attractive
aware
awestruck
awkward
bad
baffled
bashful
beaten down

belittled
benevolent
berated
betrayed
bewildered
bitter
blamed
blue
bold
bored
bothered
brave
broken
bummed
burdened
burned out
calm
capable
carefree
careless
caring
cautious
censored
centered
certain
challenged
charmed
cheated
cheerful
cherished
childish
clean
clear
clever
close
closed
clueless
clumsy
cold
comfortable
committed
compassionate
competent
competitive

complacent
complete
concerned
condemned
confident
confused
considerate
contemplative
contempt
content
controlled
convicted
cornered
courageous
cowardly
cranky
crazy
cross
crushed
curious
daring
dashed
dazed
dead
deceived
dedicated
defeated
defenseless
defensive
defiant
degraded
dejected
delicate
delighted
demoralized
dependent
depressed
deprived
deserted
desired
despair
desperate
destroyed
detached

determined
devastated
devious
devoted
different
difficulty
dirty
disappointed
disbelieving
discarded
disconnected
discontent
discouraged
disgraced
disgusted
disheartened
dishonest
disillusioned
dismal
dismayed
disobedient
disorganized
disposable
distant
distracted
distressed
disturbed
doubtful
drained
dropped
dull
dumb
eager
ecstatic
edgy
effective
embarrassed
empathetic
empty
enchanted
encouraged
energetic
energized
elated
enlightened
enraged
enriched

entertained
enthusiastic
envious
evasive
evil
exasperated
excited
excluded
exhausted
exhilarated
expectant
exploited
exposed
exuberant
faithful
fake
fantastic
fatigued
fearful
fearless
feisty
fine
flustered
foolish
forgiven
forgotten
fortunate
framed
frantic
free
friendly
frightened
frisky
frustrated
fulfilled
full
funny
furious
generous
gentle
giving
grieving
glorious
good
grateful
great
glad

gloomy
grouchy
grumpy
guarded
guilty
gullible
handicapped
happy
hateful
haunted
healthy
heard
heartbroken
helpful
helpless
hesitant
honored
hopeful
hopeless
horrible
horrified
hospitable
hostile
humble
humiliated
hurt
hysterical
idealistic
idiotic
ignorant
ignored
imaginative
immune
impatient
impelled
imperfect
impertinent
important
impressed
impulsive
inadequate
inattentive
incensed
incompetent
incomplete
incredulous
indebted

indecisive
independent
industrious
inept
inferior
inflated
informed
infuriated
inhibited
innocent
innovative
inquisitive
insane
insecure
insensitive
insignificant
isolated
insulted
intense
interested
interrogated
interrupted
intimidated
intimate
intrigued
invigorated
invisible
involved
irrational
irresponsible
irritated
irked
jaded
jealous
jinxed
jolly
jovial
joyful
jubilant
judged
judgmental
jumpy
just
justified
kidded
kind
knowledgeable

late
lazy
leery
left out
let down
liable
liberated
lifeless
light-hearted
liked
listened to
logical
lonely
loose
lost
lousy
lovable
loved
loving
lucky
mad
manipulated
mean
meditative
melancholy
merry
mischievous
miserable
misinterpreted
mistreated
misunderstood
mixed up
mocked
molested
moody
motivated
moved
mystified
naïve
nasty
needed
needy
negative
neglected
nervous
neurotic
nonchalant

nostalgic
noticed
numb
obeyed
obligated
obvious
odd
offended
old
open
oppressed
optimistic
ornery
out of control
outraged
overcome
overjoyed
overloaded
overwhelmed
overworked
owned
pampered
paralyzed
passionate
passive
patient
peaceful
peeved
pensive
perky
perplexed
persecuted
pessimistic
pestered
petrified
petty
phony
pious
playful
pleased
poor
possessive
positive
powerful
powerless
practical
pressured

private
productive
protected
protective
proud
provoked
prudish
punished
pushy
puzzled
questioned
quiet
rambunctious
reassured
realistic
rebellious
reborn
receptive
reckless
recognized
reconciled
reflective
refreshed
regretful
rejected
rejuvenated
relaxed
released
relieved
reluctant
reminiscent
remorseful
renewed
replaced
replenished
repressed
rescued
resentful
reserved
resistant
resourceful
respected
responsible
restricted
revengeful
revitalized
rich

ridiculous
right
rigid
robbed
romantic
rotten
rushed
sabotaged
sad
safe
sassy
satisfied
saved
scared
scolded
scorned
secure
seductive
self-assured
self-centered
self-confident
self-conscious
self-destructive
self-reliant
selfish
sensitive
sentimental
serene
serious
sexy
skillful
shamed
shaken
sheepish
shocked
shunned
shy
sick
silenced
silly
sincere
sinful
slandered
sluggish
small
smart
smothered

skeptical
solemn
soothed
sorry
special
spiteful
splendid
spunky
squashed
stifled
stimulated
stingy
strained
stretched
stressed
strong
stubborn
stumped
stunned
stupid
submissive
successful
suicidal
suffocated
sullen
sunk
super
superior
supported
sure
surly
surprised
suspicious
sympathetic
tacky
tactful
talented
talkative
tame
tarnished
tasteful
tearful
teased
tenacious
tender
tense
tepid

terrible	uncomfortable	warlike
terrific	unconcerned	warm
terrified	uneven	warmhearted
thankful	unfit	warned
thoughtful	unfriendly	wary
threatened	united	wasted
thrifty	unjust	weak
thrilled	unknown	wealthy
tired	unneeded	weary
tormented	unpleasant	weird
torn	unreal	whole
tortured	unruly	wild
tough	unwise	willful
tragic	uplifted	wishful
tranquil	used	witty
transformed	useless	worldly
trapped	vacant	worse
treasured	vain	worthy
trebly	vague	wounded
tremendous	valid	wrong
tricked	valued	yearning
troubled	vexed	yellow
trusted	vicious	yielding
ugly	victimized	young
unaccepted	victorious	youthful
unappreciated	violated	zany
unbalanced	vivid	zealous
unburdened	void	
uncanny	wacky	

About the Authors

John and Shawn have shared a rich and dynamic relationship for the past 33 years. Although they have been in cahoots on a good deal of their life experiences, this is their first collaborative writing project.

The recovery lessons for Shawn and his brother began at an early age since neither of the Leadem boys had to endure the pain of parental active addiction and both had ample access to their parents' recovery journeys. In fact, there were many dinnertime conversations that focused on gratitude and the joys of sober living and any questions were fair game. Shawn remembers fondly his attempts to imitate his parents by playing "going to a meeting" with his brother on their playset in the backyard as young kids and straining to listen in on campfire dialogues his parents shared with other recovering adults during their many family camping trips.

Although Shawn listened intently in these conversations and asked a myriad of questions about the consequences of addiction and the benefits of sober living it did not provide enough insight to avoid the maelstrom of addiction. But then again, insight never does result in change. In order to change one has to change. Shawn will tell you that his bank of knowledge about recovery principles and his deep appreciation for the relapse prevention strategies he witnessed in his home growing up did not prevent him from falling through the ice and into the waters of active addiction himself.

Throughout the first several years of his life, he suffered deep emotional injury from the medical traumas that he endured and despite being raised in a sober loving home Shawn chose to cope with this injury by pursuing addictive behaviors rather than by seeking the support of his family. Fortunately, Shawn experienced a "high" bottom rather early in life. He credits his early "high" bottom to having witnessed and internalized the recovery work his parents did daily to continue to fall forward. Although the external consequences he met with were not great, the torment he felt within his spirit was accessible to him because his exposure to recovery principles was more powerful than the denial present in his disease. In fact, he would find that he understood what had to be addressed in this course before the first keystroke.

Much of John's journey to learning what would need to be in a course of this kind occurred long before Shawn was born, but perhaps surprisingly to many, after John had been sober from alcohol for several years. John, by the grace of God, has never suffered a relapse from in his recovery from alcoholism since getting sober at age 18 but acknowledges that he and others had to endure great suffering for years in his early sobriety from his continual relapses in his unaddressed love and sex addiction. His "reign of romantic terror" in the early years of recovery cost him so much more than his alcoholism and drug addiction. He would come to understand the challenges of developing a relapse prevention program as he struggled to treat women and himself with dignity and respect. He often jokes that he wishes that he had co-authored this course 41 years ago because its lessons would have saved him and others a great deal of pain.

John and Shawn share over 50 years of sobriety between them and have a combined tenure in the field of addiction treatment that spans over 46 years. They are licensed clinical social workers and have multiple certifications in the field of addiction treatment. Their passion for this work has taken them into every conceivable modality known for treating addictive and co-addictive disorders. They share a common affinity to the *spiritual* principles of the 12 Steps and incorporate these principles into the work they do with others. At the core of their philosophy is a willingness to do the work they have asked others to do.

In addition to sharing the responsibilities of operating a thriving private practice, John and Shawn continue to look for ways to take their message of hope to a broader audience. This has included being hosts to workshops, presenting at national conferences, and writing books. Currently, LCCS has published two books and one is on its way. You can find *One in the Spirit: Meditation Course for Recovering Couples*, *Surveying the Wreckage: A Guide to the Fourth Step*, and *Clearing Away the Wreckage of the Past: A Task Oriented Guide for Completing Steps 4 through 7* on our website www.leademcounseling.com.

About the Artist

The cover art was provided by Julia M. Ratushny, who has an amazing gift for capturing the beauty of the New Jersey coastline in watercolor. If you are interested in seeing more of her work please visit her website at www.julieratushny.com.

Notes

Made in the USA
San Bernardino, CA
04 January 2015